THE CAMBRIDGE COMPANION TO
FREDERICK DOUGLASS

Frederick Douglass was born a slave and lived to become a best-selling author and a leading figure of the abolitionist movement. A powerful orator and writer, Douglass provided a unique voice advocating human rights and freedom across the nineteenth century, and remains an important figure in the fight against racial injustice. This Companion, designed for students of American history and literature, includes essays from prominent scholars working in a range of disciplines. Key topics in Douglass studies – his abolitionist work, oratory, and autobiographical writings – are covered in depth, and new perspectives on religion, jurisprudence, the Civil War, Romanticism, sentimentality, the black press, and transnationalism are offered. Accessible in style, and representing new approaches in literary and African American studies, this book is both a lucid introduction and a contribution to existing scholarship.

MAURICE S. LEE is Assistant Professor of English at Boston University. He is the author of *Slavery, Philosophy, and American Literature, 1830–1860* (Cambridge, 2005).

CAMBRIDGE COMPANIONS TO AMERICAN STUDIES

This series of Companions to key figures in American history and culture is aimed at students of American studies, history and literature. Each volume features newly commissioned essays by experts in the field, with a chronology and guide to further reading.

VOLUMES PUBLISHED

The Cambridge Companion to Benjamin Franklin ed. Carla Mulford

The Cambridge Companion to Thomas Jefferson ed. Frank Shuffelton

The Cambridge Companion to W. E. B. Du Bois ed. Shamoon Zamir

The Cambridge Companion to Frederick Douglass ed. Maurice Lee

VOLUMES IN PREPARATION

The Cambridge Companion to Bob Dylan ed. Kevin Dettmar

The Cambridge Companion to Malcolm X ed. Robert Terrill

THE CAMBRIDGE COMPANION TO

FREDERICK DOUGLASS

EDITED BY
MAURICE S. LEE

CAMBRIDGE
UNIVERSITY PRESS

CAMBRIDGE UNIVERSITY PRESS

Cambridge, New York, Melbourne, Madrid, Cape Town, Singapore, São Paulo, Delhi

Cambridge University Press
The Edinburgh Building, Cambridge CB2 8RU, UK

Published in the United States of America by Cambridge University Press, New York

www.cambridge.org
Information on this title: www.cambridge.org/9780521717878

First published 2009

Printed in the United Kingdom at the University Press, Cambridge

A catalogue record for this publication is available from the British Library

ISBN 978-0-521-88923-0 hardback
ISBN 978-0-521-71787-8 paperback

To
Herlan O. Loyd
(1913–2001)
and
Marjorie L. Loyd
(born 1911)

CONTENTS

NOTES ON CONTRIBUTORS

GREGG CRANE is Associate Professor of English at the University of Michigan and the author of *Race, Citizenship, and Law in American Literature* (Cambridge University Press, 2002) and *The Cambridge Introduction to the Nineteenth-Century American Novel* (Cambridge University Press, 2007).

JOHN ERNEST, the Eberly Family Distinguished Professor of American Literature at West Virginia University, is the author of *Resistance and Reformation in Nineteenth-Century African-American Literature* (1995), *Liberation Historiography: African American Writers and the Challenge of History, 1794–1861* (2004), and *Chaotic Justice: Rethinking African American Literary History* (2009). His editions of texts by nineteenth-century African American writers include *Running a Thousand Miles for Freedom; Or, The Escape of William and Ellen Craft from Slavery* (2000), William Wells Brown's *The Escape; or, A Leap for Freedom* (2001), and *Narrative of the Life of Henry Box Brown* (2008).

PAUL GILES is Professor of American Literature at the University of Oxford. His books include *Transatlantic Insurrections: British Culture and the Formation of American Literature, 1730–1860* (2001), *Virtual Americas: Transnational Fictions and the Transatlantic Imaginary* (2002), and *Atlantic Republic: The American Tradition in English Literature* (2006).

GENE ANDREW JARRETT is an Associate Professor of English and African American Studies at Boston University. He is the author of *Deans and Truants: Race and Realism in African American Literature* (2006) and the editor of several books, most notably *African American Literature Beyond Race* (2006) and, with Henry Louis Gates, Jr., *The New Negro: Readings on Race Representation, and African American Culture, 1892–1938* (2007). He is currently finishing a book on racial representation and the politics of African American literature.

BILL E. LAWSON, Distinguished Professor of Philosophy at the University of Memphis, is the co-author of *Between Slavery and Freedom* (1992) with Howard McGary and has edited numerous books: *The Underclass Question* (1992),

Frederick Douglass: A Critical Reader (1999) with Frank Kirkland, *Faces of Environmental Racism* with Laura Westra (2001), *My Bondage and My Freedom* (2002), and *Pragmatism and the Problem of Race* (2004) with Donald Koch.

MAURICE S. LEE is Assistant Professor of English at Boston University. He is the author of *Slavery, Philosophy, and American Literature, 1830–1860* (Cambridge University Press, 2005). Selected essays have appeared in *American Literature*, *African American Review*, *PMLA*, and *Raritan*. He is currently finishing a book on chance, scepticism, and belief in nineteenth-century American literature.

ROBERT S. LEVINE is Professor of English and Distinguished Scholar-Teacher at the University of Maryland. He is the author of *Conspiracy and Romance* (1989), *Martin Delany, Frederick Douglass, and the Politics of Representative Identity* (1997), and *Dislocating Race and Nation* (2008), and the editor of a number of volumes, including *The Norton Anthology of American Literature, 1820–1865* (2007) and (with Samuel Otter) *Frederick Douglass and Herman Melville: Essays in Relation* (2008).

SARAH MEER is a senior lecturer in English at the University of Cambridge, and a Fellow of Selwyn College. She is the author of *Uncle Tom Mania: Slavery, Minstrelsy, and Transatlantic Culture in the 1850s* (2005).

IFEOMA C. K. NWANKWO is Associate Professor of English at Vanderbilt University. Her research has focused on encounters between African American, Afro-Caribbean, and Latin American communities in the areas of representation, identity, and ideology. Her published work includes *Black Cosmopolitanism: Racial Consciousness, and Transnational Identity in the Nineteenth-Century Americas* (2005), "The Promises and Perils of African American Hemispherism" (in *Hemispheric American Studies*, ed. Caroline Levander and Robert S. Levine, 2008), "Charged with Sympathy for Haiti" (in *Tree of Liberty: Cultural Legacies of the Haitian Revolution in the Atlantic World*, ed. Doris L. Garraway, 2008), as well as articles in journals such as *Radical History Review*. Her current projects center on Latin Americans of West Indian descent and on US African American travelers.

ARTHUR RISS teaches US literature and culture before 1900 at Salem State College. He is the author of *Race, Slavery, and Liberalism in Nineteenth-Century American Literature* (Cambridge University Press, 2006) and is currently at work on a project linking the US Reconstruction period to contemporary debates over biotechnology.

VALERIE SMITH is the Woodrow Wilson Professor of Literature in the Department of English and Director of the Center for African American Studies at Princeton University. She is the author of *Self-Discovery and Authority in Afro-American Narrative* (1987) and *Not Just Race, Not Just Gender: Black Feminist Readings* (1998), as well as numerous articles on African American literature and visual culture. At present, she is completing a book on the Civil Rights Movement and cultural memory.

JOHN STAUFFER is Chair of the History of American Civilization and Professor of English and African and African American Studies at Harvard University. Among the leading scholars of the Civil War era and antislavery, he is the author or editor of seven books and more than forty-five articles, including *Giants: The Parallel Lives of Frederick Douglass and Abraham Lincoln* (2008); *The Writings of James McCune Smith* (2006); *The Problem of Evil: Slavery, Freedom, and the Ambiguities of American Reform* (with Steven Mintz, 2006); and *The Black Hearts of Men: Radical Abolitionists and the Transformation of Race* (2002), which won four major awards, including the Frederick Douglass Book Prize, the Avery Craven Book Award, and the Lincoln Prize Runner-Up. His essays have appeared in *Time Magazine*, *The Times Literary Supplement*, *The New York Times Book Review*, *The Huffington Post*, *Raritan*, *New York Post*, and *21st: The Journal of Contemporary Photography*.

MAURICE O. WALLACE is Associate Professor of English and African and African American Studies at Duke University. Author of *Constructing the Black Masculine: Identity and Ideality in African American Men's Literature and Culture, 1775–1995* (2002), he teaches African American literary and cultural theory, nineteenth-century American literature, and gender studies. His essays have appeared in *American Literary History*, *Journal of African American History*, and several critical anthologies.

ACKNOWLEDGMENTS

The same month that this volume went to the printers, Barack Obama became President of the United States. In his Inaugural Address – as in his other major speeches – Obama placed himself within America's longstanding struggle for equality and freedom. Frederick Douglass is one of Obama's forefathers, and it is a privilege to help readers engage Douglass's work at such a momentous time in United States history. Thanks to Ray Ryan of Cambridge University Press for approaching me regarding the project. Thanks to all the contributors for bringing their expertise to bear on Douglass's immense achievements. I am especially grateful to John Stauffer, Robert S. Levine, and Gene Jarrett for timely advice during the planning stages of the volume. John Barnard was also of great help in preparing the chronology and index. More broadly, I would like to thank the teachers who first led me to the study of slavery and African American literature. Clayborne Carson and the late Jay Fliegelman introduced me to Douglass and the history of civil rights in America. In graduate school, Richard Yarborough and Eric Sundquist took me deeper into both subjects. This volume would not have been imaginable without the lifelong contributions of scholars who established the study of Douglass. Many are acknowledged in the chapters that follow, though here I will mention Benjamin Quarles, Philip Foner, John Blassingame, and Henry Louis Gates, Jr. More personally, thanks to my excellent colleagues in the English department at Boston University for their support. And many thanks and much love to my ever-growing family: Marisa, Nico, and Matteo; Mom, Andrew, Yuko, and Jameson; Don and Linda Milanese and their extended family. To quote from Obama's Inaugural Address – and to think about the demands that Douglass places on his readers – it takes much support to remain "faithful to the ideals of our forebears, and true to our founding documents."

CHRONOLOGY OF DOUGLASS'S LIFE

1818 Frederick Augustus Washington Bailey, son of Harriet Bailey, a slave, is born in Talbot County on the eastern shore of Maryland. His father is never identified but is widely thought to have been his mother's white master, Aaron Anthony.

1824 After being raised in relative comfort by his grandmother, he is taken to the Wye River plantation of Edward Lloyd, where Anthony lives and works as general overseer. Rejoins his younger siblings Perry, Sarah, and Eliza. Befriended by Lucretia Anthony Auld.

1826 Sent to Baltimore to live with the family of Hugh Auld, a shipbuilder and brother of Lucretia's husband, Thomas Auld. Serves as companion and protector to young Tommy Auld.

1827 At Douglass's request, Sophia Auld begins teaching him to read until Hugh Auld objects. Sent back to Talbot County for the disposition of Anthony's property. He is awarded to Thomas Auld, who returns him to service with Hugh and Sophia in Baltimore.

1828–30 Works in shipyard and secretly continues his studies.

1831–32 Meets Charles Lawson, a free African American who helps him to a religious conversion. Along with his continued Bible study, he obtains a copy of *The Columbian Orator*.

1833 Sent back to Thomas Auld at St. Michaels in Talbot County. Continues his studies and organizes lessons in religion and literacy for other African Americans. Sent to Edward Covey, a notorious "breaker" of slaves.

1834 Fights Covey to a stalemate, a major turning-point in his life.

1835   Works as a fieldhand for William Freeland. Organizes Sunday school and reading lessons for fellow slaves.

1836   Plots a failed escape with five other slaves. Returns to Baltimore, where he begins training as a ship caulker.

1837   Continues his education through the East Baltimore Mental Improvement Society, and resumes teaching. Meets Anna Murray, a free black woman working in Baltimore.

1838   Hires out his own labor until Auld rescinds his permission. With financial assistance from Murray, escapes on September 3, taking a train to Wilmington, then a steamer to Philadelphia. Arrives in New York on September 4. Introduced to David Ruggles, secretary of the New York Vigilance Committee. Douglass and Murray are married on September 15. Moves to New Bedford, where he changes his name to Douglass and joins the African Methodist Episcopal Zion Church.

1839   Subscribes to William Lloyd Garrison's *The Liberator*, and attends antislavery speeches by Garrison, Wendell Phillips, and others. Douglass is licensed to preach and speaks frequently at his church and other meetings. Daughter Rosetta is born on June 24.

1840   His first son, Lewis Henry, is born in New Bedford on October 9.

1841   Speaks in New Bedford and at the convention of the Massachusetts Anti-Slavery Society in Nantucket, and becomes a general agent of that organization. Travels with prominent abolitionists, including John A. Collins, Garrison, and Phillips, speaking against slavery and northern racism.

1843   Travels with Charles Lenox Remond, Collins, and other abolitionists on the One Hundred Convention project. Attacked by a mob in Indiana, where his right hand is broken and permanently damaged. Attends National Convention of Colored Citizens in Buffalo.

1844   Because of his surpassing eloquence, white audiences begin to doubt his veracity and authenticity. Initial conflict arises between Douglass and his Anti-Slavery Society mentors, who press him to limit his speeches to the facts of his experience. Begins work on first autobiography.

1845–46   Final composition and publication of *The Narrative of the Life of Frederick Douglass, An American Slave, Written By Himself.*

The book is an immediate success, but the publicity puts him at risk for capture and rendition. In August 1845, embarks on an extended tour of England, Scotland, and Ireland. In 1846, together with Garrison, Douglass lectures widely on antislavery. Without his knowledge, British abolitionist friends Anna and Ellen Richardson raise the necessary funds to purchase his freedom from Hugh Auld, who had received the title to Douglass from his brother Thomas. Douglass defends the payment in a letter to *The Liberator*.

1847   Returns to the United States in April. With money from his English friends, purchases a printing press in Rochester, New York. In December, the first issue of *The North Star* appears.

1848   Continues lecturing in support of *The North Star*. Attends women's rights convention, where he speaks in favor of Elizabeth Cady Stanton's call for suffrage. Begins campaign to desegregate Rochester schools. Meets John Brown in Springfield, Massachusetts. Begins ongoing assistance to fugitive slaves fleeing to Canada.

1849–50   Breaking with Garrisonian ideology, he writes that the Constitution is not an inherently proslavery document. Argues strenuously against the Compromise of 1850, especially its reinvigorated Fugitive Slave Law.

1851   *The North Star* merges with Gerrit Smith's *Liberty Party Paper* to become *Frederick Douglass' Paper*.

1852   Delivers the address, "What to the Slave Is the Fourth of July?" Campaigns for Gerrit Smith, who wins a seat in Congress as an independent.

1853   Writes "The Heroic Slave." Split between Douglass and the Garrisonians widens.

1854   Denounces the Kansas–Nebraska Act.

1855   Completes and publishes his second autobiography, *My Bondage and My Freedom*, which meets with instant success, selling 15,000 copies in two months.

1856   Supports Gerrit Smith for President. Later endorses the Republican nominee, John C. Frémont, as the only viable antislavery candidate.

1858   Begins publication of *Douglass' Monthly*. Praises Lincoln for his "House Divided" speech. Continues working to end northern segregation and capital punishment, and to promote women's rights.

1859   John Brown and his followers attack and occupy a federal arsenal at Harpers Ferry, Virginia. Despite his opposition to the plan, Douglass is implicated. Goes to Canada and then England for a lecture tour arranged prior to Brown's raid.

1860   Returns to the United States. Suspends publication of *Frederick Douglass' Paper*, but continues to publish the monthly. Expresses support for Lincoln and the Republican Party. Attends the Radical Abolition convention and is named as a party elector for New York State. South Carolina secedes from the Union on December 20.

1861   On April 12, a Confederate attack on Fort Sumter begins the Civil War. Douglass calls for the arming of slaves and free blacks. Criticizes Lincoln for his conciliatory attitude toward border states.

1862   Praises the abolition of slavery in the District of Columbia. Urges Great Britain not to recognize the Confederacy. Lincoln issues the Emancipation Proclamation, declaring all the slaves in the Confederacy, but not border states, to be free.

1863   Recruits for the Massachusetts 54th Infantry, the first black regiment in the Union army. Sons Charles and Lewis join the regiment. Meets with Lincoln to advocate equal pay, opportunity, and protection for black soldiers.

1864   Continues to criticize the Lincoln administration for unequal treatment of black soldiers and failure to support black suffrage, but endorses the president for re-election.

1865   Eulogizes Lincoln after his assassination on April 14. Joins Senator Charles Sumner and other radical Republicans to advocate national black suffrage.

1866–69   Splits with women's rights activists, including Stanton and Susan B. Anthony, in prioritizing black men's suffrage over women's suffrage. Supports Ulysses S. Grant for the presidency in 1868.

1870   Becomes editor (and eventually owner) of *The New Era*, which he renames *The New National Era*. Moves to Washington, DC.

1871   Sent by President Grant as envoy to the Dominican Republic with the commission on annexation.

1872   Fire destroys Rochester home, along with the archives of *The North Star, Frederick Douglass' Paper*, and *Douglass' Monthly*. Campaigns for Grant's re-election.

1874   Tries and fails to save the failing Freedman's Savings and Trust Company. *The New National Era* also fails.

1876   Campaigns for Republican Presidential candidate Rutherford B. Hayes.

1877   Disputed election results lead to the Compromise of 1877, which gives Hayes the White House, but removes northern troops from the South, effectively ending Reconstruction and leading to drastic political losses for African Americans. Hayes appoints Douglass US marshal for the District of Columbia. In June, Douglass returns to St. Michaels, where he meets with the 82-year-old Thomas Auld.

1879   Douglass delivers the principal eulogy for William Lloyd Garrison at the memorial service in Washington, DC.

1880–81 Backs Republican James A. Garfield. Garfield appoints Douglass as Recorder of Deeds for the District of Columbia. Writes and publishes his third autobiography, *Life and Times of Frederick Douglass*.

1882   New edition of *Life and Times* is published. Neither edition is a success. After suffering a stroke in July, Anna Murray Douglass dies on August 4.

1884   Marries Helen Pitts, a white woman twenty years his junior.

1886–87 Resigns the office of Recorder. Travels to England, Scotland, Ireland, Italy, Greece, and Egypt.

1888–89 Supports successful candidacy of Republican Benjamin Harrison. Appointed consul general to Haiti.

1890–91 Involved in tense negotiations over American naval rights in Haiti. When Haiti rejects the US proposal, Douglass is accused in the press of excessive sympathy with the Haitians.

1892   Lectures at Booker T. Washington's Tuskegee Institute. Befriends Ida Wells, a black journalist and anti-lynching activist. Publishes an expanded version of *Life and Times*.

1893   Serves as Haitian commissioner and lectures on Haitian independence at the World's Columbia Exposition in Chicago. Criticizes exclusion of blacks from the Exposition. Organizes performance by the young poet Paul Laurence Dunbar.

1895   On February 20, after addressing the National Council of Women in Washington, DC, Douglass collapses at home and dies of heart failure that evening. His body lies in state in Washington, and he is mourned and eulogized across the country.

CITATIONS

The following abbreviations are used parenthetically throughout this volume to refer to Douglass's writings:

N   Frederick Douglass, *Narrative of the Life of Frederick Douglass, An American Slave, Written By Himself* (1845) in *Frederick Douglass: Autobiographies*, ed. Henry Louis Gates, Jr. (New York: Library of America, 1994).

MB   Frederick Douglass, *My Bondage and My Freedom* (1855) in *Frederick Douglass: Autobiographies*, ed. Henry Louis Gates, Jr. (New York: Library of America, 1994).

LT   Frederick Douglass, *Life and Times of Frederick Douglass* (1881, 1892) in *Frederick Douglass: Autobiographies*, ed. Henry Louis Gates, Jr. (New York: Library of America, 1994).

FDP   *The Frederick Douglass Papers, Series One: Speeches, Debates, and Interviews*, 5 vols., ed. John W. Blassingame (New Haven: Yale University Press, 1979–92).

LW   *The Life and Writings of Frederick Douglass*, 5 vols., ed. Philip S. Foner (New York: International Publishers, 1950–75).

MAURICE S. LEE

Introduction

When Frederick Douglass in 1851 changed the name of his newspaper from *The North Star* to *Frederick Douglass' Paper*, he joked, "I shall lose my reputation for being unstable if I don't change soon" (LW 2:223). Change is indeed a major feature of Douglass's life and writings, as is his sensitivity to his reputation in an often-critical public eye. Douglass rose to fame with the extraordinary success of his 1845 autobiography, *Narrative of the Life of Frederick Douglass, An American Slave, Written By Himself* (1845). The book, which forever altered Douglass's life, is itself a carefully crafted record of personal transformations – from Douglass's loss of childhood innocence under the brutality of chattel bondage, to his battle with the slave-breaker Covey (which Douglass describes as a "turning-point in my career as a slave" [N 65]), to his escape in 1838 into what he later called the "nominal" freedom of the North (LW 1:279), to his rebirth as a speaker in the American Anti-Slavery Society under the leadership of the white evangelical William Lloyd Garrison. After traveling through Great Britain in 1845–47 and having his freedom purchased by abolitionist friends, Douglass distanced himself from Garrison's influence and founded the newspaper that would eventually take his name, thus announcing himself as the most prominent black leader and writer in the English-speaking world.

Douglass's transformations would continue. He became increasingly militant with the coming of the Civil War, defending John Brown's 1859 raid on Harpers Ferry and recruiting African American soldiers for the Union Army. After the war, he made an uneasy transition from radical reformer to political appointee, holding noteworthy positions in Republican administrations during and after Reconstruction. By the time of his death in 1895, Douglass was an international figure recognized as an orator, writer, statesman, and representative of his race. A main purpose of *The Cambridge Companion to Frederick Douglass* is to examine as comprehensively as possible Douglass's diverse achievements, which occur within broad historical contexts, take multiple literary forms, draw from a wealth of intellectual traditions, and together have presented an ongoing challenge to Douglass scholars for over a century.

Historical Contexts

Even a cursory glance at the nineteenth century suggests that Douglass was hardly alone in experiencing radical change. When he was born into slavery in Maryland in 1818, Thomas Jefferson, Napoleon, and Sir Walter Scott were alive. When he died preparing for a speech in 1895 in his home in Washington, DC, Franklin Delano Roosevelt and James Joyce were teenagers and Hitler was six years old. During Douglass's lifetime, the United States grew from a twenty-state nation of small-scale economies and local political allegiances to a forty-four-state empire poised to expand beyond its continental borders. Railroads, telegraphs, corporations, and a powerful federal government linked the growing country together, while the rise of women's rights, immigration, Darwinism, industrialism, urbanization, and public education further altered American thought and culture. These developments influenced and in many cases were influenced by Douglass's social activism, which included the struggle not only for black freedoms, but also for the rights of women and Chinese immigrants. J. T. Jenifer, pastor of the AME Church in Washington, DC, exulted in his eulogy for Douglass: "[H]ow full his life! How completely rounded out! How interwoven in the warp and woof of American history!"[1]

As Jenifer suggests, the history of nineteenth-century America cannot be told without reference to the slavery controversy and what was later called the "negro problem," nor can the history of African Americans be told without reference to Douglass's writings. Douglass participated in major phases of the struggle for black freedom: the growth of abolitionism from a radical fringe group to a powerful reform movement; the national crisis that erupted over chattel bondage following the Fugitive Slave Law of 1850; the Civil War and its culmination in the emancipation of all slaves; the heady days of Reconstruction and its tragic decline into segregation and terrorism. To those who think that the history of race relations in America is one of consistent and perhaps inevitable improvement over time, Douglass's life shows that the struggle for civil rights is full of dramatic victories and discouraging setbacks alike. In his fifty years as a public figure, Douglass saw the legal status of African Americans change from property with no rights that whites were bound to respect, to citizens equally protected under the law (at least in theory), to a caste suffering from widespread racism and lynching (and who were infamously defined as "separate but equal" one year after Douglass's death in the US Supreme Court case *Plessy v. Ferguson*). As the landscape of the civil rights struggle changed, so too did some of Douglass's positions and methods, though at the core of his work is an unwavering dedication to the fulfillment of democratic ideals.

Literary Forms

Douglass's main weapons in the fight for freedom were words, both spoken and written. At a time when oratory was second only to poetry as a respected literary form, Douglass was best known as a speaker of electrifying eloquence and charisma. Douglass also published three autobiographies, edited his own newspapers, authored a novella ("The Heroic Slave" [1853]), and even wrote a bit of verse. Equally impressive, the scope of his style is as broad as the generic range of his writings. In his introduction to Douglass's second auto-biography, *My Bondage and My Freedom* (1855), the African American abolitionist James McCune Smith praised Douglass's "logic, wit, sarcasm, invective, pathos, and bold imagery" (MB 134), while the black intellectual Alexander Crummell compared his "delicate, beauteous, poetic sentiment" to the lyricism of William Wordsworth.[2] For a sense of Douglass's protean styles and influences, one can refer to very different examples: the sentimental, novelistic descriptions of his grandmother in the *Narrative* and *My Bondage and My Freedom*; the outraged irony and jeremiad intensity of his widely reprinted speech, "What to the Slave Is the Fourth of July?" (1852); the scholarly logic of his scientific oration, "The Claims of the Negro Ethnologically Considered" (1854); the black oral traditions such as slave songs and subversive humor that often echo in his speeches.

In addition to his linguistic genius and extraordinary ambition, one expla-nation for the range of Douglass's work is that his political efforts brought him into contact with a diverse array of listeners. Some of the audiences of his speeches were segregated by gender and race, while others were what the period called "promiscuous" – mixed and therefore especially challenging. Douglass also contended with skeptical listeners, particularly early in his career when foes and even friends resented so articulate, brilliant, and inde-pendent an ex-slave. Unlike writers who published but did not speak, Douglass did not simply imagine the demands of his various listeners: he faced them repeatedly during five decades of orating in which he was lauded, jeered, and even physically attacked (in fact, his hand was permanently damaged from fighting-off a mob during one of his speeches).

As for his writing, Douglass's journalistic work prompted frequent and immediate replies from readers, and Douglass often responded in print to the most hostile critiques of his editorials. Douglass's autobiographies came under much scrutiny, especially the *Narrative*, whose authorship and factual accuracy became subjects of debate – in part because Douglass was so polished a writer, and also because other slave narratives had been shown to be ghostwritten or fabricated. Considering the hundreds of speeches that Douglass gave throughout Great Britain and the United States, and given the intense intertextual dynamics of racial debates in nineteenth-century transatlantic print culture, it makes sense that Douglass learned to present his views in multiple registers, to transform his literary voice so as to move as many listeners as possible.

Intellectual Traditions

A similar logic of transformation applies to Douglass's generous intellectual commitments. Douglass wrote of slavery in an 1860 letter, "There is scarcely one single interest, social, moral, religious, or physical[,] which is not in some way connected with this stupendous evil" (LW 2:488). And in his third autobiography, *Life and Times of Frederick Douglass* (1881, 1892), he wrote that in order to address the race problem comprehensively, "I should be profoundly versed in psychology, anthropology, ethnology, sociology, theology, biology, and all the other ologies, philosophies and sciences" (LT 939). Douglass was being only partly hyperbolic, for the topic of race in the nineteenth century cut across disciplinary boundaries during a period when modern academic fields were becoming increasingly defined. We do not know the full extent of Douglass's reading: he was largely self-taught, left no explicit record of his studies, and his personal papers and library were destroyed in a fire in 1872. Nonetheless, his speeches and writings reflect an ongoing process of intellectual growth as he continued his self-education in (among other things) history, philosophy, literature, natural science, and law. Benjamin Quarles, the first scholarly biographer of Douglass, called him a "many-sided man" with a "multiplicity of interests," though Quarles also regarded Douglass's learning as "broad rather than deep."[3]

It is true that Douglass was not a scholar but a reformer fighting on many fronts. As much as he respected specialized learning, he also emphasized the value of common sense and the practical consequences of ideas. Speaking about the death of Abraham Lincoln, a figure Douglass knew and a fellow leader whose wisdom transcended academic knowledge, Douglass claimed, "[M]ost men are taught by events" and "have little time to give to theories" (FDP 4:108). Douglass recognized early in his life that questions of racial justice cannot be reduced to philosophical abstractions or single areas of study. As a thinker who in many ways anticipated cultural pluralism and its current incarnation, multiculturalism, Douglass knew that contributions from diverse perspectives are required in the ongoing pursuit of freedom.

Accordingly, his multifaceted career invites studies such as the volume at hand. Douglass even models for those who read him a kind of interdisciplinary approach.

Scholarly Contexts

The history of Douglass's critical reception is itself a narrative of transformations. In some ways, the first important studies of Douglass came from Douglass himself, if only because he published his life story three times (four if one counts the expanded version of his *Life and Times*). Anticipating the potential skepticism of his readers, Douglass included many supporting facts in his autobiographies, even in the *Narrative* – a risky decision in that Douglass was still a fugitive slave subject to capture and rendition. Douglass's autobiographies are always personal in their perspective and voice, but they increasingly resemble the "great man" histories of the nineteenth century as they become less psychologically immediate and more focused on public events. Part of the brilliance of Douglass's self-presentations was how skillfully he controlled his public image so as to preclude potential attacks. Douglass was adept at anticipating objections, defending weaknesses in his argument, and appealing to the democratic and Christian ideals of nineteenth-century United States culture. Yet if Douglass wrote his life into history, his legacy has proven to be far from assured.

Scholarship on Douglass in the fifty years after his death is relatively scant and uneven when judged by modern standards. Histories of the United States from the time tended to simplify or elide the experiences of blacks, in part because many post-Reconstruction Americans wanted to forget painful problems of race as sectional reconciliation and white solidarity proceeded at the expense of civil rights.[4] This is not to say that Douglass was forgotten. As is still the case today, he was the subject of books for students and lay readers, while general works of African American history such as John Cromwell's *The Negro in American History* (1914) and Carter G. Woodson's *The Negro in Our History* (1922) included sketches of Douglass's life. Such books, however, are mainly interested in overarching historical narratives, and – like early popular biographies of Douglass by the African American writer Charles Chesnutt and black leader Booker T. Washington (who probably used a ghostwriter) – they draw so heavily on Douglass's autobiographies as to be more hagiography than history.

It is as if Douglass told his life story so well that no one made the effort to examine it critically, a situation exacerbated by the fact that Douglass's vast writings were not collected until the mid-twentieth century. Vernon Loggins's literary history *The Negro Author* (1931) was the first book to examine

Douglass's oratory, journalism, and correspondence alongside his autobiographies. But even as Loggins emphasized the need for a scholarly edition of Douglass's writings, he felt that "such a collection will in all probability never be possible."[5] Loggins was correct that some of Douglass's works are almost surely lost forever, not only because editions of his newspapers remain missing due in part to the 1872 fire, but also because many of his speeches do not survive or only exist in transcripts hastily scrawled by journalists attending the event. However, Loggins was wrong about the possibility of a scholarly collection. A turning point in Douglass studies came in 1950 when Philip Foner addressed what he later called the "deplorable" state of Douglass historiography by publishing the first volume of *Life and Writings of Frederick Douglass*, a selection of Douglass's speeches, articles, and correspondence that would eventually reach five volumes.[6] Foner's work helped bring to light the dynamism and diversity of Douglass's thinking; and along with Quarles's 1948 biography, it encouraged scholars to look beyond the Douglass presented in the autobiographies.

Another important aspect of early Douglass scholarship is a tradition of literary criticism that Loggins both drew from and advanced. Initially, studies of Douglass tended to focus on his oratorical skills, a topic that was much debated during Douglass's life. As always, Douglass sought to shape the discussion of his work: *My Bondage and My Freedom* includes McCune Smith's lengthy praise of Douglass's oratory, while selections from Douglass's speeches appear in the appendix of the book. Newspaper accounts of Douglass's oratory often commented on his performance and style. And fitting for a man whose life was changed by reading Caleb Bingham's *Columbian Orator* (1797), Douglass appeared frequently in anthologies of speeches – from C. M. Whitman's compendium *American Orators and Oratory* (1883) to early twentieth-century textbooks edited by such notable literary figures as Julia Ward Howe, Thomas Wentworth Higginson, Alice Dunbar-Nelson, and Chesnutt. Benjamin Brawley's *The Negro in Literature and Art* (1910) also focused on Douglass's speeches, while two early biographies – Frederic May Holland's *Frederick Douglass, the Colored Orator* (1891) and James M. Gregory's *Frederick Douglass the Orator* (1893) – further indicate how closely Douglass was associated with the art of speech.

In the early twentieth century, Douglass was still far from receiving the kind of literary attention afforded to contemporary white writers such as Emerson, Hawthorne, and Longfellow. And by the mid-twentieth century, Douglass's place in American literary history was even less prominent. As many critics have noted, one reason for this is that an increasingly professionalized literary establishment created an exclusionary canon that tended to privilege formal unity over sociopolitical content.[7] F. O. Matthiessen's definitive *American Renaissance* (1941) never mentions Douglass, despite the fact that many of Matthiessen's subjects (including Emerson, Thoreau, Melville, and Whitman) share ideological, aesthetic, and in some cases personal connections with Douglass. Other scholarly works from the period by Van Wyck Brooks, Vernon Parrington, and R. W. B. Lewis similarly ignore Douglass's achievements, even in chapters on antislavery literature and antebellum politics. Little suggests that Douglass was intentionally excluded on account of his race, but it is difficult to deny a conclusion that Douglass himself painfully learned: though eloquence and truth may have no color, race matters in how black writers are read – or not read.

Another reason for Douglass's waning literary reputation in the mid-twentieth century has more to do with genre than racial discrimination as literary criticism moved away from oratory as a primary object of study. *The New Negro* (1925), an influential Harlem Renaissance collection edited by the black intellectual Alain Locke, includes sections on African American poetry, fiction, drama, and music but has little interest in the oratorical forms for which Douglass had been most celebrated. William Stanley Braithwaite's contribution to *The New Negro*, "The Negro in Art and Literature," even goes so far as to devalue Douglass's autobiographies: "Frederick Douglass's story of his life is eloquent as a human document, but not in the graces of narration and psychologic portraiture." Braithwaite takes Douglass as an example of how "the race problem … dissipated the literary energy of many able Negro writers," showing that white critics were not alone in attempting to separate aesthetics and politics at the expense of authors like Douglass.[8] Loggins's 1931 book and J. Saunders Redding's *To Make a Poet Black* (1939) are more complimentary of Douglass's autobiographies. But even when they treat his writings as literary texts (and not solely as historical documents), their discussions remain relatively unsophisticated when compared with later scholarship.

A radical change in the literary reputation of Douglass began in the 1970s with the rise of black studies programs and political approaches to literary interpretation. No single scholar or text can be said to have instigated the renaissance of Douglass studies. Important essays on Douglass appear in collections on African American literature edited by Dexter Fisher and Robert Stepto, as well as by Deborah McDowell and Arnold Rampersad. Henry Louis Gates, Jr.'s *Figures in Black* (1987) includes two influential chapters on Douglass and also acknowledges three previous projects that helped clear the way for understanding Douglass as a writer of immense linguistic complexity: Peter Walker's *Moral Choices* (1978), Dickson Preston's *Young Frederick Douglass* (1980), and John Blassingame's introduction to *The Frederick Douglass Papers* (an ongoing, multivolume project begun in 1979 that, under the current direction of John McKivigan, is super-ceding Foner's *Life and Writings* as the authoritative source of Douglass's work). As a result of these and other efforts, Douglass's autobiographies, particularly the *Narrative*, came to eclipse his oratory, especially as scholars turned their attention to the slave narrative tradition, most notably examined in William Andrews's *To Tell a Free Story* (1986).

Theoretical advances in literary studies also shaped readings of Douglass's texts as scholars drew on Marxist, psychological, feminist, new historical, and post-structural methods. Widely considered during his life a representa-tive of his race, Douglass by the end of the 1980s had become an author representative of much more – the slave narrative genre, African American literature in general, multicultural interpretation, and the politics of canon revision. At the same time that William McFeely's 1991 biography confirmed Douglass as a major historical figure, Douglass's prominence in literary studies culminated in two essay collections that brought together a host of influential scholars: Eric Sundquist's *Frederick Douglass: New Literary and Historical Essays* (1990) and Andrews's *Critical Essays on Frederick Douglass* (1991). No longer an occasionally studied orator or a purely historical subject, Douglass within a century of his death had become a canonical writer whose *Narrative* brought him into the highest ranks of United States literary history.

The last two decades have further secured and expanded Douglass's repu-tation to a point where Douglass scholarship reflects his diversity so well as to escape easy generalizations. The *Narrative* continues to be examined from generic, rhetorical, and psychological perspectives, while racial identity, poli-tical ideology, and linguistic mastery remain important foci. At the same time, some critics now consider *My Bondage and My Freedom* to be Douglass's most telling life story, if only because a more autonomous, more experienced Douglass directly addresses such controversial subjects as racism in the North (and the antislavery movement), black political power, and violent resistance. *Life and Times of Frederick Douglass* is still the least read of Douglass's autobiographies, though Douglass's role in the Civil War and Reconstruction is beginning to receive needed discussion, especially as critics challenge the notion that important literature was not written during the Civil War. Renewed interest in oratory, not simply as a literary form but as an influential cultural practice, has returned Douglass to his standing as a speaker, while growing interest in African American print culture, spurred in part by access to the nineteenth-century black press through internet databases, has brought new attention to Douglass's important editorial work.

More than ever before, *all* of Douglass's writings seem deserving of serious study, often requiring scholars to engage in interdisciplinary work. Douglass has been increasingly situated within new intellectual contexts, including nineteenth-century legal history and theory, racial science, and philosophical traditions (political, moral, and metaphysical). The recent turn toward religion in nineteenth-century studies has made Douglass's complicated views of Christianity especially compelling, while the continuing integration of African American and women writers with authors from the "old" canon puts Douglass in significant conversations with Romanticism and sentimentality. Perhaps most importantly, the paradigm shift toward transnationalism in United States literary studies has both advanced and been advanced by recent work on Douglass, whose life and interests cannot be kept within the borders of the United States, particularly given the international routes of slavery, abolitionism, and imperialism.

As with many great writers, Douglass is enriched – not diminished or excluded – by changing critical priorities. His wide-ranging commitments and modes of expression continue to make him the most important black writer of the nineteenth century, even if his representative status is rightfully fading away as critics recognize that no single voice can encompass the diversity of nineteenth-century African American texts. But while Douglass is neither a metonymic figure nor the leader of a monolithic tradition, he remains at the center of many recent scholarly developments. Our understanding of Douglass's life and writings is still – and will remain – in a process of change. *The Cambridge Companion to Frederick Douglass* seeks to describe and advance such transformation.

Overview of Chapters

The following chapters need not be read in order, but they tend to move from general to more specific topics, and they take a roughly chronological shape. In chapter 1, "Douglass's Self-Making and the Culture of Abolitionism," John Stauffer examines a fundamental background for Douglass's life and work – his experiences within the abolitionist movement in the United States and Great Britain. Focusing on the complicated dynamics between various strands of antislavery activism – and, accordingly, between Douglass and his closest associates and friends – Stauffer discusses the personal and political contexts for Douglass's major achievements.

Moving from history to issues of genre and text, Robert S. Levine in chapter 2 discusses how Douglass artistically shaped his public and private identity through his autobiographical writings. As much as Douglass sought a stable selfhood in the face of racist practices that would deny him an identity, Levine shows how Douglass was "constantly in the process of reinventing himself."

Rhetorically, politically, and psychologically complex, Douglass's autobiographies and the changes they register justify their longstanding centrality in the study of Douglass.

In chapter 3, "Douglass as Orator and Editor," Sarah Meer argues that Douglass's reputation need not rest solely on his autobiographical work. For Meer, Douglass's efforts as a lecturer and journalist are inextricably linked in a national and international public sphere increasingly connected by technological advances and the growing desire for news. Taking "What to the Slave Is the Fourth of July?" as a main case study, Meer shows that Douglass's celebrated speech does not simply reflect his exceptional oratorical genius; it also draws on a fully elaborated tradition in the antislavery press of taking Independence Day as an occasion to attack the hypocrisy of American slavery.

Chapters 4 and 5 discuss the intersection of religion and politics in Douglass's work. Using materials from throughout the career, John Ernest in "Crisis and Faith in Douglass's Work" addresses Douglass's "increasingly complex and sometimes inscrutable views on religion." While Douglass is often taken to be skeptical of religion and increasingly secular in his thinking, Ernest argues that Douglass was "a religious leader not in spite of the ongoing crisis he experienced but because of it." In "Violence, Manhood, and War in Douglass," Maurice Wallace agrees with Ernest that Douglass does not turn toward secularism in any complete sense. For Wallace, Douglass's growing militancy, most forcibly represented in his discussions of John Brown, can be understood as a "muscular Christian militancy" that waxes with the Civil War but has deep roots in Douglass's private and public life.

Chapters 6 through 8 situate Douglass within three related intellectual contexts, all of which generally address the question: how does one know – and more importantly, convince others – that slavery is wrong? In "Human Law and Higher Law," Gregg Crane describes the legal landscape of the slavery debate, aligning Douglass with such higher law advocates as William Seward and Thoreau. Crane argues that Douglass, particularly in his writings on the Constitution, "insisted that American law must be founded on universal ethical norms" best established, not through religious conviction, but through "political dialogue and public consensus." Arthur Riss in chapter seven, "Sentimental Douglass," offers a somewhat different sense of the principles of Douglass's abolitionism. For Riss, Douglass does not simply deploy sentimental discourses of sympathy, home, and family to achieve his political goals. More radically, Douglass represents sentimentality as "an enabling condition rather than merely a representational mode" in that the very notion of loving human relations is unthinkable for the subject in bondage. In chapter eight, "Douglass among the Romantics," the philosopher

Bill E. Lawson discusses Douglass in terms of Romanticism in general and American Transcendentalism in particular. With special focus on "The Heroic Slave" and using Emerson's distinction between Locke and Kant, Lawson argues that Douglass rejects the empiricist notion that humans are shaped entirely by their experience. Instead, Douglass champions a Transcendentalist position emphasizing the innate moral faculties of all people regardless of color or station.

Chapters 9 and 10 both reflect the recent shift toward transatlantic and cisatlantic approaches to Douglass. In "Douglass's Black Atlantic: Britain, Europe, Egypt," Paul Giles shows how Douglass's foreign travels shaped his expanding political vision and hybrid artistry. Douglass's overseas experiences not only gave him a new sense of freedom, they helped him to recognize "the complex, interlocking nature of social and economic power." As a thinker who never felt quite at home anywhere, Douglass's travels – physical and intellectual – unsettle the sense of Douglass as a United States figure and frame what Giles calls his "art of estrangement." Ifeoma Nwankwo also sees Douglass's work as marked by international dislocations. In "Douglass's Black Atlantic: The Caribbean," Nwankwo focuses on Douglass's "twice-doubled consciousness": he is torn in W. E. B. Du Bois's classic sense of being black in a country that disowns him, but he is also swayed by competing allegiances to blacks outside the United States. As Nwankwo shows, Douglass's relations to the British West Indies and Haiti are especially complicated, particularly given his position as US consul to Haiti and the entanglements of US slavery with Caribbean history.

Some of the foregoing chapters discuss Douglass's writings after the Civil War, but only Gene Jarrett in chapter 11, "Douglass, Ideological Slavery, and Postbellum Racial Politics," focuses solely on Douglass's career after the abolition of chattel bondage. For Jarrett, Douglass's work for racial uplift after emancipation forced him to confront "ideological slavery," what Douglass called "the unwritten law" that continued to oppress African Americans in the post-Reconstruction era. As Jarrett shows, Douglass advocated his cause in official legal and governmental forums, but he also worked in less formal domains – conventions, the women's rights movement, the black press, and the field of public education. Jarrett's discussion of Douglass's evolving thought leads to this volume's final essay. Emphasizing Douglass's shifting place within scholarly traditions over the last few decades, and drawing provocative connections between Douglass's thought and Barack Obama's presidential campaign, Valerie Smith shows that the legacy of Frederick Douglass continues to be shaped today in new and powerful ways.

NOTES

1. *In Memoriam: Frederick Douglass*, ed. Helen Douglass (Philadelphia, PA: J. C. Yorston, 1897), 26.
2. *Ibid.*, 217.
3. Benjamin Quarles, "Douglass: The Crowning Years," *Journal of Negro Education* 24:4 (Autumn 1955), 442; Benjamin Quarles, *Frederick Douglass* (Washington, DC: Associated Publishers, 1948), 343, ix.
4. David Blight, *Race and Reunion: The Civil War in American Memory* (Cambridge, MA: Harvard University Press, 2003).
5. Vernon Loggins, *The Negro Author: His Development in America to 1900* (Port Washington, NY: Kennikat Press, 1931), 139.
6. Philip S. Foner, *Frederick Douglass: A Biography* (New York: Citadel Press, 1964), 5.
7. For this argument with special reference to Douglass, see Russell J. Reising, *The Unusable Past: Theory and the Study of American Literature* (New York: Methuen, 1986), 256–72; and John Carlos Rowe, *At Emerson's Tomb: The Politics of Classic American Literature* (New York: Columbia University Press, 1997), 96–123.
8. William Stanley Braithwaite, "The Negro in Art and Literature," in *The New Negro*, ed. Alain Locke (New York: Touchstone, 1997), 37.

I

JOHN STAUFFER

Douglass's Self-Making and the Culture of Abolitionism

Introduced to the Abolitionists

It is difficult to overestimate the influence of abolitionist organizations on Frederick Douglass. In the fall of 1838, after fleeing slavery and settling in New Bedford, Massachusetts, abolitionists offered him a crucial source of hope, uplift, and self-transformation. A few months after moving to New Bedford, he began reading *The Liberator*, the Boston organ of the American Anti-Slavery Society, edited by William Lloyd Garrison. He subscribed a few months after moving to New Bedford even though he couldn't afford it, and paid the $2 annual fee in installments.

The Liberator was the most influential protest paper in American history. It relied on the Declaration of Independence and the Bible as sacred texts and called for an immediate end to slavery and equal rights for all people. It envisioned a heaven on earth in which the government of God replaced human government. It advocated nonviolence, declaring that revolution would be achieved through moral suasion alone. And it refused to compromise: "I will not equivocate – I will not excuse – I will not retreat a single inch," Garrison had vowed in the first issue of *The Liberator* in January 1831. He remained true to his word. To offset this message of breathtaking idealism, Garrison employed a style of "extraordinary physicality": in his pages oppressors trembled, nations quaked, statues leaped, and victims bled. While the Romantic poets had "spiritualized the natural world," Garrison made palpable the moral repugnance against slavery. He spoke to Douglass's heart.[1]

The publication of *The Liberator* outraged a nation whose citizens generally had no desire to end slavery. Human bondage had been a fact of life for millennia, and most Americans believed that ending slavery immediately was madness. At best, most white Americans saw slavery as a necessary evil, much like pollution today: you might be able to control it, but abolishing it required an act of God and lots of time. Most white Americans also believed that the Bible defended slavery in more places than it opposed it. Many Southerners, drawing on scripture and philosophers ranging from Aristotle and St. Augustine to the Mississippi divine James Smylie, declared that slavery benefited society, masters, and slaves. Southerners suppressed antislavery literature and unsuccessfully tried to arrest Garrison. South Carolina Senator John C. Calhoun vainly tried to pass a national law banning the circulation of all abolitionist writings and images. Even in the North, abolitionists were condemned as fanatics. In 1835 Garrison was almost lynched in Boston, and throughout most of the decade mobs of "respectable" citizens, from bankers and lawyers to merchants, attacked abolitionist meetings.

By the end of the 1830s, abolitionists were not quite as despised, even though they remained a fringe minority. This was because many white Northerners blamed the financial panic of 1837 and the subsequent horrible depression on the "Slave Power" – the South's ruling elite. They believed that slavery depressed prices in free society and thus threatened their own livelihoods. Additionally, the famous congressional Gag Rules prohibited any discussion of slavery in the nation's Capitol, thus identifying abolitionism with civil liberties.[2]

Douglass read *The Liberator* as devoutly as he read his Bible. He had been unusual as a slave in that he had learned how to read and write, but *The Columbian Orator* (1797), a popular elocution manual for young boys, had given him an introduction to the subject of rhetoric. Now he learned the language of abolitionism; he acquired a sophisticated vocabulary for combating slavery and began using punchy verbs to awaken his listeners. "The paper became my meat and drink. My soul was set all on fire," he wrote, quoting Garrison, his mentor.[3]

The Liberator inspired Douglass to attend abolitionist meetings. Despite working all day and often all night as a common laborer, he was able, through the meetings, to develop his oratory and debate with new friends. At one meeting in 1839 he and a group of New Bedford black abolitionists lashed out at the American Colonization Society, which shipped free blacks to the African colony of Liberia as a conservative solution to the "problem" of blacks in America. And they praised Garrison for advocating "immediate and unconditional emancipation" (LW 1:25).[4]

Douglass finally heard Garrison speak at a meeting in New Bedford on August 9, 1841. He had become something of a "hero worshipper" (MB 362), having read Thomas Carlyle's influential new book on heroes, and he was not disappointed: "no face and form ever impressed me with such sentiments," Douglass said (LW 1:26).

The next day Douglass accompanied Garrison and forty black and white abolitionists to Nantucket for a convention, and he was urged to speak. With over 500 people attending, the majority of them white, it was the largest audience by a factor of ten that he had ever addressed. He was so nervous that he trembled with fear, and his fright recalled memories of slavery: "The truth was, I felt myself a slave" (N 96). But after speaking for a few minutes he recovered his sense of freedom and the words flowed.

Garrison took the stage next, riffing off Douglass's speech: "Have we been listening to a thing, a piece of property, or to a man?"

"A man! A man!" came the united response.

"Will you succor and protect him as a brother man?"

"Yes!" they shouted with such force that the walls and roof of the hall "seemed to shudder," according to one reporter.[5]

Douglass was stunned by the performance. The audience seemed to become "a single individuality," the image of Garrison's "own soul" (MB 365). When Douglass spoke again at the evening session, he tried out some of Garrison's techniques. Now it was Garrison's turn to be amazed. Douglass's speech "would have done honor to Patrick Henry" (LW 1:27). He was especially struck by Douglass's control over his rich baritone voice, like a singer achieving sublime power over his listeners.

Before the convention adjourned, the general agent of the American Anti-Slavery Society invited Douglass to be a paid lecturer. Douglass was initially reluctant, but he agreed to a three-month renewable contract at an annual salary of $450, equivalent to about $34,000 in today's money. Little did he know that he had found his calling and was about to embark on a remarkable career. He would later note that public speaking was the most effective form of protest and his greatest accomplishment as an artist and activist: "I hardly need say to those who know me, that writing for the public eye never came quite as easily to me as speaking to the public ear" (LT 938).

Growing Dissension

The American Anti-Slavery Society needed Douglass more than Douglass needed it. In 1840 the Society had split over differences in opinion about politics and women and was losing members and money. Garrison and his followers opposed voting and largely ignored political debates. They interpreted the Constitution as a proslavery document, considered American government incurably corrupt, and advocated disunion from the slave republic. They also demanded that women be allowed to have leadership roles in the American Anti-Slavery Society.

One group of dissenters, believing in the efficacy of the ballot box, formed the Liberty Party in order to nominate antislavery candidates and seek change through political action. A smaller group, opposing women's rights, organized the American and Foreign Anti-Slavery Society, which prohibited "promiscuous" meetings in which men and women both spoke. After the breakup, Garrison and his followers refused to accommodate dissenters, and each group went its separate way. The upshot of the schism was that the American Anti-Slavery Society saw its membership drop in half and its annual income plummet from $47,000 to $7,000. More than ever, the Society needed a charismatic orator to champion its cause.

It also needed someone who could speak about slavery firsthand. Southerners flooded the market with pamphlets, books, and images that depicted slaves as happy and content and masters as benevolent and fatherly. They accused abolitionists of never having seen slavery. Only Southerners could speak authoritatively about the institution, they argued, adding that Northern wageworkers were far more oppressed than slaves.

Partly in response to such criticism, Northern reformers wanted to hear from a slave what slavery was like. But most fugitives affiliated with the American Anti-Slavery Society were reluctant to become lecturers for fear of exposing themselves and being recaptured. Those willing to take such risks did not meet the Society's strict standards for lecturing, which required charisma and the endurance to withstand constant travel and frequent attacks. Douglass was the first ex-slave to become a full-time lecturer for the Society.

Immediately he went on the road. Usually Douglass traveled with John Collins, a veteran white lecturer. They traversed New England in rude coaches or on the railroad, sleeping in abolitionists' homes and speaking in churches, barns, schools, taverns, or on the town green when no building could be found. When Douglass covered a town by himself, racial prejudice was more pronounced and he often had trouble securing a venue and promoting his lecture. This happened at Grafton, Massachusetts, so he walked up and down Main Street ringing a dinner bell and crying out, "*Notice! Frederick Douglass, recently a slave, will lecture on American slavery, on Grafton Common, this evening, at 7 o'clock*" (LT 669). The strategy worked: a large audience came to hear him and the next day a church opened its doors to him.

Douglass also fought prejudice on the railroads. In September 1841, while traveling with Collins on the Eastern Railroad, the conductor kicked him out of the cabin and into the freight car used for blacks. Two weeks later they boarded another Eastern Railroad car at Lynn and again sat together. The same conductor tried to separate them, and this time Douglass stayed put.

The conductor rounded up a half-dozen toughs to "snake out the damned nigger," who ejected them but in the process ripped out the floor bolts and destroyed the seat. Douglass and his comrades continued protesting such segregation, and eventually the Massachusetts railroad companies relented, abolishing Jim Crow cars.[6]

From the beginning Douglass was a great success as a lecturer. This was an era in which public speaking was one of the few forms of entertainment, equivalent to professional sports or popular music today. In these early speeches he talked about his life as a slave, adding levity to the grim subject matter with humor, sarcasm, and mimicry. He dressed formally and paid close attention to how he was seen as well as heard, sometimes asking a sexton to turn up the gaslights so that people could see him better. He referred to his back being "covered with scars" and sometimes bared it, but to protect himself he withheld the names of his former masters and the locations where he had toiled (FDP 1:3). Since Garrisonians opposed violent resistance, he downplayed his fighting prowess and his knowledge that power often needed to be met with physical force. Audiences and reporters alike were spellbound by the form and content of his stories. In December 1841, just three months after starting his new career, one journalist effusively described his performance: "This is an extraordinary man. He was cut out for a hero ... He has the 'heart to conceive, the head to contrive, and the hand to execute.' ... As a speaker he has few equals" (LW 1:48).

Douglass's performances yielded results. He toured Rhode Island in late 1841, helping to give black men the vote under the state's constitution. His success in Rhode Island highlighted the fine line that existed between public opinion and law. Increasingly, Douglass wanted to couple moral suasion with political action to achieve the desired ends.

In 1843 Douglass and a group of lecturers embarked on an ambitious One Hundred Convention Tour that began in New Hampshire and then moved west through Vermont, upstate New York, and down into Pennsylvania, Ohio, and Indiana. The performers traveled in pairs, though at times Douglass was left to abolitionize a town all by himself. In Buffalo, the venue was a deserted old post office and his audience a handful of cab drivers, whips in hand and dirt covering their clothes. When Douglass's white colleague saw these "ragamuffins" he took the first steamer to Cleveland without even bothering to give a lecture, leaving Douglass to "do" Buffalo alone (LT 674). Douglass spoke every day in the ramshackle old post office to audiences that "constantly increased in number and respectability." Within two weeks his listeners had grown from 5 to 5,000 and no venue was large enough to hold them. His last Sunday there he spoke in the park to one-third of the city's population, the power of his word inspiring the multitude.

The western leg of the One Hundred Convention Tour did not go so well, however. At Pendleton, Indiana, Douglass came as close as he ever would to being murdered. During the first day's meeting, a mob threatened to attack them. As a result, Pendletonians banished the abolitionists to the woods, where they built a platform from which to speak. On the second day some thirty backwoods boys, led by a young tough in a coonskin cap, attacked Douglass and his co-lecturers.[7]

The thugs tore down the speaking platform and hit one abolitionist in the mouth, knocking out several teeth. Another lecturer, William A. White, a recent Harvard graduate and a new convert to abolitionism, suddenly disappeared. Douglass, thinking White was in serious danger, picked up a club and went after the thugs. He knew he was violating Garrison's principle of nonviolence and the racial code that said a black man should never attack a white man. But he didn't care; such principles were irrelevant when a comrade's life was in danger. Now the thugs were out for murder: "Kill the nigger, kill the damn nigger," a few of them yelled. Douglass fled for his life, but the gang leader overtook him and clubbed him, breaking Douglass's hand and knocking him down, and then raised his club for another blow, this one aimed at Douglass's head. But White, who had not been hurt and saw Douglass fall, came to the rescue, body-blocking the tough and stopping "his murderous pursuit." Other gang members began pummeling White, until the townspeople, who had been watching, broke up the riot.[8]

Despite such bonds of comradeship, Douglass felt that most white abolitionists were not immune to the prejudice that blanketed the country. He received about half the pay of white lecturers even though he was the most effective speaker in the organization. His white colleagues treated him as a spectacle or symbol rather than as a person: "I was generally introduced as a *'chattel'* – a *'thing'* – a piece of southern *'property'* – the chairman assuring the audience that *it* could speak" (MB 366). He hated the way some of his white colleagues patronized him: just "give us the facts," John Collins told him; "we will take care of the philosophy" (MB 367). "People won't believe you ever was a slave, Frederick, if you keep on this way," another white colleague warned. "Better have a *little* of the plantation manner of speech than not; 'tis not best that you seem too learned."

Such advice felt like a slap in the face. Some of this tension was a result of envy. The backlash occasionally took racist forms, from public reprimands to one private letter from a leading Boston abolitionist that referred to Douglass as "an unconscionable nigger."[9]

These ignoble examples should not diminish the heroic interracial efforts that led to the abolition of Jim Crow cars in Massachusetts, or the state's repeal in 1843 of a ban on black–white marriages. Abolitionists accomplished what few people in American history have been able to do: integrate parts of society. One hundred years later, segregation and anti-miscegenation laws would remain facts of life in American society.[10]

In one sense, Douglass's colleagues were right to try to contain him. By 1844, after steeping himself in such authors as Byron, Burns, Shakespeare, Carlyle, Emerson, and Milton, he sounded nothing like a slave and audiences began accusing him of never having been one. Not giving details about where he came from further fueled doubts about his authenticity and threatened his career. And so he "threw caution to the wind" and wrote his life story, naming names, dates, places, creating a rogue's gallery from his days as a slave on the Eastern Shore of Maryland and in Baltimore (LW 1:59). Having rehearsed his life story for years on the lecture circuit, he knew what to say and how to say it, and he completed the manuscript during the winter months of 1844–45. When his friend Wendell Phillips, another brilliant orator, read it, he told Douglass that if he were him he "would throw it into the fire" (MB 368).[11]

Douglass ignored the advice. In May 1845 the American Anti-Slavery Society published *Narrative of the Life of Frederick Douglass, An American Slave, Written by Himself*, with introductions by Garrison and Phillips that vouched for its veracity. Selling for fifty cents, it was a hard-hitting, lyrical, and ironic page-turner that soon became an international bestseller. Within three years it went through 11,000 copies in the United States and nine editions in Britain, and by 1850 30,000 copies had been sold. Reviewers in Britain and Ireland lauded its "native eloquence," and one American reviewer called it "the most thrilling work which the American press ever issued – and the most important" (LW 1:60). Douglass became, like his new hero Lord Byron, famous almost overnight.[12]

But with fame his freedom was now in great jeopardy. Numerous slave-owners in Baltimore and on the Eastern Shore, including his masters Thomas and Hugh Auld, read the *Narrative*, despite laws prohibiting its circulation in Maryland and elsewhere in the South. The Aulds were out-raged by Douglass's portraits of them. Thomas publicly called Douglass a liar and Hugh sought revenge, vowing to "spare no pains or expense in order to regain possession of him" and "place him in the cotton fields of the South."[13]

But Douglass was already safe in the British Isles when Hugh issued his threat. He fled there three months after publishing his narrative, seeking "refuge from republican slavery in monarchical England," as he put it (MB 370). He spent almost two years in England, Ireland, and Scotland, speaking to ever-larger audiences about the nature of American slavery and gaining thousands more converts to the cause.

Douglass fell in love with England and came close to staying there permanently. He made a number of close friends, was feted by the British public, and for the first time in his life experienced an absence of racism. From "the instant I stepped upon the shore and looked into the faces of the crowd around me, I saw in every man a recognition of my manhood, and an absence, a perfect absence, of everything like that disgusting hate with which we are pursued in" America, he said (FDP 2:59). He could walk into a hotel, restaurant, or railcar without causing a fracas. And he could pass someone on the street without prompting a look of scorn. He went so far as to suggest that being black was a social advantage in Britain: "I find I am hardly black enough for British taste, but by keeping my hair as woolly as possible I make out to pass for at least half a Negro at any rate," he half-jokingly wrote one friend (LW 1:136). And he began to treat August 1, the anniversary of British West Indian emancipation, as more sacred than the Fourth of July.

Douglass did not turn a blind eye to Britain's social problems, however, especially its rampant poverty. He realized that while social stratification in America stemmed primarily from racial distinctions, in Britain it came from class; and he forged alliances with Chartists, who advocated equal rights for the poor and laboring classes. He also acknowledged that the absence of racism stemmed in large part from the fact that so few blacks lived there.[14]

The British Isles highlighted for Douglass problems in America. He came to believe that the greatest obstacle to abolitionism was neither the wealth generated by slavery, nor the Constitution and laws defending it, but the horrible prejudice against blacks. Racism enabled slave-owners to feel good about themselves; it purged any guilt that came from treating humans as oxen and sex objects.

What finally convinced Douglass to return to the United States was his sense of duty to his fellow blacks and his desire to end the scourge of racism. "I have no love for America," he announced (FDP 2:60). "I have no patriotism. I have no country." But in loving England he did not hate America: "I love humanity all over the globe." What he hated were American laws, churches, newspapers, and legislatures that defended slavery. While he was abroad the United States had annexed Texas as a slave state and made war with Mexico in order to acquire more slave territory. Douglass wanted to destroy these bulwarks of oppression, wanted to rip the Constitution into "a thousand fragments" and rebuild the government from the ground up in order to fulfill the principles of freedom and equality in the Declaration. He wanted, in short, to import into America some of the humanity he had witnessed in England.

When Douglass arrived in Boston on April 20, 1847, he was a new man. He was legally free, for his British friends had purchased his freedom. He was famous throughout Britain and America. And he was ready to move to

Rochester to start a newspaper, away from the influence of his former employer.

The news of his intended move outraged Boston abolitionists. Garrison, who considered Douglass his protégé and found out about it second hand, felt like a spurned lover and never forgave him. The rift widened to include most other Boston abolitionists, who already considered Douglass an apostate. They had opposed the purchase of his freedom because it recognized the right "to traffic in human beings" and compromised abolitionist principles (LW 1:72). They had wanted Douglass to publicly "disown" his manumission.[15] Now they considered it "absurd" for an ex-slave, "brought up in the very depths of ignorance," to pretend that he could be a successful editor (MB 390). A fugitive orator who bared his back to shocked audiences was one thing; an editor who enlightened educated readers on the principles of liberty, justice, and humanity was something else entirely!

New Affiliations

Douglass's newspaper, *The North Star*, was a four-page weekly modeled on Garrison's *Liberator*. He borrowed from his former mentor by employing a punchy, fast-paced and physical style. But where Garrison was unrelenting in his attacks, Douglass loved irony, humor, and ambiguity, and so his prose sounded more genteel. In content too Douglass both borrowed from and moved beyond his mentor. Like *The Liberator*, *The North Star* sought universal emancipation and black uplift without ignoring other reform movements such as women's rights, temperance, and labor. But whereas Garrison downplayed politics, Douglass foregrounded it. In its variety of content and voices, *The North Star* imagined a new community that transcended the nation-state and envisioned "all rights for all," which later became the paper's motto.

Douglass had no experience as a printer and editor and initially struggled as a journalist. He received considerable support in Rochester, a hub of political abolitionism and feminism. His office became a central stop on the Underground Railroad: according to one estimate, he helped about 400 fugitives gain their freedom. He gave an eloquent speech in support of female suffrage at the first women's rights convention in 1848 at Seneca Falls, sixty miles from Rochester. "I know of no place in the Union where I could have located at that time with less resistance or received a larger measure of sympathy and cooperation," he said.[16]

Despite community support, *The North Star* initially floundered. Aside from his lack of experience as an editor, Douglass faced a number of hurdles. One was that he failed to enlist as many black subscribers as he had hoped. Another, greater, obstacle stemmed from factions within the abolitionist movement coupled with resentment from former white allies. *The North Star* sought to bridge the divide between Garrisonian nonresistance and the Liberty Party and attract readers from both groups. It was wholly independent in an age in which most papers were aligned with a specific party or association. As a result, neither group provided the necessary base of support. On top of this, Douglass's former Boston colleagues boycotted his paper, and a few went so far as to write letters to Douglass's British friends instructing them *not* to subscribe.

Despite these trials, Douglass slowly established a base of influential readers. Harriet Beecher Stowe and Lucretia Mott were early subscribers, as was Lady Byron, the poet's widow. New friends from upstate New York signed on, as did old friends from Britain.

Two friends in particular set Douglass on the path to financial security. One was Julia Griffiths, an Englishwoman who had helped purchase his freedom. After learning that his paper was in jeopardy, she moved to Rochester to help. She had a brilliant business sense and raised thousands of dollars by organizing antislavery fairs, making personal appeals for money and subscriptions, and creating a crucial base of support among women readers. She also taught Frederick the art of editing, marking up his editorials "with careful blue-penciling." Soon he learned how to write quickly and confidently without mistakes. "Think what editing a paper was to me before Miss Griffiths came," he remarked a few years later. "I had not learned how to spell; I wrote slowly and under embarrassment – lamentably ignorant of much that every schoolboy is supposed to know."[17]

If Julia Griffiths taught Douglass grammar and business skills, then Gerrit Smith transformed his political views and remade his paper. From Peterboro, near Syracuse, Smith was one of the nation's wealthiest men and greatest philanthropists. He had helped found the Liberty Party and gave away about $8 million worth of land and other assets, mostly to poor blacks ($600 million in today's currency). A few days after Douglass launched his paper, Smith welcomed him to the state with a gift of forty acres and soon began sending money. He seemed almost instinctively to know when Douglass needed help, for timely letters arrived with a check for $100 here or $200 there. He was unlike any other white man that Douglass had met, for he listened to blacks, trusted them, empathized with them, and respected what they had to say. While Garrison had treated Douglass like a son, Smith became a friend and ideal colleague. Douglass found that he could argue with and oppose Smith on important issues without recrimination.[18]

The Constitution was one such issue. When they met, Douglass still clung to the Garrisonian belief that the Constitution was proslavery and corrupt. In fact Garrison publicly burned it, calling it "a covenant with death" and "an agreement with hell." But Gerrit Smith endorsed it as a thoroughly antislavery document. He and a few other theorists argued that natural law, or God's law, was incompatible with slavery and thus overrode any human law that defended it. Instead of reading the Constitution from the perspective of the *past*, and thus having to deal with the long tradition of proslavery laws emerging out of it, they tried "to discern what the Constitution *might* be."[19]

Smith's interpretation of the Constitution was more than utopian; it was anarchic. It dispensed with seventy years of legal precedent. And it encouraged people to fit the Constitution into their preconceived beliefs and define natural law according to their own laws.[20]

Initially Douglass called Smith's constitutional argument crazy. In 1849 he admitted that the Constitution, "strictly construed," was not proslavery (LW 1:352). But he emphasized that the Framers had made it a slaveholding weapon. Smith's constitutional doctrine viewed government as "nothing better than a lawless mob, acting without any other or higher authority than its own convictions" (LW 1:375). For if a government could ignore the original intentions of its Constitution "in one point, it may do so in all." There would be "no limit, or safety, or certainty" in how the Constitution was interpreted and applied. Douglass was wedded to a model of law based on original intent (LW 1: 376).

That changed over the next two years. Douglass frequently debated Smith on their different conceptions of law, and by early 1851 Douglass came around to Smith's view. "I am sick and tired of arguing on the slaveholders' side of [the Constitution]," he said (LW 2:149–50). He still believed that the Framers intended certain guarantees for slavery, even if most of them had hoped for slavery's ultimate extinction. No matter. He was ready to "fling to the winds" the Framers' intentions and legal precedent. Now he worried only about the *morality* of creating your own legal rules "to defeat the wicked intentions of our Constitution makers." Smith put these worries to rest, effectively telling him that the law was "*always becoming*," in a state of constant evolution. Douglass loved this conception of law, for he too was always becoming, remaking himself.[21]

A few months later, in June 1851, he turned his paper into an organ of Smith's National Liberty Party, the successor of the Liberty Party, and changed its name to *Frederick Douglass' Paper*. The partnership made excellent sense, for Smith offered financial security through monthly subsidies in return for greater exposure of his party's platform. And Douglass retained considerable autonomy.

Meanwhile, William Lloyd Garrison felt betrayed when he found out about Douglass's embrace of political abolitionism. "There is roguery somewhere," he announced, and he immediately struck *Frederick Douglass' Paper* from the list of approved papers he sent his readers (LW 2:54). Garrison and his Boston colleagues openly accused Douglass of selling his soul and prostituting his mind to Smith's purse-strings. Initially Douglass ignored this slander and tried to patch up their differences, but eventually he lashed back.[22] For the next decade, the man he had once worshipped, and who had done so much for his early career, refused to speak to him.

The Compromise of 1850

Significantly, Douglass's constitutional conversion coincided with the Compromise of 1850, a series of six laws passed by Congress that were intended to solve the sectional crisis over slavery. The Fugitive Slave Act was the most outrageous part of the Compromise of 1850. Replacing the previous law of 1793, it denied suspects the right to a jury trial or even a hearing before a judge, and it excluded their testimony. It appointed special commissioners, who were authorized to send the suspect immediately into slavery "without stay or appeal." And commissioners received a bonus for condemning suspects to bondage ($10 instead of only $5 for finding them innocent). Any and all citizens in a community could be called on to hunt down alleged fugitives, subject to a $1,000 fine if they refused. Anyone caught aiding a fugitive faced a fine and prison term.[23]

The law transformed public opinion in the North. It made free soil "hunting ground for southern kidnappers"[24] and convinced countless Northerners that they could no longer wash their hands of slavery. It inspired Harriet Beecher Stowe to write *Uncle Tom's Cabin*, whose impact was so profound that President Lincoln reportedly called Stowe "the little woman who wrote the book that started this great war." And it sparked a mass exodus of Northern blacks to Canada. A number of influential Northern statesmen, including William Seward, Salmon P. Chase, and Charles Sumner, called the law unconstitutional and urged people to resist it.[25]

Douglass's response to the Fugitive Slave Law created a considerable stir. In 1852 he was invited to the National Convention of the Free Soil Party, which sought to prevent the spread of slavery into the territories. He announced, to much applause and laughter: "The only way to make the Fugitive Slave Law a dead letter is to make half a dozen more dead kidnappers" (FDP 2:390). When he added that "slaveholders not only forfeit their right to liberty, but to life itself," the applause became more solemn.

If slavery was a kind of living death, as Douglass had sometimes suggested, he now demanded Old Testament retribution. The "lines of eternal justice" needed to be brightened with the blood of tyrants (FDP 2:391). This was God's law, he argued; and when human laws destroyed human rights, God's government needed to be erected in its place. He referred to Gerrit Smith's constitutional doctrine and said he was "proud to be one of [Smith's] disciples" (FDP 2:392).

Douglass downplayed his militancy when speaking to women, however. A month before his Pittsburgh talk, Rochester's Female Anti-Slavery Society had invited him to deliver the 1852 Fourth of July Address. His speech that day is probably his best known, and rhetorically it is masterful, employing a "double reversal." He opens by comforting his mostly white listeners, many of whom were women, making them feel proud and hopeful about "your nation" (FDP 2:360). The pronoun "your" foreshadows the sudden shift in tone that comes midway through: "What have I, or those I represent, to do with *your* national independence?" (FDP 2:367). And then for the next hour he berates them, dramatizing the national sins of slavery and racism. The second reversal comes near the end: "I leave off where I began, with *hope*," he says (FDP 2:387). The speech is a jeremiad, a song of lament seeking to *restore* the ideals of the Founders. But unlike his other great speeches of the era, there is no talk of retribution or of killing kidnappers.[26]

Radical Abolitionism

In late June 1855 Douglass acted on his revolutionary rhetoric. At City Hall in Syracuse, he helped found the Radical Abolition Party, the successor of the National Liberty Party. In many respects Radical Abolitionists grew out of the same tree that created Lincoln's Republican party that same year: the conservative branch of the Liberty Party evolved into the Free Soil Party, which grew into the Republican Party; and the radical branch of the Liberty and National Liberty Parties became the Radical Abolition Party. Both parties hated slavery, but Republicans, believing that the Constitution protected slavery in the states, advocated its nonextension, while Radical Abolitionists urged an end to it everywhere.

The Radical Abolition Party was aptly named. At its inaugural convention, members embraced immediate and universal abolition; full suffrage for all Americans regardless of sex or skin color; the redistribution of land so that no one would be rich and no one poor; and violent intervention against the Slave Power. And they relied on "pentecostal visitations" (messages from God) to help them pave the way to their new free world.[27]

A few hundred people attended the convention, including three close friends of Douglass. Gerrit Smith, the party's chief organizer, was there. So was John Brown, a lean, grey-eyed fifty-five-year-old militant whom Douglass had befriended soon after moving to Rochester. James McCune Smith was the third friend present. A frequent contributor to Douglass's newspaper, he was the nation's foremost black intellectual and its first black physician. Like Douglass, McCune Smith had lived in Britain, having received his BA, MA, and MD degrees from the University of Glasgow after being rejected by American colleges owing to his race. McCune Smith chaired the convention, itself a revolutionary act, for the next time a black man chaired a national political convention was in 1988.[28]

The party's true colors emerged during John Brown's speech. A year earlier the Kansas–Nebraska Act had become law, repealing the Missouri Compromise and opening Northern territories to slavery. It effectively turned Kansas into a battleground between proslavery and antislavery emigrants. In his speech Brown quoted Hebrews 9.22, reminding his listeners that "without the shedding of blood there is no remission of sin." He appealed for money and guns to bring with him to Kansas, and his speech electrified his listeners. Most members agreed that armed resistance was "the only course left to the friends of freedom in Kansas," prompting Douglass to ask for contributions, which yielded Brown about $60 and a few guns.[29]

The fruits of this convention could be seen a year later, when Radical Abolitionists again met at City Hall in Syracuse to nominate candidates. Gerrit Smith became the party's presidential candidate and Douglass was nominated as Vice President. A Smith–Douglass ticket did not carry, though, partly because both men were New Yorkers, and the delegates, needing geographic diversity, elected Samuel McFarland of Pennsylvania as Smith's running mate. Douglass and his comrades were under no illusions that Smith could get elected. In fact Douglass supported the Republican John C. Frémont, the dashing young western explorer and California's first senator. Even Gerrit Smith supported Frémont, giving him $500. Their immediate goal was to agitate against slavery, help elect Frémont, and push Republicans toward a more radical antislavery stance.

The convention was again quite spirited, for six days earlier (May 22) Charles Sumner, the abolitionist senator from Massachusetts, had been bludgeoned almost to death on the Senate floor by Preston Brooks, an arrogant young congressman from South Carolina. Sumner had been quietly working at his desk when Brooks, who had been drinking, entered the Senate chamber and without warning began pummeling Sumner on the head with a cane made out of gutta-percha, a heavy wood with the density of lead. He hit him so hard his cane snapped in two. Sumner, blinded by blood and trapped at his desk that was bolted to the floor, valiantly struggled to rise and ripped the desk from the floor before collapsing. The provocation for the attack was Sumner's recent "Crime against Kansas" speech, which accused slaveholders of raping the virgin soil of Kansas. Brooks was defending Southern honor, and people throughout the South were now sending him commemorative canes, silver pitchers, and gold plates for a deed well done.[30]

Things were even worse in Kansas. Missouri "Border Ruffians" and other Southerners were fighting a terrorist war against antislavery emigrants. On May 21, the day before Sumner's beating, about 750 Border Ruffians, many of them drunk, attacked the town of Lawrence, an antislavery stronghold. They destroyed the newspapers, burned and looted homes, and blew up the Free State Hotel. Some of them carried flags or banners that said "Southern Rights," "THE SUPREMACY OF THE WHITE RACE," and "ALABAMA FOR KANSAS."[31]

Civil war had begun in Congress and Kansas.

Radical Abolitionists called for immediate retaliation. Frederick Douglass summarized the prevailing mood of his party: liberty "must either cut the throat of slavery or slavery would cut the throat of liberty," he announced to great applause.[32]

These were precisely the sentiments on which John Brown had acted four days earlier, soon after learning about the assault on Sumner and the sack of Lawrence. On the night of May 24, he and seven men, including four sons and a son-in-law, entered the proslavery settlement along Pottawatomie Creek, and hacked to death with broadswords five unarmed settlers. One victim was decapitated and another's windpipe "entirely cut out."[33]

Frederick Douglass knew that Brown had gone to Kansas to be a warrior and had encouraged him to go. When he eventually found out the details of the Pottawatomie massacre, he morally justified Brown's actions by saying it was "a terrible remedy for a terrible malady," not unlike "the execution of a murderer" (LT 744). In a brutal environment one needed to be brutal or die.

As for the legal justification of their warfare, Radical Abolitionists relied heavily on the writings of former president John Quincy Adams. As early as 1836, in response to belligerent Southerners, Adams had argued that Congress and the President, under the war powers clauses of the Constitution, could end slavery in the states. Douglass and Radical Abolitionists latched onto this interpretation of war powers, but with a crucial revision: they defined *slavery* as a state of war. This meant that Congress and the president were obliged to free the slaves right now and end the civil war raging in the slave states. But since they did nothing, it was the "highest obligation" of the people of the free states to make war on slavery in order to preserve the peace and save the Union.[34]

Radical Abolitionists were only the first group to act on Adams's constitutional use of war powers. Immediately after Confederate troops fired on Fort Sumter in April 1861, Charles Sumner, who had been Adams's protégé, walked as fast as he could to the White House (he had only recently recovered from his beating) and told Lincoln "that under the war power the right had come to him to emancipate the slaves." Union generals John C. Frémont,

David Hunter, and Benjamin Butler also tried to use the war-power theory in their military campaigns. Congress drew on the same source to pass the Confiscation Acts of 1861 and 1862, which authorized the Union army to confiscate (and in the case of the 1862 Act, to emancipate) slaves of disloyal masters. And of course Lincoln issued the Emancipation Proclamation by the power vested in him "as Commander-in-Chief of the Army and Navy of the United States *in time of actual armed rebellion* against authority and government of the United States, and *as a fit and necessary war measure* for suppressing said rebellion." Frederick Douglass and his comrades had established an important precedent.[35]

In less than twenty years, Douglass had evolved from an unknown slave to become the most famous black man in the Western world, a household name, and one of the nation's greatest orators and writers. The American Anti-Slavery Society, British and Rochester abolitionists, the National Liberty Party, and the Radical Abolition Party were in essence his family, school, and community, nurturing his talent and ambition. From them he learned how to use words as weapons and to promote weapons with words. Language (specifically rhetoric) became his coat-of-arms, protecting him from the scourge of racism in the country. And Douglass's words, not the bloodshed of the Civil War, ultimately ended slavery. He and his comrades articulated an antislavery interpretation of the Constitution that grew in influence and popularity until it became military law and was then enshrined in the Constitution.

Douglass transformed himself with the nation. He is the preeminent self-made man in American history, but his understanding of self-making differed dramatically from its popular usage today. Beginning in the 1850s, one of his signature speeches was called "Self-Made Men," which he delivered over fifty times. He revised it as he evolved, but the heart of the speech described how men and women could better their condition through luck and pluck, environment, and self-reliance coupled with reliance on God. The *goal* of self-making, however, was to improve society rather than get rich. While it might be comforting to imagine a heaven that was free from all wars and wrongs, real self-made men waged war on evil "so that the will of God may be done on earth as in heaven" (FDP 3:291). In remaking the self, you reformed society and worked tirelessly to realize a heaven on earth.

NOTES

1. William E. Cain, ed., *William Lloyd Garrison and the Fight Against Slavery: Selections from* The Liberator (Boston: Bedford Books, 1995), 72 (quoted); Henry Mayer, *All on Fire: William Lloyd Garrison and the Abolition of Slavery* (New York: St Martin's Press, 1998), 112 (quoted).

2. John Stauffer, *The Black Hearts of Men: Radical Abolitionists and the Transformation of Race* (Cambridge, MA: Harvard University Press, 2002), 117–18; Richard H. Sewell, *Ballots for Freedom: Antislavery Politics in the United States, 1837–1860* (New York: Oxford University Press, 1976), 101–6.
3. Mayer, *All on Fire*, 120 (quoted).
4. "Communications. Great Anti-Colonization Meeting in New-Bedford," *The Liberator*, March 29, 1839.
5. Mayer, *All on Fire*, 306 (quoted).
6. *Ibid.*, 307 (quoted); William S. McFeely, *Frederick Douglass* (New York: W. W. Norton, 1991), 92–93.
7. *Ibid.*, 108–12.
8. William A. White, "The Hundred Conventions," September 22, 1843, *The Liberator*, October 13, 1843 (quoted).
9. Edmund Quincy to Caroline Weston, July 2, 1847, Boston Public Library, reprinted in Robert K. Wallace, "Douglass, Melville, Quincy, Shaw: Epistolary Convergences," *Leviathan: A Journal of Melville Studies* 6:2 (October 2004): 64.
10. David Brion Davis, *Inhuman Bondage: The Rise and Fall of Slavery in the New World* (New York: Oxford University Press, 2006), 260.
11. LW 1:59 (quoted); MB 217 (quoted).
12. McFeely, *Frederick Douglass*, 116–17.
13. Dickson J. Preston, *Young Frederick Douglass: The Maryland Years* (Baltimore, MD: Johns Hopkins University Press, 1980), 170–74, 230n24.
14. Richard Bradbury, "Frederick Douglass and the Chartists," in *Liberating Sojourn: Frederick Douglass and Transatlantic Reform*, eds. Alan J. Rice and Martin Crawford (Athens: University of Georgia Press, 1999), 169–86.
15. Quoted from Tyrone Tillery, "The Inevitability of the Douglass–Garrison Conflict," *Phylon* 37:2 (1976), 137–49 at 142.
16. Benjamin Quarles, *Frederick Douglass* (1948; reprint, New York: Da Capo, 1997), 119; Howard W. Coles, *The Cradle of Freedom: A History of the Negro in Rochester, Western New York and Canada* (Rochester, N. Y: Oxford Press, 1943), 127 (quoted).
17. *Ibid.*, 158 (quoted); Quarles, *Frederick Douglass*, 87.
18. Stauffer, *Black Hearts*, 155–58, 160–62; LW 2:210.
19. Cain, *William Lloyd Garrison* , 36 (quoted); William M. Wiecek, *The Sources of Antislavery Constitutionalism in America, 1760–1848* (Ithaca, NY: Cornell University Press, 1977), 18 (quoted), 27–39, 205–27, 249–75.
20. Stauffer, *Black Hearts*, 38–39.
21. Robert Cover, *Justice Accused: Antislavery and the Judicial Process* (New Haven, CT: Yale University Press, 1975), 6 (quoted).
22. Douglass to Gerrit Smith, May 21, 1851, Gerrit Smith Papers, Syracuse University.
23. Allan Nevins, *Ordeal of the Union*, Vol. 1: *Fruits of Manifest Destiny, 1847–1852* (1947; reprint, New York: Collier Books, 1992), 380–82 (quotation from 381).
24. *Ibid.*, 36.
25. *Ibid.*, 386; Joan D. Hedrick, *Harriet Beecher Stowe: A Life* (New York: Oxford University Press, 1994), vii.
26. One reason why "What to the Slave Is the Fourth of July?" is so well known is because it lacks the militancy of his other great speeches of the era. White Americans like their black heroes virtuous and nonviolent.

27. *Proceedings of the Convention of Radical Political Abolitionists* (New York: Central Abolition Board, 1855), 3, 44–45; Stauffer, *Black Hearts*, 8–14, 22–27.

28. Stauffer, *Black Hearts*, 10; Peter Boyer, "Ron Brown's Secrets," *New Yorker*, June 9, 1997, 67.

29. Richard J. Hinton, *John Brown and His Men* (New York: Funk and Wagnalls, 1894), 19; "Radical Political Convention," *National Anti-Slavery Standard*, July 7, 1855; Stauffer, *Black Hearts*, 13–14.

30. David Herbert Donald, *Charles Sumner*, Part 1 (1960; reprint, New York: Da Capo Press, 1996), 293–94.

31. David S. Reynolds, *John Brown, Abolitionist* (New York: Alfred. A. Knopf, 2005), 156–57.

32. Frederick Douglass, quoted in *Radical Abolitionist* 1:12 (July 1856): 100.

33. *New York Herald*, June 8, 1856 (quoted); Reynolds, *John Brown*, 154–57, 171–73.

34. Stauffer, *Black Hearts*, 26.

35. David Herbert Donald, *Lincoln* (New York: Simon and Schuster, 1996), 388 (quoted); Lincoln, "Final Emancipation Proclamation," in *Abraham Lincoln: Great Speeches* (New York: Dover, 1991), 99 (quoted).

2

ROBERT S. LEVINE

Identity in the Autobiographies

Douglass published three autobiographies during his lifetime – *Narrative of the Life of Frederick Douglass, An American Slave* (1845), *My Bondage and My Freedom* (1855), and *Life and Times of Frederick Douglass* (1881, 1892). The first of the autobiographies draws considerably on the conventions of the slave narrative; the second and third are more expansive autobiographies, though still somewhat indebted to the slave narrative tradition of describing in documentary fashion the journey from slavery to freedom. But Douglass is no mere documentary realist. Most notably in his accounts of his resistance to the slave-breaker Covey, he tells the same story differently in his autobiographies, depending on the larger truths he wishes to underscore at the time of composition. Douglass's autobiographical narratives provide a rich resource for his biographers, as well as for historians of slavery, abolitionism, and the politics of race in nineteenth-century American culture. Perhaps most importantly, they provide insights into Douglass's evolving sense of his representative identity and his artistry of self-presentation. In all of the autobiographies, Douglass skillfully crafts an image of himself as a heroic black man and a model for the race, whose energy, will, and intelligence helped him to rise from his obscure origins in slavery to become the representative black leader of his time. But there are also mysteries of identity in the autobiographies, a sense that he never quite knows or comes to terms with his racial or private identity. Thus Douglass is constantly in the process of reinventing himself. Identity is never stable in Douglass; it is tied to the contingencies of the historical moment and to the problematics (and challenges) of the autobiographer's art.[1]

The *Narrative*

Nowhere are these problematics more apparent than in Douglass's first autobiography, the *Narrative*, which draws most fully on the conventions of the slave narrative. Because slave narratives were nearly always published by white abolitionists, the critic John Sekora has argued that they can best be understood as "white envelopes" with "black messages" – texts in which black voices and perspectives are constrained or "enveloped" by the white sponsors.[2] There are clear indications that Douglass himself was concerned about the constraints placed on his first autobiography by William Lloyd Garrison, the white abolitionist who "discovered" him in New Bedford in 1841, signed him on as a lecturer in his Massachusetts Anti-Slavery Society, and published the *Narrative* in 1845. Douglass would formally break with Garrison in 1851, and in his 1855 *My Bondage and My Freedom* he elaborates his political differences with the man. But he also makes clear in his second autobiography that even when aligned with the Garrisonians, he felt that Garrison and his white colleagues condescended to him in urging him simply to "*narrate* wrongs" in his speeches, while he "felt like *denouncing* them" (MB 367). In the *Narrative* Douglass does much more than narrate wrongs. He also displays his ability to analyze the events he describes, presenting slavery in the United States as a powerful cultural force that makes resistance on the part of the slaves an overwhelming if not impossible prospect. At the same time, Douglass presents himself as a sort of black Benjamin Franklin, a master of self-reliance, whose hard work, energy, and creativity help to lift him from slavery to freedom. As in all of his autobiographies, he also depicts himself in spiritual terms as a black leader who shares traits with Moses, Jeremiah, and Christ. But even in this first autobiography, supposedly constrained by his white sponsors, Douglass reveals his confusions about his personal identity, his indebtedness to the black slaves for his knowledge about slavery, and his Romantic desires for a spiritual connection to nature in ways that have little to do with the burden of black Garrisonian leadership that he takes up in the *Narrative*'s closing scene.

The *Narrative* begins with prefatory testimonials by the white abolitionists Garrison and Wendell Phillips, suggestive of the classic "white envelope" of the conventional slave narrative. Garrison focuses on his first encounter with Douglass in August 1841 at a Garrisonian antislavery meeting in Nantucket, Massachusetts. Although he condescendingly asserts that Douglass needs "nothing but a comparatively small amount of cultivation to make him an ornament to society and a blessing to his race" (N 4), for the most part he celebrates Douglass's magnificent oratorical abilities, his links to the American Revolutionary tradition, and his aura of having been "consecrated" (N 3) by God for the antislavery struggle. Phillips offers similar high praise, terming the *Narrative* a "declaration of freedom" (N 12) in the tradition of the Declaration of Independence.

There is much in the *Narrative* that follows up on Garrison's and Phillips's representation of Douglass as an exemplary black leader in the spiritual tradition of consecrated Biblical patriarchs and in the political tradition of American Revolutionaries. But Douglass begins his autobiographical narrative in the understated and somewhat conventional way of the slave narrative, with the simple documentary statement: "I was born in Tuckahoe, near Hillsborough, and about twelve miles from Easton, in Talbot county, Maryland" (N 15). There is nothing in the opening chapter about representative leadership, nothing about his heroic rise from slavery to freedom. Instead, there are confessions of dislocation and confusion. Douglass knows that his father is white but is unsure of exactly who he is; he barely knows his mother and barely grieves when he learns of her death; he is not even sure of his age. Anticipating (or influencing) Harriet Beecher Stowe's efforts to link white readers to black slaves by showing how slavery undermines the family, Douglass crafts this understated opening so that he sounds as much like an orphan out of a Charles Dickens novel as a former slave narrating his life history. His anger remains beneath the surface (there are no David Walker-like declamations against slavery in these opening paragraphs), and it is only at the end of the first chapter that he depicts one of the "bloody scenes that often occurred on the plantation" (N 20), describing how he watched his master Aaron Anthony whip his Aunt Hester in a scene that disturbingly hints at rape. Through the circular structure of the opening chapter, from birth to rape, Douglass to a certain extent enacts his discovery of how he came into being, as his very existence depended (so this dramatic moment suggests) on the rape of his mother (a blood relative of Hester) by a master who may in fact have been Anthony. Fear, anxiety, guilt, and uncertainty about identity, racial or otherwise, mark this opening chapter.[3]

In the next several chapters, Douglass displays his analytical abilities, as he describes not only his own childhood on Colonel Lloyd's slave plantation but also the workings of the institution of slavery itself, such as the slaves' need to use deceit on a daily basis and the psychological interdependencies of the white masters and black slaves. By evincing his own powers of reflection, Douglass draws on Scottish commonsense traditions in order to demonstrate, against the grain of the emerging racist science of the period, and the Garrisonians' own racialist paternalism, that blacks are just as capable as whites of rational thought and feeling.[4] But Douglass's account of the murder of the resistant slave Demby, who is instantly shot dead for disobeying the overseer Gore, exhibits the equally large truth that, as desirous as the slaves may be of achieving their freedom, slavery functions as a total institution offering virtually no hope for those who choose resistance.[5]

Drawing on the tradition of the spiritual autobiography, Douglass suggests that one reason he does not suffer the fate of a Demby is that God tests him with afflictions but ultimately watches over him.[6] Although the *Narrative* is indebted to Benjamin Franklin's autobiography in tracing Douglass's eventual escape to freedom by dint of hard work, there is an equally powerful effort on Douglass's part to represent himself as a spiritual leader who, in the manner of Moses and Christ, has been consecrated by God. The centrality of the providential to his rise is underscored when Douglass describes how he is sent from Maryland's Eastern Shore to Baltimore, where, like Franklin after moving from Boston to Philadelphia, he has new opportunities for agency and mobility. As he explains to his readers, he regards the seeming happenstance that he, of all of the slaves, was chosen for Baltimore as "the first plain manifestation of that kind providence which has ever since attended me" (N 36). That said, Douglass's exemplifications of Franklinian forms of uplift, self-making, and possessive individualism remain crucial to the limning of his identity in subsequent chapters.[7] Like Franklin, Douglass learns through imitation, trickery, and hard work, teaching himself to read and write after Hugh Auld forbids his wife, Sophia, to continue with her lessons. Though he proclaims that he sometimes "envied my fellow-slaves for their stupidity" (N 42), he assumes a leadership role when he is back on the plantation, where, in the spirit of Franklin, he sets up his own school, and, in the spirit of Patrick Henry, attempts to lead a revolutionary escape. Foiled in his efforts, he is sent back to Baltimore, where, again like Franklin, he hopes to lift himself by making money as a caulker, only to see his wages turned over to his master. When he escapes to the North, he embraces Franklinian ideals of free labor even as he confronts the realities of white racism and soon takes up his consecrated role as black abolitionist leader.

And yet Douglass's identity is more complicated than the Franklinian/consecrated leadership narrative might suggest. Although he generally presents himself as superior to the illiterate blacks, he remarks early, and importantly, in the *Narrative* that his first intimation of the evil of slavery came not when he watched his Aunt Hester being whipped, and not when he began to read abolitionist writings in *The Columbian Orator* (1797), but rather when, as a child, he listened to his fellow slaves sing their sorrow songs. It is to those songs, he says, that "I trace my first glimmering conception of the dehumanizing character of slavery ... Those songs still follow me, to deepen my hatred of slavery, and quicken my sympathies for my brethren in bonds" (N 24). Here, the slaves teach Douglass and not the other way around. To be sure, he depicts himself as an exceptionally self-reliant man when he uses defensive force to rebel against the slave-breaker Covey. But in that well-known scene, which Douglass sets up by stating "you shall see how a slave was made a man" (N 60),[8] he is not completely on his own (and in accounts in the subsequent autobiographies, he does emphasize the help of his fellow slaves). After Douglass displays his brutalized body to the unmoved Thomas Auld, it is the slave Sandy who gives him a root that supposedly will protect him from further assaults from Covey. Though Douglass rejects the superstition and eventually fights back primarily on his own, the solidarity offered by Sandy clearly has helped to strengthen his resolve.

In addition to disclosing his indebtedness to the slaves, Douglass expresses his more private longings in a manner that is not completely in accord with his presentation of himself as a representative leader. Just prior to rebelling against Covey, he gazes at the sailboats on the Chesapeake Bay and delivers his great apostrophe on mobility and freedom:

> You move merrily before the gentle gale, and I sadly before the bloody whip! You are freedom's swift-winged angels, that fly round the world; I am confined in bands of iron! O that I were free! ... O God, save me! God, deliver me! Let me be free! Is there any God? ... There is a better day coming. (N 59)

Alternating between hope and despair, between appeals to God and to his godly inner divinity, Douglass in this crucial passage in effect writes into being his own divine individuality. This is Douglass at his most Emersonian, with the spiritual expressiveness working against the portrait of Douglass as the single, representative black leader. In true Emersonian fashion, his desires for freedom are disconnected from the mechanics of social reform, focusing instead on the self, but with the implication that the self as imagined here speaks to the larger Godhead shared by all of the slaves (and indeed all of humanity).[9]

Douglass concludes the *Narrative* with his discovery of William Lloyd Garrison. In turn, Garrison discovers Douglass, and the *Narrative* comes full circle, as Douglass assumes the identity of black abolitionist that Garrison had celebrated in his prefatory remarks. In the final paragraph of this first autobiography, Douglass tells of being inspired by his reading of Garrison's antislavery newspaper, *The Liberator*, to attend "an anti-slavery convention at Nantucket, on the 11th of August, 1841," the very convention Garrison refers to in his prefatory remarks. While there, Douglass feels moved to participate, and though still thinking of himself as a slave amidst white people, he speaks for "a few moments," suddenly experiencing "a degree of freedom." That freedom reveals to him his new vocation and aspects of the representative identity that have been an important part of the *Narrative*: in the manner of Jeremiah, he speaks out against the evils of slavery; and in the manner of Christ, he takes up the "severe cross" to become a black antislavery leader at whatever the price. In the final sentence of his first autobiographical narrative, he presents himself as a Moses-like black leader who has been working in tandem with Garrisonian abolitionists since 1841 in order to help lead his people to freedom: "From that time until now, I have been engaged in pleading the cause of my brethren – with what success, and with what devotion, I leave those acquainted with my labors to decide" (N 96). Still, despite the congruence here between his and Garrison's conception of his role as a black Garrisonian abolitionist, there is a tense irresolution in the overall *Narrative* as Douglass attempts to speak both with and through such an identity. The confused sense of genealogical relations of the opening chapter, the fraternal connections he feels toward the black slaves when they sing their sorrow songs, the liberatory possibilities that he perceives in literacy, and the Romantic yearnings expressed in the Chesapeake apostrophe all suggest a Douglass who cannot easily be constrained, or explained, by the identity that is highlighted at the close of the *Narrative*.

My Bondage and My Freedom

Within two years of the publication of the *Narrative*, Douglass would begin the process of breaking with Garrison by choosing to publish his own newspaper, *The North Star*, against Garrison's objections. As he reports in the 1855 *My Bondage and My Freedom*, in the early 1850s he publicly declared his belief in the antislavery nature of the US Constitution (Garrison had argued that it was proslavery), his commitment to political abolitionism (Garrison had argued against participating in the electoral process), and his conviction of the limits of Garrisonian moral suasion in a culture that actively does violence to blacks (MB 391–92). He would therefore need to represent himself as something other than a Garrisonian abolitionist in any subsequent autobiography. In the account of his defensive but still violent resistance to Covey, and in his habit throughout the *Narrative* of offering analysis of the events he describes, Douglass had already begun to stray from the fold, and in *Bondage* he asserts in the strongest possible terms the importance of blacks taking the leadership role in the interrelated struggle for black elevation in the North and the liberation of the slaves in the South (MB 398). As the Exodus-inspired title of his second autobiography might suggest, he crafts his identity as a black Moses in accord with a more insistently racialized vision of his connections to the larger African American community.

In the introduction to *Bondage*, for instance, the free black physician and political philosopher James McCune Smith hails Douglass as "a Representative American man" (MB 132), but he also very specifically emphasizes Douglass's role as a black leader whose "energy, perseverance, eloquence, invective, sagacity, and wide sympathy ... [are] indebted to his negro blood" (MB 136). Much more than in the *Narrative*, which presents Douglass as relatively distant from his black genealogical roots, Douglass in *Bondage* depicts himself as inspired by his mother. The woman who is barely mentioned in the

Narrative is presented in the second autobiography as a model of hard work, intelligence, and "earnest love of knowledge" (MB 156) – a figure who also helps Douglass to advance his message to his free black readers on the importance of temperance.[10] Challenging white racists' claims that classical civilizations were exclusively white, he even connects his mother to ancient royalty. Remarking on her "deep black, glossy, complexion" (MB 152), Douglass, long after her death, notes resemblances between his mother and the image of an Egyptian king in James Cowles Prichard's *The Natural History of Man* (1845). With a good deal of pride, then, he states:

> I am quite willing, and even happy, to attribute any love of letters I possess, and for which I have got – despite of prejudices – only too much credit, *not* to my admitted Anglo-Saxon paternity, but to the native genius of my sable, unprotected, and cultivated *mother* – a woman, who belonged to a race whose mental endowments it is, at present, fashionable to hold in disparagement and contempt.
>
> (MB 156)

He writes with pride about other blacks in the slave South as well, such as the rebellious Nelly, whose physical resistance to the cruel overseer Sevier anticipates (and arguably helps to influence) his own resistance to Covey, and the religious Uncle Lawson, who helps him with spiritual matters.

But it is the emphasis on his mother's intelligence that best speaks to another important aspect of Douglass's changing rhetorical aims in the representation of his identity in *Bondage*. In the *Narrative* he had defied the Garrisonians by analyzing and not simply describing key events; and in *Bondage* he is even more insistent on analysis, which is why the second autobiography is nearly four times longer than the first, even though it contains only a few chapters that move beyond the chronological endpoint of the *Narrative*. Much of the added material displays Douglass as a thinking, reflective being whose representative intelligence, as Douglass himself says in his prefatory remarks, confutes white racist notions that blacks are "naturally, inferior; that they are *so low* in the scale of humanity, and so utterly stupid, that they are unconscious of their wrongs, and do not apprehend their rights" (MB 106). That reflective voice contributes to a change in the narrative texture of the second autobiography as well. Instead of describing his journey from slavery to freedom in its full immediacy, Douglass now regards that journey from his perspective as an intellectual black leader of the 1850s, and thus depicts himself as a subject in history who himself can be critically examined. This revised historical perspective is signaled right from the start in the titles of the opening three chapters: "The Author's Childhood," "The Author Removed from His First Home," and "The Author's Parentage." There is also much self-quotation from the *Narrative* in *Bondage*, along with self-conscious remarks on those passages, so that here, too, Douglass could make clear that the independent black leader of the 1850s is somewhat different from the Garrisonian author of the 1840s. For instance, when he works with his earlier account of the providential nature of his removal to Baltimore, he intersperses the original passage with his more "adult" sense that in his 1845 rendition he may have over-emphasized the "consecrated" status that Garrison had insisted on in his preface. Putting past and present into dialogue, he writes:

> I may be deemed superstitious and egotistical, in regarding this event as a special interposition of Divine Providence in my favor; but the thought is a part of my history, and I should be false to the earliest and most cherished sentiments of my soul, if I suppressed, or hesitated to avow that opinion, although it may be characterized as irrational by the wise, and ridiculous by the scoffer. (MB 213)

What comes across in this playful look at himself in history is that the greatest scoffer of all may be the more mature Douglass of 1855.

Douglass not only revises and reflects upon individual passages in the *Narrative*, he also changes whole scenes so that they would better accord with his revised identity as a post-Garrisonian leader who has developed even closer connections to the blacks that he hopes to inspire. In his account of his rebellion against Covey, for example, Douglass portrays himself as considerably more skeptical of Garrisonian nonviolence: "[I]f he [the slave] kills his master, he imitates only the heroes of the revolution" (MB 248). Douglass does not go so far as to kill his master, but when he fights back, he depicts himself as engaged in more than simply self-defensive violence, giving Covey's cousin Hugh a blow "which fairly sickened my youthful assailant" (MB 284). Douglass also presents this key moment of resistance (as he would in *Life and Times*) as no longer about his individual manly heroism but rather about working in tandem with the slave Caroline and the black hired man Bill Smith in overcoming Covey. "We were all in open rebellion, that morning" (MB 285), he says. This sense of black solidarity extends to subsequent chapters, as Douglass refers to the slaves on Freeland's plantation as "a band of brothers" (MB 320) and later, in the North, speaks of his desire to work with his "sable brothers" (MB 398). Douglass may well be a representative leader along the lines of a black Moses, but in the 1855 revision of his life story he de-emphasizes his exceptionality and points to the important influence of black women (his mother, Nelly, and Caroline) and black men on his emergence as a representative black leader.

And yet, as in the *Narrative*, there are complications and dislocations in the identity that Douglass has crafted in *Bondage*. He may well think of himself as a Mosaic leader in fraternal relation to his fellow blacks, but there are numerous mentions of his homelessness, rootlessness, and continued Romantic yearnings consistent with the Chesapeake apostrophe that he reprints in *Bondage*. Douglass may align himself with his mother, but that does not mean he has a strong sense of familial identity. "Slavery does away with fathers, as it does away with families" (MB 151), he writes, with the implication that he will always be orphaned. Bereft of a family, he presents himself, even as a slave, as desirous of transcendental meaning beyond the merely material. As a boy, he is fascinated by a ladder ascending to an "upper apartment" of his grandmother's "log hut, or cabin" (MB 141) and loves the relative freedom of running wild on the plantation; as a young man, he revels in the imaginative freedom opened up by reading and (as in his Chesapeake apostrophe) finds himself yearning after "the smiles of nature" which he finds "in every calm, ... in every wind, and ... in every storm" (MB 227). When he eventually escapes, he happily describes himself "in a flying cloud or balloon, (pardon the figure,) driven by the wind" (MB 349), though as the figure suggests, the happy access to mobility comes with a sense that he lacks agency and that freedom itself may be illusory, resembling a "quick blaze, beautiful at the first, but which subsiding, leaves the building charred and desolate" (MB 350). Douglass conveys despair and confusion in a letter that he sends to Garrison from England and reprints in *Bondage*: "I have no end to serve, no creed to uphold, no government to defend; and as to nation, I belong to none" (MB 372). To a certain extent Douglass recuperates his identity when he agrees to be purchased by a benefactor, thus giving him the freedom to return to the United States to work for black uplift and emancipation. But even as he speaks to that mission, he mystically invokes Psalms 68:31, "'Ethiopia shall yet reach forth her hand unto God'" (MB 398), in a way that subsumes his identity to a larger black diaspora taking little heed of nation and representative leadership. The Ethiopianism at the end of *Bondage* looks forward to the sympathetic embrace of Haiti at the end of the expanded 1892 edition of *Life and Times*, where Douglass similarly suggests an uncertainty about national allegiances and vocation.

Life and Times

Twenty-six years after *My Bondage and My Freedom*, Douglass published a new, updated version of his autobiography, *Life and Times of Frederick Douglass*, which attempted to shore up his identity as an African American leader. The 1881 autobiography covers some of the same ground as the *Narrative* and *Bondage*, and then provides hundreds of pages on Douglass's public activities from the 1850s to 1880. In the spirit of James McCune Smith's

1855 introduction to *Bondage*, the African American jurist George
L. Ruffin writes in his introduction that Douglass is "a self-made man"
(LT 470) whose life "has been a complete vindication of the colored
people," particularly their potential to attain "high intellectual position"
(LT 472). Though Ruffin characterizes *Life and Times* as a success story, it
is important to note that by 1881 Douglass had been much vilified, by
whites and blacks alike, for his involvement with the Republican Party. The
most prominent African American political appointee in post-Civil War
Republican administrations, Douglass was criticized by senator Charles
Sumner and others for supporting president Ulysses S. Grant's failed efforts
to annex Santo Domingo during the early 1870s. A few years later, after
accepting the presidency of the Freedman's Bank, he became the scapegoat
when that institution went bankrupt. In the third version of his autobiography, which was probably motivated by a desire for self-vindication,
Douglass discusses his role on the Santo Domingo commission and his
presidency of the Freedman's Bank, depicting himself as a thoroughgoing
patriot whose love of country goes hand in hand with his desire to see the
elevation of his black brethren.

The identity Douglass rhetorically fashions for himself in *Life and Times*,
then, has multiple facets: he continues to present himself as both a representative and an exemplary African American whose life history confutes
notions of black inferiority and offers a model for black uplift. As in the
earlier autobiographies, he continues to present himself as an intellectual
who does not simply recount events but analyzes them as well. What is new
to the 1881 *Life and Times* is Douglass's emphasis on his identity as a loyal
national subject. Consistent with this aim, Douglass portrays himself as an
instant and unwavering supporter of the presidency of Abraham Lincoln,
despite having published numerous essays in his newspaper castigating
Lincoln for his seeming racism and his willingness to capitulate to the
South. Although he had written in the September 1861 *Douglass' Monthly*
that "unless a new turn is given to the conflict, and that without delay, we
might as well remove Mr. LINCOLN out of the President's chair, and
respectfully invite JEFFERSON DAVIS or some other slaveholding rebel to
take his place,"[11] in the 1881 *Life and Times* Douglass depicts the new
president as a heroic liberator, who, from the moment he was elected, sought
"to exclude slavery from the territories of the United States ... with a view to
its ultimate extinction" (LT 766). Douglass may have been under attack
during the 1870s, but Lincoln, as presented in *Life and Times*, regarded
Douglass as one of the great men of the age. According to Douglass, Lincoln
remarked during their first interview in the White House that "there is no
man in the country whose opinion I value more than yours" (LT 804). In the

vivid account of the Lincoln–Douglass relationship in *Life and Times*, it is Douglass who plays the key role of bringing black troops into the Union army, and it is Douglass who ensures that Lincoln will remain true to the emancipatory aims of the Civil War. In the wake of Lincoln's assassination, Douglass essentially attempts to assume the mantle of the most celebrated leader of the time.[12]

In this spirit, Douglass presents himself during the post-Civil War years as embodying Lincoln's principle of malice toward none (even as he is regularly subjected to the malice of others). Amidst his accounts of his political squabbles of the 1870s, Douglass describes two moving moments with his former owners and their families. As William L. Andrews has argued, these sentimental postbellum accounts provide models of interracial reconciliation (something that simply was not happening in the culture) by underscoring that whites and blacks alike were victimized by slavery and now had an equal stake in recuperating the South as an integral part of the US nation.[13] Both are deathbed scenes in which whites declare their antislavery beliefs, along with their admiration (and affection) for Douglass. In the first of these scenes, the now-married daughter of Lucretia Auld, who was seven or eight when Douglass escaped from slavery, tells Douglass of how she has long treasured his account in the *Narrative* of her mother. Touched by an interview in which a white woman says she is "ready to die" now that she has seen the former slave of her father, Douglass declares: "I esteem myself a good, persistent hater of injustice and oppression, but my resentment ceases when they cease, and I have no heart to visit upon the children the sins of their fathers" (LT 832). Nor does he have the heart to visit resentment upon the fathers themselves. In a powerful chapter on his 1877 meeting with the dying Thomas Auld, Douglass describes a warm encounter between the former master and former slave who at long last can talk honestly with one another. Douglass apologizes to Auld for suggesting in the *Narrative* that Auld had cruelly treated Douglass's grandmother, and Auld declares that had he been in Douglass's position, "I should have done as you did" (LT 877). A great-grandson of Colonel Lloyd also welcomes Douglass during a meeting that leaves Douglass "deeply moved and greatly affected" (LT 880). In the year that the federal government was withdrawing troops from the Southern states and in effect declaring the end of Reconstruction, Douglass uses his identity as race leader and Lincoln-inspired patriot to underscore the continued possibilities for interracial reconciliation.

As hopeful as these scenes may be, Douglass raises fresh questions about his racial and national identity in the thirteen chapters added to the expanded 1892 edition of *Life and Times*.[14] Peter Walker has influentially argued that the reconciliation scenes reveal Douglass's "hopeless secret desire to be white,"[15] but it is worth noting that Douglass once again links his black mother to the image of black African nobility in Prichard's *Natural History of Man*, reasserting the claim that his "love of letters" can be attributed "to the native genius of my sable, unprotected, and uncultivated mother" (LT 484). Race becomes more complicated in the 1892 expanded edition, for in 1884, two years after the death of his African American wife Anna, Douglass married Helen Pitts, a white woman who had worked as his secretary when he was Recorder of Deeds in Washington, DC. The marriage was greeted with considerable controversy: Douglass was attacked by blacks and whites (including Helen's family) for marrying someone outside of his "race." In response, Douglass in the 1892 *Life and Times* aggressively challenged essentialist notions of race, cagily beginning the new section added to the 1881 edition by listing the various questions he is repeatedly asked about his racial status and marriage:

> In what proportion does the blood of the various races mingle in my veins, especially how much white blood and how much black blood entered in my composition? ... Whether I considered myself more African than Caucasian, or the reverse? Whether I derived my intelligence from my father, or from my mother, from my white, or from my black blood?   (LT 940)

The implication of this rhetorical opening is that Americans can address their race problems only after they realize the intellectual and moral bankruptcy of such questions.

As in the earlier chapters of *Life and Times*, Douglass continues to describe his public life as a political appointee and his ongoing work for black elevation. But in the new section these identities come into conflict, as the text culminates with a detailed account of Douglass's diplomatic service in Benjamin Harrison's administration as Minister Resident and Consul General to the Republic of Haiti. Appointed in 1889, Douglass resigned in 1891 after he was accused of deliberately sabotaging US efforts to obtain a naval base in Haiti because of his alleged sympathies for a black nation. Although he insists that as a black man he could be loyal to the United States, Douglass by the end of his account of the controversy seems more sympathetic to Haiti, condemning the United States for its long history of racist paternalism toward the black republic and its "peculiar and intense prejudice against the colored race" (LT 1039). In an 1891 letter to Secretary of State James G. Blaine, in which he effectively resigned from his position, Douglass conveys his hopes that Haiti will have "been able to refuse the lease requested by the United States without effecting our relations to that great country."[16] The "our" of that letter is ambiguous, and anticipates the remarkable closing sentence of the 1892 *Life and Times*:

> I have been the recipient of many honors, among which my unsought appoint-
> ment by President Benjamin Harrison to the office of Minister Resident and
> Consul-General to represent the United States at the capital of Haïti, and my
> equally unsought appointment by President Florvil Hyppolite to represent Haïti
> among all the civilized nations of the globe at the World's Columbian
> Exposition, are crowning honors to my long career and a fitting and happy
> close to my whole public life. (LT 1045)[17]

In the final sentence of his final autobiography, Douglass puts his US and
Haitian honors in an equivalent balance, and thus to some extent suggests a
collapse of key aspects of his representative identity as a US nationalist and
leader of African Americans. That "collapse" is anticipated in chapters just
prior to his account of his diplomatic work in Haiti, when Douglass describes
a tour of England, France, Italy, Greece, and Egypt that he undertook from
October 1886 to May 1887 with his wife, Helen. The tour, he says, had "an
ethnological purpose" (LT 1006), insofar as he sought to find evidence of
racial hybridity in Europe that would counter what he terms "the steady
march of the slave power toward national supremacy since the agonies of the
war" (LT 981). But in his account of his travels, he does something more than
simply offer lessons about race. In Egypt, at age seventy, he climbs "to the top
of the highest Pyramid" (LT 1012), where he achieves a sublime vision of the
"millions on millions that lived, wrought, and died there" (LT 1013); and
then upon returning to Rome, he contemplates the limits of human ambition
and power in a manner consistent with what he intimated in Egypt:

> The lesson of the vanity of all things is taught in deeply buried palaces, in fallen
> columns, in defaced monuments, in decaying arches, and in crumbling walls; all
> perishing under the silent and destructive force of time and the steady action of
> elements, in utter mockery of the pride and power of the great people by whom
> they were called into existence. (LT 1015)

In the final chapters of Douglass's 1892 autobiography, and thus at the
conclusion of his cycle of autobiographies, he hints at the limits of his
representative identity as race leader, the vanity and futility of human actions,
the tenuousness of nations and institutions, and the mocking reality of death.
On the level of sheer politics, Douglass also seems dumbfounded in 1892 by
the persistence of white supremacy and notions of race over the nearly fifty
years from his first to his last autobiography. Whether he is gazing at the
Chesapeake or imagining himself in a balloon with no set destination, there
are complexities of desire and anxiety that inform all of the autobiographies
and suggest the possibility of the imminent collapse of any particular construction of identity at any particular moment. In that light, perhaps the most
heroic aspect of Douglass's efforts to write himself into being as a heroic black

leader is his faith in writing itself. There is something Whitmanian in his perpetual inventions and reinventions of the identity that we have come to call Frederick Douglass. Like Whitman, the contradictory Douglass contains multitudes and secrets and waits for us to assume what he had assumed.

NOTES

1. For discussions of representativeness in Douglass's writings and politics, see Waldo E. Martin, Jr., *The Mind of Frederick Douglass* (Chapel Hill: University of North Carolina Press, 1984), 253–78; Wilson J. Moses, "Where Honor Is Due: Frederick Douglass as Representative Black Man," *Prospects* 17 (1992): 177–89; Robert S. Levine, *Martin Delany, Frederick Douglass, and the Politics of Representative Identity* (Chapel Hill: University of North Carolina Press, 1997); and John Stauffer, "Frederick Douglass's Self-Fashioning and the Making of a Representative American Man," in *The Cambridge Companion to the African American Slave Narrative*, ed. Audrey Fisch (Cambridge: Cambridge University Press, 2007), 201–17. On connections between slave narratives and the art of autobiography, see Robert S. Levine, "The Slave Narrative and the Revolutionary Tradition of American Autobiography," in *The Cambridge Companion to the African American Slave Narrative*, ed. Fisch, 99–114.
2. John Sekora, "Black Message / White Envelope: Genre, Authenticity, and Authority in the Antebellum Slave Narrative," *Callaloo* 32 (1987): 482–515.
3. For a different reading of the scene that emphasizes Douglass's alliance with Anthony, see Jenny Franchot, "The Punishment of Esther: Frederick Douglass and the Construction of the Feminine," in *Frederick Douglass: New Literary and Historical Essays*, ed. Eric J. Sundquist (Cambridge: Cambridge University Press, 1990), 141–65. On gender and sexuality, see also Hester Blum, "Douglass's and Melville's 'Alphabets of the Blind,'" and David Van Leer, "A View from the Closet: Reconcilable Differences in Douglass and Melville," both in *Frederick Douglass and Herman Melville: Essays in Relation*, ed. Robert S. Levine and Samuel Otter (Chapel Hill: University of North Carolina Press, 2008), 257–78, 279–99.
4. On the importance of Scottish commonsense philosophy to Douglass as a philosopher of race, see Maurice S. Lee, *Slavery, Philosophy, and American Literature, 1830–1860* (Cambridge: Cambridge University Press, 2005), 93–132.
5. Arthur Riss argues that the *Narrative*, which is generally taken as a paradigmatic liberal text, also develops a counter-narrative on the limits of personal action and self-definition; see *Race, Slavery, and Liberalism in Nineteenth-Century American Literature* (Cambridge: Cambridge University Press, 2006), esp. 164–69.
6. For a discussion of connections between the spiritual narrative and the slave narrative, see Yolanda Pierce, *Hell without Fires: Slavery, Christianity, and the Antebellum Spiritual Narrative* (Gainesville: University of Florida Press, 2005).
7. On the influence of Franklin on Douglass's autobiographical writings, see Rafia Zafar, "Franklinian Douglass: The Afro-American as Representative Man," in *Frederick Douglass: New Literary and Historical Essays*, ed. Sundquist, 99–117.
8. For an important discussion of how the valorization of Douglass's exceptionality contributes to a "critical valorization of physical struggle" (205) in the slave narrative, at the expense of different strategies developed by female authors, see

Deborah E. McDowell, "In the First Place: Making Frederick Douglass and the Afro-American Narrative Tradition," in *Critical Essays on Frederick Douglass*, ed. William L. Andrews (Boston, MA: G. K. Hall & Co., 1991), 192–214.

9. On the influence of Emerson on Douglass, see Stauffer, "Frederick Douglass's Self-Fashioning," 205.

10. On the importance of temperance and black elevation to Douglass's conception of his identity in *Bondage*, see Levine, *Martin Delany, Frederick Douglass*, 99–143.

11. Douglass, "The Progress of the War," *Douglass' Monthly* 4 (September 1861): 513.

12. For comprehensive accounts of the Douglass–Lincoln relationship, see James Oakes, *The Radical and the Republican: Frederick Douglass, Abraham Lincoln, and the Triumph of Antislavery Politics* (New York: W. W. Norton & Company, 2007); and John Stauffer, *Giants: The Parallel Lives of Frederick Douglass and Abraham Lincoln* (New York: Twelve, 2008).

13. William L. Andrews, "Reunion in the Postbellum Slave Narrative: Frederick Douglass and Elizabeth Keckley," *Black American Literature Forum* 23 (1989): 5–16. On the importance of sentimentalism to Douglass's other autobiographies, see Stephanie A. Smith, "Heart Attacks: Frederick Douglass's Strategic Sentimentality," *Criticism* 34 (1992): 193–216; and Elizabeth Barnes, "Fraternal Melancholies: Manhood and the Limits of Sympathy in Douglass and Melville," in *Frederick Douglass and Herman Melville*, ed. Levine and Otter, 233–56.

14. Though the title page, reproduced in the Library of America volume, lists the publication date as 1893, the expanded *Life and Times* was published in fall 1892.

15. Peter F. Walker, *Moral Choices: Memory, Desire, and Imagination in Nineteenth-Century American Abolition* (Baton Rouge: Louisiana State University Press, 1978), 247.

16. Douglass to James G. Blaine, June 27, 1891, in *A Black Diplomat in Haiti: The Diplomatic Correspondence of US Minister Frederick Douglass from Haiti, 1889–1891*, ed. Norma Brown, 2 vols. (Salisbury, NC: Documentary Publications, 1977), 2:244.

17. On Douglass and Haiti, see Ifeoma Nwankwo, *Black Cosmopolitanism: Racial Consciousness, National Identity, and Transnational Ideology in the Americas* (Philadelphia: University of Pennsylvania Press, 2005), 129–52; and Robert S. Levine, *Dislocating Race and Nation: Episodes in Nineteenth-Century American Literary Nationalism* (Chapel Hill: University of North Carolina Press, 2008), 200–18.

3

SARAH MEER

Douglass as Orator and Editor

Major developments in communications unfolded in the mid-nineteenth-century United States, and Frederick Douglass played a central part. The demand for both lectures and newspapers escalated rapidly between 1800 and 1850, aided by improvements in education and technology, including steam presses, railways, and better roads. The status and numbers of editors and lecturers grew to match. Both lectures and newsprint fed an increasing need for information and opinion, and celebrity in one was often linked to appearances in the other.[1] Douglass's pre-eminence in these two great nineteenth-century media would have made him remarkable even without his autobiographies; they also comprised the "great schools" in which Douglass's contemporary Jan Marsh Parker said Douglass received his education: "Methodism, Garrisonianism, Journalism, Political Campaignism."[2]

Douglass's rhetorical ability was exceptional even in an age when politics, churches, revivals, and the great reform movements of the 1840s (not the least of which was the antislavery campaign) produced charismatic speakers. All over New England and far into the West, town lyceums held winter lecture courses, and by the 1840s the lyceum circuit drew huge audiences and provided a lucrative living for professional lecturers.[3] Douglass distinguished himself first in the pulpit, then as a promoter of abolition, temperance, and women's rights. He became a lyceum star with speeches on topics like "Self-Made Men," "Santo Domingo," and "Our Composite Nationality"; and he gave the first scholarly commencement address by an African American, presenting "The Claims of the Negro Ethnologically Considered" at Western Reserve College in 1854.[4] In this, and in speeches on the denial of literacy to slaves, Douglass not only challenged the racial assumptions of his contemporaries, but, in James Perrin Warren's words, cleared "a cultural space in which [African Americans could] speak and write."[5]

Douglass was also a central figure in the antislavery press, itself part of an American newsprint explosion. In the first half of the nineteenth century, American consumption of newspapers awed foreign visitors, and so did the huge number of titles: as many as 3,000 by 1860.[6] The outpouring was attributed to a democratic interest in public affairs, and to the exigencies of an expanding nation, where practical men did not have time to read more substantial material. In the tradition of Benjamin Franklin, prominent nineteenth-century editors included Noah Webster, William Cullen Bryant, Charles A. Dana, Horace Greeley, Walt Whitman, and Margaret Fuller. The antislavery movement and the press also shared a martyr in Elijah P. Lovejoy, the editor of the *Alton Observer* murdered by an Illinois mob in 1837 for publishing an abolitionist paper.

Perhaps because Douglass's complete runs of *The North Star* and *Frederick Douglass' Paper* were destroyed by fire in 1872, and the papers are relatively inaccessible in print, Douglass's newspaper work has received much less attention than his speeches and lectures. Nevertheless, from 1847 until well into the 1860s, Douglass's lecturing and editing were inextricably linked – financially, as Douglass's star-power as an orator helped underwrite the costs of publishing his papers, and intellectually, as ideas and interests migrated from one enterprise to the other. Moreover, Douglass's newspapers reveal the speeches as enmeshed in broader antislavery conversations: in the cumulative concerns of correspondents' reports, readers' letters, and comments on other papers, we glimpse not a lone orator, but a thinker engaged in a dense discursive context.

Douglass as Orator

Many African Americans were impressive speakers in the mid-nineteenth century, both as participants in antislavery campaigns and as preachers and general reformers, among them Sojourner Truth, Samuel Ward, Charles Remond and J. W. C. Pennington. Some appearances offered as much spectacle as eloquence, like Henry Brown's stage demonstrations of the box in which he had himself mailed out of slavery, but many elicited something like the "electrical" effect Harriet Beecher Stowe attributed to Sojourner Truth.[7] Even beside his contemporaries, however, Douglass was recognized as extraordinary.

Black churches were a formative influence on the young Douglass; he himself became a Sabbath school leader and later preached at the African Methodist Episcopal Zion Church in New Bedford.[8] He also practiced debating with free black companions in Baltimore, and the first book he bought was Caleb Bingham's *The Columbian Orator* (1797), a late eighteenth-century primer that inculcated public speaking skills alongside literacy and republican values. These rhetorical influences helped form Douglass as a speaker, and also as a writer.[9]

Although he had already preached in New Bedford, Douglass's debut before a white audience took place at Nantucket in August 1841. He gave three speeches in the course of a two-day antislavery meeting, and was asked at the close to become a full-time lecturer for the Massachusetts Anti-Slavery Society. Douglass later spoke of the sense of freedom this accolade brought him, and within a few months he was discussing racial prejudice in the North, moral suasion versus politics, the dissolution of the Union, and the immorality of returning escaped slaves. In just a few years he would be on Irish platforms discussing calls for the repeal of that country's union with Great Britain, and in Scotland protesting at the Free Church of Scotland's connection with proslavery churches in the United States. These topics not only reflect Douglass's independence (he rejected white colleagues' urging to restrict himself to the "facts," while they took care of the "philosophy"), they also suggest how much Douglass's public speaking contributed to his intellectual development. The antislavery work was intensely stimulating to this intelligent and self-educated young man: "I was now reading and thinking. New views of the subject were presented to my mind ... I was growing, and needed room" (MB 367).

Contemporary accounts of these early speeches marvel at Douglass's physical presence at the podium. The recurring term "manly" registers not only a strong sense of Douglass's masculinity (what one critic goes so far as to call "sex-appeal"[10]) but in the 1840s had a class connotation as well: part of Douglass's impact, and one of the reasons why some listeners found it hard to believe that he had been a slave, was his gentlemanly demeanor. Even in the free states, Douglass's polish amounted to a political argument in itself – against segregation and prejudice, as well as slavery. As the *Salem Register* put it: "He was a living, speaking, *startling* proof of the folly, absurdity and inconsistency (to say nothing worse) of slavery. Fluent, graceful, eloquent, shrewd, sarcastic, he was, without making any allowance, a fine specimen of an orator" (LW 2:55).

Although Douglass was initially hired to produce graphic accounts of life as a slave, he was soon forging arguments indebted both to the neoclassical literary taste of *The Columbian Orator* and his mentor William Lloyd Garrison, and to the techniques of repetition, parallelism, and contrast that he had learned from the preachers.[11] Homely imagery and diction were deployed along with apocalyptic hyperbole and denunciation. Above all, Douglass was a mesmerizing performer – by turns amusing, indignant, and bitterly sarcastic, adroitly eliciting humor and pathos. James Monroe described his most popular set-piece, the "Slaveholder's Sermon," as a "brilliant example of irony, parody, caricature, and *reductio ad absurdam* all combined."[12] At a time when white actors regularly mocked black preachers on the stage, Douglass reversed the mimicry, skewering "the holy tone of the [slaveholding] preacher – the pious snuffle – the upturned eye – the funny affectation of profound wisdom." That keen observation and robust sense of humor were also deployed in his account of the white girl who said she saw heaven in a religious trance, but when asked about its black inhabitants exclaimed, "Oh! I didn't go into the kitchen!"[13]

Douglass himself experienced these kinds of attitudes as an antislavery lecturer, sometimes suffering violent physical attacks by proslavery mobs, and often facing discrimination on transport and in hotels. The job was exhausting: long uncomfortable journeys, away from his family, speaking in halls and tents and out in rainy fields. In Britain between 1844 and 1846, Douglass also struggled against the distrust of antislavery colleagues. During the 1850s, however, lecturing was a vitally important part of his livelihood: after the Civil War, he earned between fifty and a hundred dollars for lyceum appearances. It was also integral to his work against slavery and for civil rights.

Douglass as Editor

Abolitionist papers formed a central part of the struggle, at least as important as lectures and other publications. The activities were closely linked: books, pamphlets, and copies of speeches were advertised in the papers; speeches were reprinted; items in papers were in turn discussed at meetings. In 1853 Wendell Phillips attacked a *Frederick Douglass' Paper* editorial in a speech; the paper reprinted it, along with the piece in question and a comment; *The Liberator* reported on this too (FDP 2:446, 2:449, 2:450). Circulated to readers, such reports brought the public worlds of the meeting and the lecture into the private home. They fostered a sense of shared endeavor and discussion, publishing and commenting on letters, as well as resolutions taken by meetings and items clipped from other papers. These included opponents' newspapers republished for ironic or indignant effect, just as Theodore Weld's 1839 book *American Slavery As It Is* used advertisements from Southern papers to expose the casual brutality of slave-owning society.

Newspapers played a crucial role in Douglass's career. He first gleaned the word "abolitionist" from *The Baltimore American*, and he was a passionate reader of *The Liberator*, the antislavery paper Garrison published in Boston, before he ever heard Garrison speak. In the 1840s, he himself wrote for *The Liberator* and the American Anti-Slavery Society's New York paper the *National Anti-Slavery Standard*. Douglass also assisted the two black editors of *The Ram's Horn*, an antislavery weekly produced in New York in 1847–48.[14] In London he caused an outcry with a letter to *The Times* denouncing the officers who denied him a berth on the *Cambria* despite his first-class ticket. His ambition to start his own paper exacerbated his differences with the Garrisonians, and when his white British supporter Julia Griffiths helped him run it, her presence in the Douglass home caused scandal. After the break with Garrison, *The Liberator* attacked Douglass, and featured items from his paper in the column usually used to deride proslavery editorials: "The Refuge of Oppression."

Since *Freedom's Journal* in 1827, there had been a number of black-run papers, most very short-lived.[15] In 1845–46, Douglass came increasingly to believe he could produce an antislavery paper of his own. Despite the Garrisonians' fears that he would draw black readers from *The Liberator*, in 1847 Douglass moved to Rochester, recruited Martin Delany and W. C. Nell as co-editor and publisher (respectively), and set up *The North Star* with equipment bought by British supporters. The masthead of the first issue proclaimed: "Right is of no Sex – Truth is of no Color – God is the Father of us all, and we are all Brethren." Douglass's format was similar to *The Liberator*'s (and that of other antislavery weeklies). There were four pages of seven columns: the first reported speeches from antislavery meetings, conventions, or to Congress. The second and sometimes the third contained editorial commentary, and the third and fourth included extracts from other sources, announcements, advertisements, letters, and also literary material – reviews, poetry, and serialized novels. Despite constant financial struggles, Douglass's paper would survive for over a decade: renamed *Frederick Douglass' Paper* in 1851, it ran until 1860, and its sister *Douglass' Monthly* from 1859 until 1863. Between 1870 and 1874 he also edited the *New National Era*. William McFeely argues that becoming an editor made Douglass a gentleman, a member of a profession; he asked a correspondent to address him as "Mr. Editor, if you please."[16] John Sekora has shown that the new role also had a significant impact on his 1855 autobiography.[17]

Many contemporaries felt that Douglass was even more effective as an editor than as a speaker (LW 1:93). He was more actively antislavery than other black editors, and a keener advocate for women's rights. He was also more interested than white antislavery rivals in racial uplift, education, and "mental culture" (LW 1:92).[18] In the 1890s, Douglass believed that black editors had "demonstrated, in a large measure, the mental and literary possibilities of the colored race" (LW 4:468). Readers praised his paper not only for speaking for Northern black people, but also for publishing their own words on its letters page.[19] Despite the fact that few of the initial subscribers were African American (and even in 1848, there were five times as many white subscribers on a mailing list of 700), Douglass's contemporaries recognized that the paper was an important institution for African

Americans. Contributor William Johnson pleaded in 1854 that it was "the duty of every colored man and woman to sustain Frederick Douglass and his paper" (LW 1:84).[20] Within a few years of Douglass's beginning his "work [in New Bedford] with my paper," black travelers told him "that they felt the influence of my labours when they came within fifty miles" (LT 708). Philip Foner noted in 1950 that the paper's regular black correspondents from other cities were "an outstanding feature," and for historians "a significant source of information on life among the free Negroes of the United States and Canada" (LW 1:92). Such correspondents must also have inspired pride, strengthened communities, and helped foster a sense of shared African American culture.

In addition, Douglass's papers solidified international networks. There was a long tradition of links between British and American antislavery organizations, but many British activists had a special regard for Douglass, which his papers helped develop into a sense of an international community. The initial funding for the press and many later donations came from British supporters; Griffiths assisted in person between 1849 and 1855. Douglass wrote items specifically addressed "To My British Anti-Slavery Friends," or pointed out what would "be more surprising to my English readers than to Americans" (LW 2:480). From June 1858 Douglass produced a special British edition of *Douglass' Monthly*, for which Griffiths wrote a column called "Letters from the Old Country" (LW 1:91). Douglass also serialized Charles Dickens's novel *Bleak House* in 1852–53, a sign, as Elizabeth McHenry argues, that his paper aimed to foster a sophisticated and enquiring readership, but also evidence of Douglass's international perspective and participation in what Meredith McGill calls the American "culture of reprinting."[21] *Frederick Douglass' Paper* may have reframed Dickens even more radically: in Britain *Bleak House* was accused of harboring an anti-abolition message, but Douglass offered quite a different reading by juxtaposing it with discussions of antislavery novels and speeches.[22]

The scale and variety of Douglass's work as editor was as demanding as his life as an antislavery lecturer. His duties included not just producing and soliciting copy, organizing and editing material, but the physical mechanics of printing – setting type, laying out pages, manning the press, and mailing out – as well as the unrelenting grind and worry of the finances. The papers also increasingly provided a discursive context for the lectures. Douglass's speeches are too often read as heroic exceptionalism, ignoring their relationship to discussions already enjoying a lively airing in reform circles. In *The North Star* and *Frederick Douglass' Paper*, Douglass's antislavery colleagues were exploring the same arguments that emerged in his speeches; they tried similar rhetorical tactics, and sometimes pressed them even further than he did.

The Fourth of July

Probably the most anthologized of Douglass's speeches is the talk he gave at Rochester, New York in July 1852: "What to the Slave Is the Fourth of July?" In its contrast of national ideals and shortcomings, it belongs to the tradition of the American jeremiad. William McFeely has called it "perhaps the greatest antislavery oration ever."[23] It also illustrates the under-examined relationship between Douglass's oratory and his newspapers.

The ironic force of the speech comes from its play with the listener's expectations of July Fourth rhetoric. Douglass rehearses the narrative of the Revolution with a troubling coolness, then holds its celebration, while slavery exists, to be a cruel hypocrisy. Although it would be easier to arouse sympathy by appealing to shared sentiments, the speech insists on the alienation of African Americans from this national story, confronting white listeners with their privilege. Douglass projects a sense of detachment that is only reinforced by the occasional acknowledgment of what he shares with his audience and what comes to seem an ironic repetition of the phrase "fellow-citizens." He asserts that he is "not wanting in respect for the fathers of this republic" (extraordinarily muted praise on such an occasion), but he insistently uses "your," rather than "our," and makes a bitter quip that must have made a nineteenth-century audience wince: "I leave, therefore, the great deeds of your fathers to other gentlemen whose claim to have been regularly descended will be less likely to be disputed than mine!" His allusion to illegitimate descent links the Founding Fathers with unacknowledged children, that word "regularly" a reminder that many African Americans were indeed descended "irregularly" from white Revolutionaries. Although later the speech castigates the American churches for supporting slavery, there is an echo of the preacher admonishing the backslider: "[Y]ou have no right to wear out and waste the hard-earned fame of your fathers to cover your indolence." He compares them to Jacob's children, boasting of their ancestor "when they had long lost Abraham's faith and spirit." The speech's most biting assertion follows: "The rich inheritance of justice, liberty, prosperity and independence, bequeathed by your fathers, is shared by you, not by me. The sunlight that brought light and healing to you, has brought stripes and death to me. This Fourth July is *yours*, not *mine*."[24]

That Douglass implicates his listeners in the speech is striking, and so is the isolation he constructs for himself. By asking him to speak on the national holiday, the Rochester Ladies' Anti-Slavery Society had implicitly recognized its ironies for a former slave. But his questions insist on a distinction between white and black Americans, asserting that while slavery existed African Americans could never fully or comfortably be "fellow-citizens": "[W]hy am I called upon to speak here to-day? What have I, or those I represent, to do with your national independence?" This is performative – Douglass is once again dramatizing his role as "living, speaking, startling proof." But Douglass's grammatical self-positioning in the speech as alone – a single black "I" addressing a white plural "you" – raises interesting questions about his claim to "represent" other African Americans.

In its sense of acute disengagement, "What to the Slave?" has been held to reflect Douglass's 1851 shift from anti-Constitution Garrisonianism to political abolition – the view that the Constitution was a liberating document, and that emancipation could be achieved through the political system. In the speech, Douglass pays Garrison the compliment of quotation (from the first issue of *The Liberator* and Garrison's 1845 poem "The Triumph of Freedom") but he refers the audience to the opposing arguments of Lysander Spooner, William Goodell, and Gerrit Smith, and declares that "the Constitution is a glorious liberty document." This is suggestively ambivalent, just as the speech not only attacks the Fourth and emphasizes Douglass's distance from the Founders, but also praises the Constitution.

What the speech may indicate about Douglass's relationship with the black community is just as striking. Many Northern blacks shared Douglass's new position, particularly as the Northern secession Garrison advocated would have abandoned the Southern slaves. Douglass's editorial activity had also brought him closer to the black community; as James McCune Smith declared, "[O]nly since his Editorial career has he [seemed] to become a colored man!"[25] Nevertheless, it might be speculated that the speech's alienated patriotism, its image of a people who are fully sensible of the inspiring history of an Independence that excludes them, reflects not only the partially severed threads attaching Douglass to the Garrisonians, but also Douglass's incomplete connection with black antislavery networks. David Blight has described Douglass's position in the 1850s as relatively lonely, having to represent "slaves, freedmen and the black elite," while being, as Douglass described the black intellectual, "debarred by his color from congenial associations with whites ... equally cast out by the ignorance of the blacks."[26]

Some of Douglass's rhetoric could be put down to genre. Fourth of July speeches became a tradition after 1776 (there are three in *The Columbian Orator*), and it was quite conventional in them to contrast the Founders' ideals with their unworthy descendants.[27] William Lloyd Garrison made several antislavery Fourth of July addresses, and frequently referred on other occasions to the special hypocrisy that the Fourth of July must represent to a slave. Between 1842 and 1852 Douglass himself had been called to make seven Fourth of July orations. Douglass delivered his talk on July 5 because in 1852 the Fourth fell on a Sunday, but earlier in the century, colonizationists and free blacks had organized "anti-Fourth" protest-celebrations on July 5. Thus Douglass's question, "[W]hy am I called upon to speak here today?" was posed strategically, reframing a familiar problem for an audience who should not need the lesson.

Douglass's Papers on the Fourth of July

Douglass looks far less isolated and his argument less exceptional if "What to the Slave Is the Fourth of July?" is read alongside his newspapers. Long before Douglass's Rochester speech, the Fourth of July was a frequent topic in *The North Star* and *Frederick Douglass' Paper*. Here we glimpse other, more antagonistic audiences that help explain Douglass's confrontational stance in his speech, but we also see that his position was less lonely than he suggested. Indeed, some writers took Douglass's argument further, claiming that as well as slavery, Jim Crow laws (racial segregation) tarnished the celebration. Like Douglass, they expressed ambivalence about American institutions and recognized both the liberating possibilities and the lies gathered up in the idea of the Fourth of July.

Douglass was already calling the Fourth an "anniversary of American hypocrisy" in 1848 ("theirs is a white liberty"), but many other contributors to his papers reflected on the holiday.[28] They denounced "Clap-trap" oratory on the Fourth, lamented America's neglect of black Revolutionaries, and reprinted a speech declaring America would not be free until it had abolished the evils of slavery, alcohol, "bondage" to party or sect, and the "prejudices of complexion, of class and of sex."[29]

Even the painful perspective of Douglass's "What to the Slave?" was pre-empted in an 1848 poem by John Westall, "Feelings of a Slave on the Fourth of July."[30] Where Douglass's speech offers a conventional account of the anniversary's significance before distinguishing his own position with almost a Du Boisian double-consciousness, Westall's poem adopts a relatively simple voice, merely looking on at the "gladness I cannot share" and dreaming of following *The North Star* to freedom. And yet, like Douglass's speech, he hints at a genealogical claim to the American holiday: "Within my veins the proudest blood / Of proud Virginia rolls." This is the same suggestion that Douglass makes more obliquely in his "regularly descended" jibe, and in other respects Douglass's papers demonstrate that he was working variations on themes his paper's readers would have recognized, and perhaps expected.

The North Star even brought the grounds of complaint closer to home. An article on the "Black Laws" of Ohio called the state's constitutional claims "rhetorical flowers employed only to deck the expanding ideas of the Fourth of July orators."[31] This protest against Jim Crow laws takes almost the same tactic Douglass does in his speech, observing that the rhetoric of justice, liberty, and equality falls "as unmeaning sounds upon the ear" when "we find used the word white as the only qualification necessary to possess and enjoy the rights of citizenship." Although Douglass in his great speech had asserted that the Fourth of July belonged only to whites, he did so on the grounds of Southern slavery: this correspondent went much further in attacking the laws of a free state as a mockery of constitutional principles. Equating Northern disenfranchisement with slavery itself, the correspondent compared free blacks with "the slave who dreams pleasantly of liberty and freedom, but awakes to feel more keenly the blow from the driver's lash." Douglass blamed slavery for his distance from his audience; this writer traced slavery's tentacles into Ohio law.

While Douglass's speech presumes a separation from his audience, an 1850 report from Cincinnati gives a sense of a genuinely antagonistic public. Repeatedly heckled by two Louisville men, Douglass surmised that it was a volatile time of year to address the topic of slavery: "[S]o soon after the fourth of July, when the great deeds of our venerated and revolutionary sires were fresh in every man's memory, it was difficult to speak with any force or faithfulness without giving offence to some patriotic souls."[32] Douglass's dry observation here shows how beautifully these two Southerners justify his 1852 speech: if "patriots" are uncomfortable hearing about slavery near the Fourth, if the holiday *is* somehow incompatible with antislavery work, then yes, it represents "white liberty" – "yours not mine."

Even less overtly hostile audiences were tellingly uncomfortable with abolitionist July Fourth speeches: in 1854 Douglass reprinted the *Rochester American*'s argument against antislavery Fourth of July events, which begged that the "glorious Fourth" should not be turned "into a scene of mourning," and rejected "the substitution of an abolition excitement in place of the old and traditional celebration of our National anniversary."[33] Although the writer acknowledged the strength of antislavery feeling, he urged, "Let them have this single day at least for reviewing our past history, for reflecting upon the deeds of our patriotic sires, for contrasting our little past, with our present greatness and power, and for blessing the hand that has led us along so prosperously in the way to National eminence." Written two years after Douglass repudiated the triumphalist model of July Fourth oration, this exemplifies it. Its smugness alone helps explain Douglass's alienated stance in the speech, and its impersonal reference to abolitionists as "them," with an ambiguous relationship to "our," suggests the necessity for his "you" and "your." Douglass's paper retorted that because those "glorious" principles were mocked by the suffering of slave families and fugitives, it was necessary "to meet, in public convocation, and declare eternal hostility to the Anti-Republican system" of slavery. The Fourth of July was "yours," but *Frederick Douglass' Paper* insisted on the black community's right to use the date – and to illuminate their exclusion from it.

Elsewhere, the paper adopted patriotic Fourth of July sentiments wholesale. Celebratory Fourth poems were reprinted from other papers with ironic references to their *"incendiary* ... application to American slavery," or labeled "Is it insurrectionary? and why not?"[34] Despite the sarcasm, these conscriptions of the date to fight slavery seem even more pro-Constitution than the strategy taken in Douglass's speech. "What to the Slave?" rejected the conventional significance of the anniversary, but his paper here appropriates it. This antislavery patriotism, using the Fourth to call for freedom, coexisted in the paper with anti-Fourth abolitionism, a shifting perspective that echoes Douglass's in the 1852 speech, despite his rhetoric of isolation.

On other occasions the paper contrasted the Fourth with August 1, Emancipation Day in the British West Indies. Douglass did not mention the date in his autobiographies until 1892, but his paper documented the anniversary many times. In 1854 the paper rejoiced in a day of processions of black farmers and hairdressers staged in Columbus, Ohio, calling it "a day which looks the 'glorious' fourth completely out of countenance," and a "gala day" compensating for the Fourth, "with all its blood and blackness."[35] The cosmopolitanism of the August celebration – a day of black liberation, rather than a national holiday – was echoed in the 1848 report from a Haitian correspondent, considering the Fourth alongside Haitian festivals, and linking Haiti's independence with the European revolutions of that year.[36]

This internationalist perspective is one of the most striking things about the response of Douglass's papers to a national holiday, and again it predated "What to the Slave?" In his speech, Douglass contrasted American churches' responses to slavery with British ones, and reinforced the cosmopolitan frame of reference in the closing imagery of enlightenment stealing over the globe.[37] In his paper he made similar comparisons. Passing through Ohio's Miami Valley on July 4, 1850, he remembered his trip to Britain: "The trees reminded me of some the best cared-for woods of British noblemen. They needed little labor to make them superior in many respects to the most beautiful in 'Devonshire.'"[38] For an instant, Douglass is tempted towards an egalitarian variety of national pride: "When I thought that this fertile valley is probably owned by the hard-handed farmer, whose neat dwelling and luxuriant fields broke upon me at intervals, and varied the pleasant view, I felt that the people might well celebrate the Fourth of July." But he stops himself with the thought of the Fugitive Slave Law: "I could almost have joined with them, if I were not checked and saddened by the recollection that even this beautiful valley is but common hunting-ground for men – that even *here*, the panting slave may be chased, caught, chained, and hurled back into interminable slavery." Douglass's republican pleasure that the landscape is the work of an ordinary farmer (rather than the duke who owns its British counterpart) is spoilt by the running sore of slavery. Appealing to national feeling, only to confront it with slavery, Douglass bends the British example from a source of shared pride into a political goad. Here, as in Westall's poem and elsewhere, an item in Douglass's papers prefigures part of the 1852 speech.

Reading Douglass's speeches in the context of his newspapers might risk making his material or even his arguments seem less exceptional, as his use of the Fourth of July is revealed to be a standard antislavery tactic, already embedded in public discussions of slavery and the nation. But by seeing Douglass's oratory as part of ongoing discussions between abolitionists and their opponents, we grasp more of his contribution – not only to the antislavery movement, but also to the social, cultural, and political possibilities for African Americans in the United States. Warning Douglass against his newspaper project in 1847, Garrison wrote that it would be "quite impracticable to continue the editor with the lecturer" (LW 1:78). Not only did Douglass show that he could combine the two professions quite as well as Garrison himself, but his newspapers reveal to us a community in the process of creation: demanding freedom for the slaves as the basis of a better society altogether.

NOTES

1. Donald M. Scott, "The Profession that Vanished: Public Lecturing in Mid-Nineteenth Century America," in *Professions and Professional Ideologies in America*, ed. Gerald L. Geison (Chapel Hill: University of North Carolina Press, 1983), 12–28.
2. Quoted in William S. McFeely, *Frederick Douglass* (New York: W. W. Norton, 1991), 167.
3. Carl Bode, *The American Lyceum: Town Meeting of the Mind* (New York: Oxford University Press, 1956); Angela G. Ray, *The Lyceum and Public Culture in the Nineteenth-Century United States* (East Lansing: Michigan State University Press, 2005).
4. David B. Chesebrough, *Frederick Douglass: Oratory from Slavery* (Westport, CT: Greenwood Press, 1998).
5. James Perrin Warren, *Culture of Eloquence: Oratory and Reform in Antebellum America* (University Park: Pennsylvania State University Press, 1999), 132.
6. Frank Luther Mott, *American Journalism: A History of Newspapers in the US through 250 Years, 1690–1940* (New York: Macmillan, 1941), 167.
7. R. J. M. Blackett, *Building an Antislavery Wall: Black Americans in the Atlantic Abolitionist Movement, 1830–1860* (Baton Rouge: Louisiana State University Press, 1983); Daphne Brooks, *Bodies in Dissent: Spectacular Performances of Race and Freedom, 1850–1910* (Durham, NC: Duke University Press, 2006), 66–130.

8. William Andrews, "Frederick Douglass, Preacher," *American Literature* 54 (1982), 592–97; Gregory P. Lampe, *Frederick Douglass: Freedom's Voice, 1818–1845* (East Lansing: Michigan State University Press, 1998), 13, 33–42.

9. Shelley Fisher Fishkin and Carla L. Peterson, "'We Hold These Truths to Be Self-Evident': The Rhetoric of Frederick Douglass' Journalism," in *Frederick Douglass: New Literary and Historical Essays*, ed. Eric J. Sundquist (Cambridge: Cambridge University Press, 1990), 189–204.

10. Terry Baxter, *Frederick Douglass's Curious Audiences: Ethos in the Age of the Consumable Subject* (New York: Routledge, 2004), 135.

11. Ronald K. Burke, *Frederick Douglass: Crusading Orator for Human Rights* (New York: Garland, 1996).

12. James Monroe, *Oberlin Thursday Lectures, Addresses and Essays* (1897), quoted in Lampe, *Freedom's Voice*, 81.

13. Lampe, *Freedom's Voice*, 79.

14. Patsy B. Perry, "Before *The North Star*: Frederick Douglass' Early Journalistic Career," *Phylon* 35 (1974), 96–107.

15. Frankie Hutton, *The Early Black Press in America: 1827–1860* (Westport, CT: Greenwood Press, 1993).

16. McFeely, *Frederick Douglass*, 149–50.

17. John Sekora, "'Mr. Editor, If You Please': Frederick Douglass, *My Bondage and My Freedom*, and the End of the Abolitionist Imprint," *Callaloo* 17 (1994), 608–26.

18. Hutton, *Early Black Press*, 4, 70.

19. *Antislavery Newspapers and Periodicals*, 5 vols., ed. John W. Blassingame and Mae G. Henderson (Boston: G. K. Hall, 1980), 1:xii.

20. McFeely, *Frederick Douglass*, 153.

21. Elizabeth McHenry, *Forgotten Readers: Recovering the Lost History of African American Literary Societies* (Durham, NC: Duke University Press, 2002), 124–26; Meredith L. McGill, *American Literature and the Culture of Reprinting, 1834–1853* (Philadelphia: University of Pennsylvania Press, 2003).

22. LW 1:437; Lord Denman [Thomas, 1st Baron], Uncle Tom's Cabin, Bleak House, *Slavery and the Slave Trade* (London: Longman, 1853).

23. McFeely, *Frederick Douglass*, 173. See also Bernard W. Bell, "The African American Jeremiad and Frederick Douglass's Fourth of July 1852 Speech" in *The Fourth of July: Political Oratory and Literary Reactions, 1776–1876*, ed. Paul Goetsch and Gerd Hurm (Tübingen: Gunter Narr Verlag, 1992), 121–38; James A. Colaiaco, *Frederick Douglass and the Fourth of July* (New York: Palgrave Macmillan, 2006).

24. All quotes from "What to the Slave Is the Fourth of July?" are from LW 2:181–204.

25. Quoted in Waldo E. Martin, Jr., *The Mind of Frederick Douglass* (Chapel Hill: University of North Carolina Press, 1984), 58.

26. David W. Blight, *Frederick Douglass' Civil War: Keeping Faith in Jubilee* (Baton Rouge: Louisiana State University Press, 1989), 2, 3, 45; quoting from *Frederick Douglass' Paper*, March 4, 1853.

27. Goetsch and Hurm, introduction to *Fourth of July*, 7; Patricia Bizzell, "The 4th of July and the 22nd of December: the Function of Cultural Archives in Persuasion, as shown by Frederick Douglass and William Apess," *College Composition and Communication* 48:1 (1997), 44–60 at 47.

28. "The Fourth of July,"*North Star*, July 7, 1848.
29. "Our Influence Abroad," *Frederick Douglass' Paper*, December 22, 1854; "From Our San Francisco Correspondent," *Frederick Douglass' Paper*, July 27, 1855; "The Speech," *Frederick Douglass' Paper*, August 5, 1853.
30. "Feelings of a Slave on the Fourth of July," *North Star*, July 7, 1848.
31. "The Ohio Black Laws," *North Star*, June 2, 1848.
32. "Letter from the Editor – no 2," *North Star*, July 18, 1850.
33. "Fourth of July Celebration," *Frederick Douglass' Paper*, June 23, 1854.
34. "Song for the Fourth of July," *North Star*, July 20, 1849; "Hymn of Victory," *North Star*, July 27, 1849.
35. "First of August in Columbus, Ohio," *Frederick Douglass' Paper*, August 11, 1854; see also "West India Emancipation Day," *Frederick Douglass' Paper*, August 10, 1855; "WEST INDIA EMANCIPATION," July 20, 1855.
36. "Communications," *North Star*, August 21, 1848.
37. Paul Giles, "Narrative Reversals and Power Exchanges: Frederick Douglass and British Culture," *American Literature* 73 (2001): 792.
38. Douglass, "Letter from the Editor," *Frederick Douglass' Paper*, July 18, 1850.

4

JOHN ERNEST

Crisis and Faith in Douglass's Work

In the concluding paragraphs of his last autobiography, *Life and Times of Frederick Douglass* (1881, 1892), Frederick Douglass looks back with justifiable pride at a distinguished life of often stunning accomplishments. What he chooses to emphasize in his final paragraph is his life of service to African Americans, and his comments are both an indication of the challenges he saw and of the philosophy he promoted. Speaking of the black communities with whom he was most closely associated, at times by choice and at times by necessity, Douglass states:

> I have aimed to assure them that knowledge can be obtained under difficulties; that poverty may give place to competency; that obscurity is not an absolute bar to distinction, and that a way is open to welfare and happiness to all who will resolutely and wisely pursue that way; that neither slavery, stripes, imprisonment or proscription need extinguish self-respect, crush manly ambition, or paralyze effort; that no power outside of himself can prevent a man from sustaining an honorable character and a useful relation to his day and generation; that neither institutions nor friends can make a race to stand unless it has the strength in its own legs; that there is no power in the world which can be relied upon to help the weak against the strong or the simple against the wise; that races, like individuals, must stand or fall by their own merits; that all the prayers of Christendom cannot stop the force of a single bullet, divest arsenic of poison, or suspend any law of nature. (LT 913)

This is, of course, a demanding sense of mission presented in an equally demanding statement. Included are principles of self-reliance and self-determination, as well as various acknowledgments of the significant obstacles regularly faced by African Americans in a white supremacist nation. Poverty, enslavement, and even bullets are placed next to competency, self-respect, and determination. By presenting this list of principles in a single sentence, Douglass underscores the extent to which he views these various convictions as part of a coherent philosophy, while emphasizing as well the enormousness of the challenges involved – as if to answer those who might underestimate the overwhelming odds against African American success.

But if we take this as a philosophical statement, what are we to make of Douglass's suggestion of the ineffectuality of "all the prayers of Christendom?" Is Douglass suggesting that only self-respect, ambition, and effort can be trusted, and that Christianity plays no significant role in life's struggles? Those who read on to the sentences that follow might well think so, for Douglass is clearly critical of the role of religion in African American life. "In my communication with the colored people," he continues, "I have endeavored to deliver them from the power of superstition, bigotry, and priest-craft. In theology I have found them strutting about in the old clothes of the masters, just as the masters strut about in the old clothes of the past" (LT 913). In other words, Douglass views the religion entertained by many African Americans as an extension of slavery. Douglass does speak of the possibility of an after-life, but it is clear that his attention is on the practical challenges of the here and now. "I have urged upon them," he emphasizes, "self-reliance, self-respect, industry, perseverance, and economy, to make the best of both worlds, but to make the best of this world first because it comes first, and that he who does not improve himself by the motives and opportunities afforded by this world gives the best evidence that he would not improve in any other world" (LT 914).

Douglass was not alone in his critique of African American religious practices. Years earlier, his former colleague and fellow black abolitionist Martin R. Delany noted with pride that "the colored races are highly susceptible of religion," while also lamenting that "they carry it too far," for it leads them to rely upon unfounded hope, and "consequently, they usually stand still."[1] Douglass similarly suggests that those who do not want to stand still are tasked to take not just the first significant step but the series of steps that follow, and he was frequently critical of any religious belief that seemed to counsel otherwise.

But behind Douglass's confident advice and equally confident critique of religious beliefs and practices throughout his life are unsettled and unsettling questions about both crisis and faith. In his second autobiography, *My Bondage and My Freedom* (1855), Douglass notes that as he started his new life of "freedom" in New Bedford, Massachusetts, his damaged but still resolute Christian faith led him to seek out a church. "Among my first concerns on reaching New Bedford," he states, "was to become united with the church, for I had never given up, in reality, my religious faith" (MB 359). Having been associated with the Methodist Church during his enslavement, Douglass attended the Methodist church in New Bedford, only to discover that it practiced racial segregation even for "the sacrament of the Lord's

Supper, that most sacred and most solemn of all the ordinances of the Christian church" (MB 360). First the white congregants were served, and only afterwards did the pastor invite the black congregants to the altar, assuring them that "God is no respecter of persons." "The colored members – poor, slavish souls – went forward," Douglass reports; "I went *out*, and have never been in that church since, although I honestly went there with a view to joining that body" (MB 361). This early incident in Douglass's life of "freedom" marked the beginning of an ongoing pattern of hopes and disappointments, reminding Douglass again and again, in lessons both familiar and new, that he was a member of a society devoted not only to the system of slavery but also to the ideology and practice of white supremacy.

This pattern formed the basis of an ongoing crisis of Douglass's life, and this early experience in the Methodist Church indicates the challenges Douglass faced in thinking of himself and living his life as a man of Christian faith. Given that both religion and philosophy operate by way of public institutions and social interactions, what comfort could Douglass possibly hope to find as a Christian? What forums would be available to him to enjoy communion with other Christians and study the tenets of his faith? What conversations with those who represented the Christian faithful would fail to remind him of the deep injustices all around? Such questions placed Douglass in a pattern that extended far beyond his life, for as Hortense Spillers has argued, "In a very real sense, the black intellectual, by definition, embodies the ongoing crisis of life-worlds in historical confrontation with superior force."[2] So often considered *the* representative African American man of the nineteenth century, Douglass was representative as well in his struggle for a stable religious understanding in a world of professed Christians seemingly determined, as a character in Harriet Beecher Stowe's antislavery novel *Uncle Tom's Cabin* (1852) puts it, to "warp and bend language and ethics to a degree that shall astonish the world at their ingenuity," pressing "nature and the Bible, and nobody knows what else, into the service."[3]

Douglass came to know this world intimately, in every phase of his life, and his considerable accomplishments arose out of that intimacy with a world of duplicity, disappointment, and threatening ingenuity. And this intimate knowledge, joined with the determination to engage in that world, proved to be his greatest strength as a student of religion. Ultimately, Douglass can be identified as a man of lasting faith and a religious leader not in spite of the ongoing crisis he experienced but because of it. He worked not around but through that crisis, asserted agency by means of it, and sustained a faith in a Christianity that could be realized and maintained only by way of resistance to the violated religion that surrounded him. Crisis, one might say, was the heart and wellspring of Douglass's faith.

Douglass's complex experience of Christian faith began, as is often the case, in a rather conventional manner during his youth, but it involved from the beginning a rather unconventional relationship with religion. He began attending a Sabbath school for black children at the age of twelve, and through the church he encountered powerful preachers and mentors, leading to what one biographer has called "one of the nineteenth century's classic experiences of conversion." As William S. McFeely observes, "The familiar rhetoric describing the torment of doubt, the flash of truth, and then the coming through to faith, belies the intensity of the experience for the person achieving salvation."[4] Of course, this was the beginning of Douglass's life-long experience with "the torment of doubt, the flash of truth," and, as I will suggest, the ongoing "coming through to faith." And Douglass's early experience was important in part because what was not quite "classic" about this nineteenth-century experience of conversion was the fact that "the person achieving salvation" was also a person experiencing enslavement. Years later, Douglass would refer frequently to the ways in which slaveholders tried to use religion to keep the enslaved docile, as if, he once said, black Americans "were of a race willing to work two hundred years and take our pay in religion alone, and going to heaven when we died" (FDP 4:263). For Douglass and for many others, the experience of Christianity could not be separated from the experience of slavery. Any viable understanding of religion would have to involve freedom and, therefore, resistance to slavery as central concerns.

When Douglass arrived and settled in New Bedford, Massachusetts, in 1838, he had every reason to hope that he would be entering into a fundamentally different community of believers – and his time there proved to be, in fact, a new and formative phase in his religious life. As William Andrews has noted, while still enslaved Douglass had taken "leadership roles in clandestine religious institutions designed to teach slaves to read the Bible."[5] Although the slaveholders broke up these Sabbath schools, his experience in them remained important to Douglass. Commenting on the schools in *My Bondage and My Freedom*, he observed, "I have had various employments during my short life; but I look back to *none* with more satisfaction, than to that afforded by my Sunday school" (MB 300). In New Bedford, following his experience with the segregated church, he turned to the African Methodist Episcopal Zion (AMEZ) Church and continued his personal ministry, earning a license to work as a local preacher by 1839. What eventually was established as the AMEZ Church began in New York City in 1801 in response to the racist practices of white Methodists, and members of the church would later include such prominent activists as Sojourner Truth and Harriet Tubman, in addition to Douglass. The denomination's origins, its membership, and its sense of mission naturally gave Douglass reason to believe that he would find there a spiritual home, and indeed he valued his experience there throughout his life. "My connection with the little church," he noted in 1894, "continued long after I was in the antislavery field. I look back to the days I spent in little Zion, New Bedford, in the several capacities of sexton, steward, class leader, clerk, and local preacher, as among the happiest days of my life."[6] The Christianity that had once been distorted and obstructed by the system of slavery remained important to Douglass in freedom, and clearly he hoped to become part of a more just church devoted to that faith.

But Douglass's experiences had also prepared him to adhere resolutely to a Christianity separate from established churches. In the South, the churches with which Douglass was familiar included slaveholders among their most prominent members, forcing him to recognize that Christianity was exposed to corruption even in the so-called house of God. In the North, that same recognition led him to leave the church, an obligation not separate from his Christian faith but instead, in his view, required by it. As Douglass observes in *My Bondage and My Freedom*, when he first sought out a church community in New Bedford he had not fully appreciated the oppressive power of organized religion.

> I was not then aware [he writes] of the powerful influence of that religious body in favor of the enslavement of my race, nor did I see how the northern churches could be responsible for the conduct of southern churches; neither did I fully understand how it could be my duty to remain separate from the church, because bad men were connected with it. (MB 360)

Soon, he was forced to recognize that he could not find refuge from the corruptions of slavery even in the AMEZ Church, forcing him to the same conclusion about his religious responsibilities, though in softer tones: "I could not see it to be my duty to remain with that body, when I found that it consented to the same spirit which held my brethren in chains" (MB 362). The source of his complaint here is unclear, since the AMEZ Church was actively opposed to slavery, but having experienced "many seasons of peace and joy" with this congregation, Douglass undoubtedly was determined to look beyond submission and patience as the guiding values of Christian life.

For some of his primary biographers, Douglass's separation from Christian churches has indicated a separation from Christianity, joined with an entrance into a new form of faith, abolitionism. Benjamin Quarles, for example, suggests that "the severe criticism [Douglass] heard leveled by the [abolitionist] Garrisonians against the church weaned him away from his religious bent and led him to go through life examining religious institutions from the outside."[7] Waldo E. Martin, on the other hand, suggests that

Douglass was not weaned but fed, a process that led him to almost a second conversion experience. "His introduction to Christianity around age thirteen," Martin states, "had already whetted his religious appetite. His introduction to abolitionism soon thereafter whetted it further. Indeed, for Douglass, abolitionism quickly assumed the status of a religion, drawing upon the best Christian ideals: love, morality, and justice."[8] And as Douglass learned to join "natural rights philosophy" with his "Christian philosophy," Martin argues, his "abolitionist religion" developed accordingly.[9] For McFeely, who presents Douglass's conversion experience from the perspective of a more mature Douglass looking back on his early years, "long after his faith was gone," Douglass's adoption of the abolitionist religion was a still more decisive break with the past, for "Douglass found that he could not marry the two religions, Christianity and antislavery, though one led to the other."[10]

Of course, Douglass brought religious zeal to his new calling, becoming one of the most influential and powerful activists and orators of the abolitionist movement, but this new "religion" could not offer him any more refuge from the crisis of his life than could Christianity. As Maurice S. Lee has observed, many of Douglass's writings "tell the story of a crisis of philosophical faith."[11] Noting that Douglass once equated the force of conscience with the law of gravity, and that he therefore believed that "the end of slavery" was "as sure as the fall of Newton's apple," Lee follows Douglass's faith on its seemingly inevitable course towards despair. "What happens," Lee asks, "when apples do not drop? When the law of conscience falters?"[12] What happens indeed? And what happens, as well, when one discovers, as Douglass did regularly, that the antislavery movement itself was far from being free of racial prejudice, or, worse still, from the assumptions of white supremacy? In an article published in 1856 entitled "The Unholy Alliance of Negro Hate and Anti-Slavery," Douglass stated the case of his new "religion" quite plainly: "Opposing slavery and hating its victims has come to be a very common form of Abolitionism" (LW 2:387). In numerous other publications, Douglass was less plain but no less emphatic about the similarities between his new religion and the old.

In much of his work throughout his career, Douglass joined other activists, black and white, in calling for a Christianity attentive and responsive to the conditions and challenges that were fundamental to any understanding of an African American community. This is not to say that all African Americans were in agreement about how to understand or observe such a form of Christianity. Indeed, when Douglass seemed to give more credit to men than to God in the ongoing struggles against the system of slavery, he was sharply criticized by prominent black clergymen for promoting "human instrumentalities, unaided by Divine influence" – in effect, an abandonment of rigorous Christian faith and duty.[13] The clergy would have been more outraged still had they read the correspondence of Douglass's intimate German friend Ottilie Assing, who noted that one obstacle to their "loving and lasting friendship" was Douglass's belief in "the personal Christian God," a belief she did not share. Assing claimed that by introducing Douglass to radical German philosophy she had broken him from his former faith, what for her amounted to his "second emancipation" from enslavement.[14] Still, it is important to note that Douglass's critique of Christianity, and his understanding of both the possibilities and the dangers of human agency, were echoed by many prominent African Americans. In a novel devoted to envisioning the development of a revolutionary black community, Delany has his main character announce:

> You must make your religion subserve your interests, as your oppressors do theirs! ... They use the Scriptures to make you submit, by preaching to you the texts of "obedience to your masters" and "standing still to see the salvation," and we must now begin to understand the Bible so as to make it of interest to us.[15]

Similarly, the Reverend Samuel Ringgold Ward notes in his *Autobiography of a Fugitive Negro* (1855) the number of men who justify their actions by way of Christianity, and he asserts that the word "*religion* ... should be substituted for Christianity; for while a religion may be from man, and a religion from such an origin may be capable of *hating*, Christianity is always from God, and, like him, is love."[16] In fact, as Douglass would make forcibly clear throughout his career, there was absolutely no reason to suppose that leaving Christian churches was the same thing as leaving Christianity.[17]

Today, most scholars take note of Douglass's increasingly complex and sometimes inscrutable views on religion while also recognizing that Christianity remained a central presence in his publications and orations, which include regular references to a governing God of justice, and which include frequent and apt applications of Biblical verse. As Scott C. Williamson explains, "The standard interpretation of Douglass as a religious figure is that his evangelical roots withered in the searing light of philosophic inquiry. The movement from evangelical Methodist to religious liberal is hailed as the definitive shift in Douglass's religious life, marking the transition from the immature to the mature Douglass."[18] Often, this interpretation relies upon a very generalized overview of nineteenth-century American Christian culture, generalizations that obscure a more complex reality. Martin, for example, states that "mainstream nineteenth-century American Protestantism, notably black Christianity, encompassed a powerful sense of divine determinism in human affairs. In light of this common religious belief, the most radical and controversial aspect of Douglass's philosophy of social reform was its shift towards religious liberalism during the 1850s and 1860s."[19] Many would agree, but one cannot help but note that the clean lines of the term "religious liberalism" can keep one from looking further into Douglass's religious thought, and can encourage one to see Douglass's religion as a kind of supplement to the heart of his philosophy, or even a matter of rhetorical packaging for promoting his antislavery views in a largely Christian culture. The problem, Williamson suggests, is that "the classification *religious liberal* under-reports Douglass's enduring fondness for what he called 'the Christianity of Christ,'" and thus leads to an interpretation that "is not sensitive to the nuances of religious style nor to the gradations of religious commitment."[20] How, then, might one classify Douglass's beliefs differently – that is, in a way that is sensitive generally to these gradations and that is sensitive specifically to the nature and terms of Douglass's lifelong commitment to self-reliance, self-determination, and social reform?

One might begin by taking very seriously Douglass's ongoing criticism of slaveholding Christianity and complacent Christian churches. Douglass's numerous orations and publications unambiguously dismiss the use of religion to justify and protect the interests of the system of slavery. He frequently criticized William Meade's proslavery *Sermons Addressed to Masters and Servants* (1813), and on occasion he entertained his audiences with a parody of a slaveholder's sermon.[21] Douglass notes the serious effects of such religious practices – including his youthful belief that "the wrath of God" would follow him should he try to escape – and he notes as well the seriousness of his attempt to get his audiences to laugh at such practices (FDP 2:99). "It is this kind of religion I wish you to laugh at," he said following a parody of a slaveholding sermon, for "it breaks the charm there is about it." Douglass is more serious still in the central chapter of his 1845 *Narrative* when he presents in religious terms the struggle with a slave-breaker that left him resolved that while he might remain "a slave in form," he would no longer be "a slave in fact" (N 65). Within a few pages of this episode, he connects his resolve to his views on slaveholding religion. "I assert most unhesitatingly," he writes, "that the religion of the south is a mere covering for the most horrid crimes, – a justifier of the most appalling barbarity, – a sanctifier of the most hateful frauds, – and a dark shelter, under which the darkest, foulest, grossest, and most infernal deeds of slaveholders find the strongest protection" (N 68). Moreover, he was consistently clear that his denunciations of slaveholding religion were not limited to Southern churches:

> The church in America [he stated in an 1847 speech] is, beyond all question, the chief refuge of slavery. When we attack it [slavery] in the state, it runs into

the street, to the mob; when we attack it in the mob, it flies to the church; and, sir, it is a melancholy fact, that it finds a better, safer, and more secure protection from the shafts of abolitionism within the sacred enclosure of the Christian temple than from any other quarter whatever. (FDP 1:29)

Of course, these various statements would have little force if Douglass were dismissive of Christianity altogether, and in fact he viewed Christianity as vital to antislavery efforts. Following his parody of a slaveholding sermon, Douglass once explained his sense of the importance of faith in his antislavery work, drawing from the Bible (James 3:17) to testify to his personal beliefs:

> I dwell mostly upon the religious aspects because I believe it is the religious people who are to be relied on in this Anti-Slavery movement. Do not misunderstand my railing – do not class me with those who despise religion – do not identify me with the infidel. I love the religion of Christianity – which cometh from above – which is pure, peaceable, gentle, easy to be entreated, full of good fruits, and without hypocrisy. (FDP 2:99)

Presenting the battle against slavery as a struggle of biblical proportions, between Christian "votaries" and the religion of the "Priest and Levite," Douglass expresses his hope for a Christian revival (FDP 2:99–100). This was the battle he faced when enslaved, and he holds to the faith that encouraged his initial resistance to slavery. "The masters won't have the Bible among their slaves," he noted in 1847, "because it teaches them their right to liberty" (FDP 1:88). "It is idle to make the Bible and Slavery go hand in hand," Douglass stated in 1849, though he knew full well that the Bible was used regularly not only to support slavery but also to discourage or moderate antislavery efforts. The antislavery movement was, among other things, a theological movement – involving not only contrasting interpretations of the Bible but also the challenge of providing liberating doctrine to those who were denied both the ability to read and the freedom to act upon a liberating faith.[22] For Douglass, the failure to resist the system of slavery was a dangerous moral failure, an implicit abandonment of the religion that so many claimed as the foundation of their sense of national character and of individual identity.

Far from finding it impossible to marry Christianity and antislavery, Douglass found it impossible to divorce one from the other. The system of slavery was indeed a system, involving the nation's political, economic, and social laws and practices, and so, too, was *religion* a system invested in and corrupted by the systemic operations of slavery and race. Douglass knew that ending slavery could not be achieved without wholesale social reform. As David W. Blight observes, "Consistent with his apocalyptic outlook, Douglass yearned for events, however they might arise, that would stop time, overturn the past, and begin a new history. He wanted the old Union destroyed and a new Union re-created and rededicated. The old principles were fine, but a new history was necessary."[23] The Civil War naturally brought Douglass's religious interpretation of historical events to a point, albeit ultimately an ambiguous and unsettled point. But as Douglass understood, and as the aftermath of the Civil War proved all too conclusively, addressing the influence of slavery and racism in the church would similarly require a comprehensive reform of religion, a destruction of the old and a re-creation and rededication of basic principles. He noted once that "the noble Garrison thought that he would only have to announce to the church her duty relative to this subject [slavery] and it would rush to the rescue" (FDP 1:354). Douglass was under no such illusions. There would be no stable solution to the problem of slavery and racism without an equally ambitious re-envisioning of religion. "There is another religion," he stated in 1847, a religion that "takes off fetters instead of binding them on," and "the Anti-Slavery platform is based on this kind of religion." "This," he stated proudly, "is Anti-Slavery – this is Christianity" (FDP 1:101). For Douglass, the Anti-Slavery cause was fundamentally devoted to the reform and reinvigoration of Christianity, work that remained long after the antislavery mission was seemingly complete.

An understanding of Douglass's religious beliefs within the context of the communities he tried to serve leads one not to a generalized religious liberalism but rather to a demanding Christian activism. Because he believed that Christianity could not be realized or acted upon without freedom and civil rights, Douglass viewed his most immediate and fundamental moral responsibility to be the creation of a politically, socially, and theologically forceful community. As Reginald F. Davis has argued, Douglass in this way and others anticipated what has since become known as liberation theology, "a theology that is at the heart of the Christian tradition to eradicate economic, social, and political oppression."[24] Liberation theology emphasizes the importance of the conditions that shape the lives of the community of faith as well as the historical causes of those conditions. It is considered, indeed, a theological duty to understand what some have called "the structures of sin" – that is, to understand oppression in systemic terms and not simply as isolated and individualized incidents. Moreover, liberation theology encourages communities to seek an understanding of the systemic conditions that shape individual and communal life, and it does so as part of a central commitment to action in the here and now. A continual engagement in the world, and especially in the lives of the oppressed, is part of an ongoing process of theological reflection, development, and action central to this theology, and this was the sort of engagement that Douglass both practiced and demanded of others.

The problem, Douglass argued in 1849, is that "we think that religion is the entertainment of hope." "I know there is a hope in religion," Douglass acknowledged; "I know there is faith and I know there is prayer about religion and necessary to it, but God is most glorified when there is peace on earth and good will towards men" (FDP1:189). Douglass presented this ideal as the promise delivered by angels "when our Saviour came into the world," and he presented it as the primary test of any religion, and any individual, claiming the authority of Christianity.

Knowing how religion was failing that test, Douglass believed, was more important than vaguely hoping that it might someday live up to its ideals; and it was precisely in this way that in crisis Douglass found the grounds for faith, for the slaveholding and racist violations of religion were central to the development of his Christian beliefs. The Christian's responsibility was to address those social conditions that were obstacles to the realization and practice of active faith. Believing that "there can be no virtue without freedom" and that "there can be no obedience to the Bible without freedom," Douglass worked to change the lives of the enslaved and the oppressed, of those without freedom and those without recognized and practicable rights, and he continued that work by withholding his support for churches that failed to devote themselves to this central responsibility (FDP 1:188). In doing so, he was not subordinating religion to his other concerns but was instead working within an envisioned but largely invisible church – that is, the community of believers, and not the institutions in which they observed their beliefs. "When we see men binding up the wounds of those who fall among thieves," he observed in 1849, "administering to the necessities of the down-trodden, and breaking off the chains of the bondsmen, it is evidence enough that their works are of God, and, whatever may be their abstract notions, Christ himself lives within them; for this was his spirit" (FDP 1:188). Years later, in 1870, he would echo this view in the statement that outraged some black clergymen of the time: "I want to express my love to God and gratitude to God, by thanking those faithful men and women, who have devoted the great energies of their souls to the welfare of mankind. It is only through such men and such women that I can get any glimpses of God anywhere" (FDP 4:264). Douglass lived to see many disappointments, but out of those disappointments he saw as well an interracial and activist community whose lives indicated the development of a community of the truly faithful. The language for expressing and understanding that faith was regularly placed in the service of oppression, but the terms of oppression became the terms by which the community might know its responsibilities, discover one another as members of the rising community, and devote themselves to an active faith and a lived theology. A glimpse of God himself, Douglass discovered in the ongoing crisis of his life the terms, the opportunities, and the responsibilities of faith.

NOTES

1. Martin Robison Delany, *The Condition, Elevation, Emigration, and Destiny of the Colored People of the United States* (1852; New York: Arno Press and New York Times, 1968), 38.
2. Hortense J. Spillers, "The Crisis of the Black Intellectual," in *A Companion to African-American Philosophy*, ed. Tommy L. Lott and John P. Pittman (Malden, MA: Blackwell, 2006), 87.
3. Harriet Beecher Stowe, *Uncle Tom's Cabin; or, Life among the Lowly* (New York: Vintage Books/The Library of America, 1991), 261.
4. William S. McFeely, *Frederick Douglass* (New York: W. W. Norton, 1991), 38.
5. William L. Andrews, "Frederick Douglass, Preacher," *American Literature* 54:4 (December, 1982), 593.
6. Qutoted in Andrews, "Frederick Douglass, Preacher," 596.
7. Benjamin Quarles, *Frederick Douglass* (1948; New York: Atheneum, 1968), 23.
8. Waldo E. Martin, Jr., *The Mind of Frederick Douglass* (Chapel Hill: University of North Carolina Press, 1984), 19–20.
9. *Ibid.*, 20.
10. McFeely, *Frederick Douglass*, 38, 84.
11. Maurice S. Lee, *Slavery, Philosophy, and American Literature, 1830–1860* (Cambridge: Cambridge University Press, 2005), 121.
12. *Ibid.*, 121.
13. Quoted in Martin, *The Mind of Frederick Douglass*, 179.
14. Maria Diedrich, *Love Across Color Lines: Ottilie Assing and Frederick Douglass* (New York: Hill and Wang, 1999), 227–29.
15. Martin Robison Delany, *Blake, or The Huts of America: A Tale of the Mississippi Valley, The Southern United States, and Cuba* (Boston, MA: Beacon Press, 1970), 41.
16. Samuel Ringgold Ward, *Autobiography of a Fugitive Negro: His Anti-Slavery Labours in the United States, Canada, and England* (1855; New York: Arno Press and The New York Times, 1968), 41.
17. For an argument that explores similar grounds as the one I am presenting, but with somewhat different conclusions, see James A. Wohlpart, "Privatized Sentiment and the Institution of Christianity: Douglass's Ethical Stance in the *Narrative*," *American Transcendental Quarterly* 9:3 (September 1995), 181–94.
18. Scott C. Williamson, *The Narrative Life: The Moral and Religious Thought of Frederick Douglass* (Macon, GA: Mercer University Press, 2002), viii.
19. Martin, *The Mind of Frederick Douglass*, 175.
20. Williamson, *The Narrative Life*, ix.
21. *Sermons Addressed to Masters and Servants*, ed. William Meade (Winchester, VA: John Heiskell, 1813). For an example of Douglass's satiric sermons, see "Love of God, Love of Man, Love of Country: An Address Delivered in Syracuse, New York, on 24 September 1847" (FDP 2:97–99).
22. Debates over the scriptural grounds for slavery were quite heated in the nineteenth century, and were presented in such books as George Bourne's *A*

Condensed Anti-Slavery Bible Argument: By a Citizen of Virginia (1845) and Thornton Stringfellow's *Scriptural and Statistical Views in Favor of Slavery* (1856).

23. David W. Blight, *Frederick Douglass' Civil War: Keeping Faith in Jubilee* (Baton Rouge: Louisiana State University Press, 1989), 73. On Douglass's religious interpretation of the Civil War, see 102–21.

24. Reginald F. Davis, *Frederick Douglass: A Precursor of Liberation Theology* (Macon, GA: Mercer University Press, 2005), viii. For an excellent consideration of liberation theology in Douglass's 1845 *Narrative*, see Sharon Carson, "Shaking the Foundation: Liberation Theology in *Narrative of the Life of Frederick Douglass*," *Religion and Literature* 24:2 (Summer 1992), 19–34.

5

MAURICE O. WALLACE

Violence, Manhood, and War in Douglass

In a March 1978 address at Goshen College in Goshen, Indiana, the late John H. Yoder, distinguished Christian theologian and radical pacifist, publicly decried the nuclear arms race "as one of the simplest analogies to the monster language of the Apocalypse." He called the language of apocalypse "right" in describing the extraordinary threat of the age. "The problem is still one," he said, "that fits the apocalyptic language of dragons and angels and the sky falling down. This is a better description of what we are up against." The fitness of apocalyptic language to the imagined prospect of nuclear annihilation was no otherworldly abstraction to Yoder. Nor was it spiritualistic theologizing. Instead, Yoder understood Apocalypse to offer "a way of talking critically about *this* world."[1] He saw in the state of global affairs an untold irruption in history in the offing. More than a century earlier, Frederick Douglass shared a similarly critical vision of the state of US affairs concerning slavery and the war to defeat its interests. Like many others, North and South, Douglass discerned something millennial in the approaching Civil War. Like few others, however, Douglass slowly felt himself elected to the hastening of "the America apocalypse" with full confidence in its emancipatory ends. This chapter is about the evolution of Douglass's thought and actions from 1845 to the Civil War regarding the serviceability of war and violence to the politics of abolition and freedom. It shows how Douglass transformed a platform of Christian pacifism into one of holy violence by deploying a sociology of manhood and a theology of political radicalism better suited to the task of making the history Douglass seems to have been, everywhere and at all times, intent upon.

When *Narrative of the Life of Frederick Douglass, An American Slave* was published in May 1845, it was a risky, if compelling, vindication against Douglass's cynical contemporaries who doubted his claim, so frequently repeated in his abolitionist speeches, to have been a bondsman himself. Although the *Narrative* offered up to the reading public ample details about Douglass's life in bondage for their verification, it was precisely such verification that imperiled the escaped slave. As a fugitive from slavery and not a free man according to the law, Douglass still belonged to his Maryland master. The *Narrative* let the attentive slave-owner know precisely where to find and reclaim his self-stolen chattel. So urged on by his eminent friend and supporter Wendell Phillips, Douglass absconded again, this time much farther from the Maryland plantation of his master across the Atlantic to Liverpool, where he would begin a grand tour of the British Isles as an antislavery and temperance lecturer. With his autobiography in print four months and his fame in Europe and elsewhere growing steadily, Douglass landed in Liverpool a leading light of the US reform movement on August 28, safe from the reach of would-be slave-catchers.

Like his travels in the free states of America, the passage to the British Isles was not without event. Although brusquely relegated to a second-class cabin by American prejudice when he applied to the steamer, *Cambria*, for passage, Douglass and his traveling companion, fellow abolitionist James N. Buffum, happily avoided the face-to-face indignities that were so frequent in America. Hidden from plain sight in the steerage and, thus, shielded from public acts of racial affront, Douglass enjoyed respite from the everydayness of racial injury, but it was not to last. The night before docking in Liverpool, the captain of the *Cambria*, almost certainly at the urging of Buffum, invited Douglass to give a lecture aboard the steamer. Also on board were "several young men, passengers from Georgia and New Orleans" who, taking Douglass's speech as a direct insult to them, drunkenly protested and loudly "swore," Douglass recalled, that "I should not speak" (LT 678). Their protestations notwithstanding, Douglass descanted through jeers and undisguised contempt for several minutes, condemning slavery and renouncing its apologists determinedly. Before he could finish, two of his detractors rose to physically confront him. A melee ensued. At once tragic and comic, Douglass would remember, the scuffle was soon put down by the captain's own threats to the offending men to place them in irons, whereupon they were abruptly sobered, "and for the remainder of the voyage conducted themselves very decorously" (LT 679).

That this brief episode of would-be mutiny by a few "salt-water mobocrats" should inaugurate Douglass's first European tour is not without irony since the politics it violently dramatizes between the lines – an *international* conflict between the agents of American proslavery and those of English reformism, all white – would surface in an anti-war address delivered by Douglass to the London Peace Society nine months into his nearly two-year tour (LT 678). The war Douglass decried in his May 1846 oration was a prospective one pitting the US forces against Great Britain over the Oregon boundary. With the US presidential election of 1844, American expansionists under James Polk began aggressively agitating for a "clear and unquestionable" claim by the US to the Oregon Country, which the two interests had agreed to jointly occupy for ten years. By the early 1840s, US expansionist sentiment made further compromise with the British eminently undesirable. American jingoists rallied unbending expansionists with belligerent sloganeering: "Fifty-four Forty or Fight" heightened the tensions between the US and Great Britain while calls for war issued from a few Congressional warmongers. By the spring of 1846, the dispute was serious enough (if only symbolically) to raise worries on both sides of the Atlantic. Before "a large and excellent meeting" of Peace Society members, Douglass stood opposed to all the calls and clamor for war (LW 1:167). The "demoniacal spirit of war" subverted "the reformation and purification of the world" which the Creator had set about to realize, Douglass preached (FDP 1:263). It was a position appropriate to the meeting since the London Peace Society (originally, the Society for the Promotion of Universal and Permanent Peace), an organization founded under strong Quaker influence, had stood "principled against all war, under any pretense" since 1816.[2]

Still, Douglass's stance against war was a curious one. President Polk was, after all, a Southerner and a slaveholder, and US abolitionists had good reason to worry that, less than six months after the government admitted Texas into the Union as a slave state, the US expansion of Oregon Country might also expand slavery into the Pacific Northwest (unlikely as it seemed, given the territory's climate and natural environment militating against slavery). Since 1845, former Vice-President and South Carolina Senator John C. Calhoun had agitated aggressively against abolitionism in the legislature and later opposed admitting Oregon as a US territory "for the reason that it did not specifically provide for the introduction of slavery within its boundaries."[3] Not accidentally, then, did talk of war in England come to be imagined as "a war against the slave power of the world."[4]

In his address "My Opposition to War," Douglass acknowledged the peculiarity of an anti-war stance by a fugitive slave "when it is universally believed that a war between [England and the US] would eventuate in the emancipation of three millions of my brethren who are now held in the most cruel bonds" (FDP 1:261). That he "believed this would be the result" was not sufficient, however, to shake the pacifistic resolve in Douglass. In words hardly imaginable as those of the iconic champion of muscular emancipation valorized by Eric Sundquist, for example, who perceives Douglass as belonging to the American Revolutionary tradition,[5] the silver-tongued spokesman declared his position ever more decisively:

> [S]uch is my regard for the principle of peace – such is my deep, firm conviction that nothing can be attained for liberty universally by war, that were I to be

asked the question as to whether I would have my emancipation by the shedding of one single drop of blood, my answer would be in the negative. (FDP 1:262)

According to accounts in the London *Morning Advertiser*, London *Daily News* and London *Patriot*, "loud cheers" followed (FDP 1:262). Remarkably, neither the event of Douglass's lecture before the London Peace Society nor the text of it is recalled in the early or late literature devoted to Douglass. Perhaps because none of Douglass's autobiographies – the *Narrative*, *My Bondage and My Freedom* (1855), and *Life and Times of Frederick Douglass* (1881, 1892) – recalls the London Peace address, its mention, in ringing contrast to the universal familiarity of his orations "What to the Slave Is the Fourth of July?" (1852) and "What the Black Man Wants" (1865), has passed unnoticed even under the hands of Douglass's most meticulous biographers.[6]

That Douglass's trumpeted pacifism is recalled at all is owed in the main to the late John Blassingame's monumental publication, *The Frederick Douglass Papers, Series One: Speeches, Debates and Interviews* (1979–1992), the venerated historian's multivolume edition of Douglass's papers and manuscripts. The text of Douglass's speech collected in Blassingame is the only published version of "My Opposition to War" outside of its July 3, 1846 publication in William Lloyd Garrison's *The Liberator*. It is not merely the speech's obscurity or its pacifist fervor that surprises, however – as Blassingame pointed out, Douglass "had often argued against war" (FDP 1:xiv); the surprise of the address in London lies rather in its tension with the insurrectionary suggestion of the *Narrative*'s pivotal fray with Covey in chapter ten. Ironic as it sounds, one might say that it was in fact the generically melodramatic appeal of the *Narrative*'s climactic "main event" (and its near recapitulation onboard the *Cambria*), not his declamatory eloquence, that earned Douglass his earliest, most ready audience abroad. Did Douglass "not sense the tension between [his] pacifist stance" so passionately preached in London and the "celebration of the psychological and moral consequences of fighting Covey" that helped to inspire the English tour, as Bernard Boxill has wondered?[7] The answer to Boxill, an incongruous *yes* and *no* at once, I shall parse over the course of this essay. Suffice it to say for now that if Boxill, in his own straightforwardly titled essay, "The Fight with Covey," imagined the force of a meticulously outlined moral philosophical argument suitable to the task of explaining away the strange "tension" in Douglass's views on war and violence, I, on the other hand, prefer a somewhat different tack. I argue that the apparent paradox of *yes* and *no* at once in Douglass's double-minded ideas concerning violence, non-violence, and abolition is more properly located in the nineteenth-century situation of what, a century later, H. Richard Niebuhr would call fittingly "the double wrestle" of culture and theology.[8]

Given Douglass's care to point out, in the lines immediately preceding chapter ten, Covey's public standing as "a professor of religion – a pious soul – a member and a class-leader in the Methodist church" (N 54), it requires no stretch in interpretive imagination to see that in his row with Covey, Douglass was also wrestling with the "*slaveholding religion* of this land" and his determined faith in the "Christianity of Christ" for which he is, in the face of the devil who is Covey, emblematic (N 97). I take "the widest possible difference" Douglass insists obtains between the "partial and hypocritical Christianity" and "Christianity proper" in the *Narrative*'s doubly parodic and exhortative appendix to grow as wide with Douglass as that between pacifism and militancy. To illustrate, "My Opposition to War" stakes out ground at the furthest ideological remove imaginable from the battle cry, "Men of Color, To Arms!" (1863), that Douglass would trumpet seventeen volatile years later. In that appeal, issued to as many free men of color as might be reached by his paper, *Douglass' Monthly*, Douglass urged black men to "fly to arms, and smite with death the power that would bury the Government and your Liberty in the same hopeless grave." The once moral suasionist who declared in London his preference for slavery's "cruel bonds" to "the shedding of one single drop of blood" by the sword at last proclaimed (after Byron): "Who would be free themselves must strike the first blow. Better even to die free, than to live as slaves." Perhaps given to posturing in London, Douglass, in any case, reversed his anti-war position entirely. The Civil War, raging already for "two dreary years," called "logically and loudly" for colored volunteers, he reasoned. Recalling precisely the fistic power that was to defeat Covey, Douglass expressed the black military imperative in the metonymic terms of the nation's "powerful black hand" unfastened from its bonds and armed for "Action! action!" His pacifism long since spent, Douglass charged that to refuse to fight was to prove oneself "weak and cowardly," hardly devout as his earlier position – "I am opposed to war, because I am a believer in Christianity," he had preached (FDP 1:262). Promising the new recruits (his two sons, Lewis and Charles, would be among them) the equivalent wages, rations, and protections of white enlistees, Douglass closed "Men of Color, To Arms!" assuring prospective recruits of his authority to pledge their fair treatment and, thus, of the reliability of his leadership. As an official recruiter of black troops in Massachusetts, newly chosen by abolitionist Major George Luther Stearns, he had not only the authorization of "the General Government" to make a public guarantee of fair dealing for black volunteers, but he claimed "[m]ore than twenty years unswerving devotion to our common cause" as evidence of his trustworthiness.[9]

Perhaps not surprisingly in the context of his appeal's urgency, Douglass coolly exaggerated the character ("unswerving devotion"), if not the duration ("more than twenty years"), of his commitment to the urgency of slavery's defeat in battle, specifically, as "Men of Color, To Arms!" commends. In an October 1847 speech delivered in New York City seventeen months following "My Opposition to War" and fifteen (not yet twenty) years before "Men of Color, To Arms!", Douglass was firm in his posture against war:

> I am not a man of war. The time was when I was. I was then a slave: I had dreams, horrid dreams of freedom through a sea of blood. But when I heard of the Anti-Slavery movement, light broke in upon my dark mind. Bloody visions fled away, and I saw the star of liberty peering above the horizon. Hope then took the place of desperation, and I was led to repose in the arms of Slavery. I said, I would suffer rather than do any act of violence – rather than that the glorious day of liberty might be postponed. (LW 1:277)

Even if Douglass's opposition to slavery *per se* never abated, his view of the appropriate time and means for its end was anything but "unswerving" before 1850. According to Ronald Takaki, he felt "ambivalence" as his convictions on violence became "complicated and ... contradictory."[10] Similarly, critic Richard Yarborough described Douglass "struggling" with the "mixed feelings" he had about violence and its instrumentality in the cause of antislavery, especially in his speeches and writings between 1847 and 1860, which vacillate between lionizing physical force and valorizing acts of physical restraint.[11] But it is Boxill's sense that Douglass "*became converted* to [violent] slave resistance" that suggests, more plainly than Takaki or Yarborough, why Douglass's sensibilities concerning war and peace seemed so fitfully and fervently paradoxical.[12] In a phrase, he was facing a theological crisis, one animated by an ever deepening distrust in the absolutist doctrines of Christian non-resistance and antimilitarism he received from the tutelage of Garrison, a principal figure of the US abolitionist movement and staunch religious perfectionist. (It is worth noting, of course, that the confessional rhetoric in Douglass's account above of an original conversion *to pacifism* has yet to be critically imagined.)

From the first, Douglass, a devout man in his own right, impugned slavery as an ecclesial and theological scandal. While critics have discussed how the prefatory letters of the white abolitionists Garrison and Phillips authorize the *Narrative*, much less reflection has been given to the entirely self-authorized content of the work's appendix, a "religious indictment of the political economy of slavery," one into which, according to theologian J. Kameron Carter, Douglass "enlists theology."[13] In fact, one might take the appendix of Douglass's *Narrative* to render in explicit terms the doubly Christological and jeremiadic allegory of so much of the narrative proper, including the Covey event, wherein "the Christianity of Christ" – "Christianity proper," in other words – brings judgment upon "the corrupt, slaveholding, women-whipping, cradle-plundering, partial and hypocritical Christianity of this land" (N 97). That a theological vision subtends Douglass's representation of that decisive battle with Covey, a scene confused by the melodrama of mixed assailment and restraint, is clear enough under Carter. Duly noting the paschal echoes in Covey's striking Douglass upon the head where "blood ran freely" (N 61) in the place where a thorny crown of braided branches pierced Christ, as well as in the memory of day and time (Friday at three o'clock), just to mention two allusions to the Easter story, Carter shows Douglass to be doing theology, as it were, by insinuating the slave's analogous suffering within "the very core narrative of Christian faith." More specifically, "in bringing attention to the time of his own quasi-death," Carter argues, "Douglass unites his death with the death of Jesus on Good Friday."[14] It is, thus, the self-possession of the Prince of Peace, not the violent indignation of the unruly slave, that the professed pacifist would seem to have been concerned to emphasize at the narrative's first writing. The seeming contradiction of Douglass's anti-war speech before the London Peace Society and his valorizing the violence inherent in "the battle with Covey" is hardly the contradiction it appears to be, it turns out (N 65).

Although Douglass confesses in the *Narrative* to having bloodied Covey in their fight, it is only a phrase ("but I had [drawn blood] from him"), nearly nothing compared to the ubiquitous blood-thirst of masters and overseers everywhere depicted in the *Narrative* (N 65). Concerned as he was in the London address that emancipation should not come at "the shedding of one single drop of blood," the *Narrative* dramatizes a theology of bloodshed according to which the blood-spill of war and insurrection needlessly, and thus cruelly, repeats the sufficient suffering of (black) Christ portrayed in the *Narrative* in both Aunt Hester and Douglass himself.[15]

If certain Christological commitments may be said to subtend Douglass's early pacifism, those commitments would be powerfully challenged, and profoundly changed, by the political commitments of a new Christ-figure, John Brown, who struck Douglass forcefully as the embodiment of a more manful Christianity than he had, under the influence of Garrison and the African Methodist Church, thought theologically possible. Douglass was not alone in this, however. He shared with many of his contemporaries a sense of Brown's messianic importance. Thoreau, for instance, deified Brown as "an Angel of Light," "the savior of four millions of men." Just as Brown had impressed upon the country's most prolific advocate of nonviolent civil disobedience the righteousness of his program of violent insurgency, so did he effect in Douglass the same doctrinarian *volte-face* his martyrdom had so abruptly brought about in Thoreau, whose last word in "A Plea for Captain John Brown" must have startled thousands: "revenge."[16]

According to Douglass, he first met Brown in Springfield in 1847. To Douglass, Brown cut a figure larger-than-life. Douglass observed a "lean, strong, and sinewy" fellow, "straight and symmetrical as a mountain pine" (LT 716). Brown's eyes, he said, were "full of light and fire." His words commanded universal attention. So powerfully enigmatic were Brown's person and manner that "I never felt myself in the presence of a stronger religious influence," admitted Douglass. It was, however, the scriptural allusiveness of Douglass's assertion that Brown was "not averse to the shedding of blood" and confessed "no better use for his life than to lay it down in the cause of the slave" that secured for Brown that very Christ-likeness at which Douglass's physical descriptions of him had been hinting (LT 717, 719). The very nature of him seemed to Douglass, as to Thoreau, to verge on the divine. As suddenly as Brown had caused Thoreau to double back on (what most presume was) his own philosophical instincts concerning the impracticalities of resistance to civil government, Douglass also changed his tack: "From this night spent with John Brown in Springfield ... while I continued to write and speak against slavery, I became all the same less hopeful of its peaceful abolition. My utterances became more and more tinged by the color of this man's strong impressions" (LT 719). However "apprehensive" Douglass remained in the short term toward the political expediency of antislavery violence, Brown's messianic mystique must have seemed to Douglass like the sanction of heaven upon a shifting landscape. Already, several prominent abolitionists and churchmen including Gerrit Smith, Charles Stearns, Charles Sumner, and Theodore Parker had parted from the prevailing view of so many non-resistance advocates who avowed that the "Savior meant to inculcate the doctrine of never fighting in self-defense." Recourse to "carnal weapons under any pretext or in any extremity whatever," the view went, was to be eschewed by all who professed Christianity.[17] John Brown offered Douglass another view, one to which Douglass was fully converted at Brown's execution.

Where those sympathetic to the strict pacifism and moral suasion ideals advocated by Garrison pointed chiefly to the example of Christ's non-resistance, Brown, in bearing and speech, hinted at a different, millennialist view of Christ. For his insistence to Douglass that "[s]lavery was a state of war" (at once Lockean political analysis and battle cry) not only put martial words into the mouth of one who had the appearance of the lowly Savior, but offered itself up to the developing theology of muscular Christianity that was shortly to flower in England and the United States (LT 718). Of course, Brown's zealous view of slavery as a state of war ("He denounced slavery in look and language fierce and bitter" [LT 717]), and of the right of the slaves to physically oppose slavery's dominion could not but contain echoes of an

Armageddon eschatology, coming as it did from the eccentric warrior-preacher. More than that, though, his belief that the violent overthrow of slavery was necessary to give the slaves "a sense of their manhood" appeared informed by a theology (if not also a phylogeny) of muscular perfectionism, one that would come to be systematically articulated in the 1879 publication of Thomas Hughes's study, *The Manliness of Christ*. Brown's conviction that "[n]o people ... could have self-respect, or be respected, who would not fight for their freedom" was surely of a piece with Hughes's preachment that "constant contact and conflict with evil of all kinds [composed] the necessary condition" for Christ's achievement of "courage or manfulness."[18]

It makes sense, then, in view of Hughes, that Douglass converted to the gender-inflected principles of violent resistance since his whole career was dedicated in both explicit and implied ways to the manly perfectibility of black men in and out of slavery. If during the period prior to 1847 Douglass could be said to have been a devoted pacifist, and the years between 1847 and 1860 posit an arc, or pendulous middle phase, between devoted pacifism and an unswerving apocalyptic militancy to come,[19] then the year 1860, only months after Brown's failed attack on Harpers Ferry and little more than a year before the first skirmishes of the Civil War, marks Douglass's full and final conversion to muscular Christian militancy. In that year, not coincidentally, Douglass made John Brown the subject of two major speeches delivered in Edinburgh and Boston. Escaping arrest by Virginia authorities under suspicion of having conspired to abet Brown's raid (there was ample evidence that he was closely connected to Brown's plan, even if he was not exactly a co-conspirator), Douglass fled to Canada, then set out for a second tour of Great Britain in the immediate wake of Brown's arrest and execution. For three months afterward, Douglass, anxious to elude the agents of Southern justice, kept a low profile. By the time of his first public mention of Brown, whom he proclaimed a "noble, heroic, and Christian martyr, animated by a desire to do unto others as he should himself be done unto," a great many other leading abolitionists – Thoreau, Emerson, Lucretia Mott, Henry Ward Beecher, even a begrudging Garrison – had already praised Brown's courage many times over (FDP 3:315). While these others celebrated Brown as a sort of moral victor, however, they consistently saw his violent acts as misguided. In Edinburgh on January 30, 1860, Douglass, at some risk, and departing from the vague paternalism of his fellow abolitionists, stood by Brown entirely.

A popular figure in Edinburgh where, according to Blassingame, he spoke on more than sixteen occasions during his first tour of the British Isles in 1846, Douglass addressed the Edinburgh Ladies' and Young Men's Anti-Slavery Society (FDP 3:313n1). No longer conflicted about peace, violence, and the path to emancipation, Douglass reconciled their seeming disagreement in

Brown. Referring to Brown as "a man of peace" (counterintuitive except insofar as it recalls the Christ figure), Douglass parsed the meaning of peace scripturally (FDP 3:317). Not surprisingly, his portrait of Brown elicited some laughter (which Douglass appears to have delighted in here and elsewhere), but its irony and explanation were deadly serious:

> He was a peace man – (laughter) – but his peace principles only lead him to be peaceable towards those to whom peace was a blessing, and was really appropriate. He was not for "casting pearls before swine." (Laughter.) He was for the peace of which God himself was in favour – peace for well-doing; but he was not for a peace – as God had no such peace – to the wicked. There could be only peace where there was no oppression, injustice, or outrage upon the right. (FDP 3:317)

By the 1860 address in Edinburgh, Douglass was no longer a pacifist. A peace man of a different sort now, he had come to understand the ways in which Garrisonian non-resistance relied upon the unchallenged presumption that passivity preserved peace. But peace, Douglass was to decide, was neither the essential condition of the life of the spirit ("The human heart is the seat of constant war") nor of the slaveholding state ("Just what takes place in individual human hearts, often takes place ... between individuals of the same nation"). The very acts of enslavement and of slavery's toleration were "a perpetual chronic insurrection," Douglass argued. "John Brown did not invade a peaceful neighborhood or community," he explained. As "[e]very slaveholder in America was an insurrectionist ... with the American Government so-called at their back, ... [and] an armed band of insurgents against the just rights and liberties of their fellow-men," Brown "merely stepped in to interrupt and arrest this insurrection against the rights and liberties of mankind." And inasmuch as he did so, Brown put the lie to the advocates of non-resistance, showing non-resistance to be but a resignation to the constitutional violence of the state, a "standing insurrection," by which slavery, a second-order state violence (past the first-order coercions of law, party, police, and army), was maintained.

In Boston in December of 1860, Douglass took a more extreme position, one placing him in direct descent from Brown. There, at the Martin's Joy Street Baptist Church, with John Brown, Jr. seated on the dais behind him, Douglass spoke once more in vengeful tones of bowie knives, revolvers, the nervous sleeplessness of slaveholders and insurrection as a thing that "can be done, and will be done" (FDP 3:416). "We need not only appeal to the moral sense of these slaveholders; we have need, and a right, to appeal to their fears," he said, as if directly to obstinate moral suasionists (FDP 3:419). Perhaps no more blistering an expression of antislavery fervor was ever spoken than when Douglass averred, not without sincerity, "The only way to make the Fugitive Slave Law a dead letter, is to make a few dead slave-catchers." Like Brown, this "millennialist Douglass" saw the prospects of such an end as a species of revolutionary peacemaking.[20] In Brown, Douglass perceived the avatar of a judgment upon the South, full of the wrath and fire of heaven, and he exulted in its terrible imminence. "Douglass yearned for what we might call a politics of disorder," writes historian David Blight. "Throughout the Afro-American experience, the greatest advances for black liberation and equal rights have come during periods of political and social upheaval, and in the secession winter of 1860–61, Douglass understood that [the] political turmoil" wrought by a religious war on slavery "might facilitate black advancement" and secure a lasting manhood for the race.[21]

Occurring on the heels of Brown's Harpers Ferry raid, two more events – the one anecdotal, the other politically historical – entrenched Douglass in his own violent view of the project of radical abolitionism. As Blight generously reminds us, Douglass's John Brown speech at Martin's Joy Street Baptist was a relocation of an event previously scheduled for Tremont Temple.[22] Evoking the 1846 brawl onboard the *Cambria*, a malicious band of outraged anti-abolitionists intruded upon Tremont Temple and broke up the meeting dedicated to Brown's newly hagiographic memory. Douglass attempted to speak above the chaos mounting on the floor, but his opponents' belligerence was relentless. Scuffles "great and small" followed, the papers reported (FDP 3:402). During the fracas, a mob of men seized Douglass and tossed him down a staircase. According to the record, Douglass fought back manfully. The New York *Daily Tribune* declared that Douglass scrapped "like a trained pugilist" (FDP 3:388). Who can doubt that the impassioned militancy expressed by the hope of "a few dead slavecatchers" hours later at Martin's Joy Baptist was freshly fueled by the morning's rioting, and redoubled by the inescapable, vitalizing memory of his fistic entrance into manhood at sixteen? Perfectly riled by the time he stands to speak at Martin's Joy, Douglass's speech there is fighting mad. He speaks as if by the spirit of John Brown, dramatically abandoning John Brown, Jr. to the shadows and presuming to take upon himself, Jacob to the junior Brown's Esau, the mantle of revolutionary antislavery leadership.

The episode at Tremont Temple also staged, in spectacular microcosm, the very politics of disorder Blight has argued Douglass was yearning for all along. In a sense, Douglass had been itching for a fight, one which he hoped would instill in the hard hearts of the South's slaveholding oligarchy the fear of a vindicating God, and the brawl at Tremont Temple seemed like a provocation in that direction. And it is not unlikely that Douglass saw the chance, abruptly, to show the manhood of the race. By 1861 Douglass had abandoned the peaceful premise of moral perfectionism espoused by

Garrison (who imagined the Bible as a progressive revelation in order to reconcile the gospel's portrayal of the non-resistance of Christ to the warring God of the Old Testament) and was giving full voice to a theological perspective on perfectionism very much like Brown years earlier and Hughes in the years to come. In a speech before the Spring Street AME Zion Church in Rochester that year, Douglass felt the rumblings of war portending an "American apocalypse." War seemed a thing justified by a new theological common sense:

> Men have their choice in this world. They can be angels, or they may be demons. In the apocalyptic vision, John describes a war in heaven. You have only to strip that vision of its gorgeous Oriental drapery, divest it of its shining and celestial ornaments, clothe it in the simple and familiar language of common sense, and you will have before you the eternal conflict between right and wrong, good and evil, liberty and slavery, truth and falsehood, the glorious light of love, and the appalling darkness of human selfishness and sin. The human heart is a seat of constant war … Just what takes place in individual human hearts, often takes place between nations, and between individuals of the same nation.   (FDP 3:435)

The vision of one John stripped of "gorgeous Oriental drapery" and "shining and celestial ornaments" evokes Douglass's vision of the second John, now martyred, who, with an "air of plainness" about him, casts his long, Spartan shadow over Douglass's pro-war confession before the (black) Methodists of Rochester (LT 715–16).

By now, Douglass's militancy was not a political rhetoric alone; it was, as the *Daily Tribune* hinted at, a physical ethics. Douglass's principles, that is, were to be discerned in their bodily enactment. The image of Douglass as prize-fighter offered "a glimmer of [the] idealized, restrained combat" characterizing boxing,[23] which Douglass had not only valorized previously in his 1845 *Narrative* and in the novella "The Heroic Slave" in 1853, but which, just months later, he would extend to portray the kind of fight potential in black men, "dead slavecatchers" notwithstanding, who could be relied upon to engage valiantly in battle if given leave to enlist.

While the event of the Boston altercation has generally received only scant notice, none of Douglass's most serious scholars have failed to observe how crucially the election of 1860 figured upon Douglass's attitude toward violence and freedom. Although Douglass was buoyed by the Republican win, the failure of a universal suffrage referendum in the state of New York where, in Rochester, he made his home quickly disillusioned him. Lincoln's apparent disinclination to forcefully renounce slavery within the first months of his election further frustrated the country's most preeminent race man and caused him to doubt if there was will enough to put down slavery in the

South. Soon enough, the political signs of the time – the secession threat, Republican platitudes, presidential cowardice, the failed referendums – convinced Douglass that nothing short of some violent upheaval of governmentality, some eschatological rebirth of nation and state, would bring slavery's demise in the South. No more of the mind to "act for the abolition of slavery through the Government" rather than "over its ruins," Douglass came to yearn for a new Union altogether in the months before Fort Sumter.[24] Writes Blight: "He wanted the old Union destroyed and a new Union re-created and rededicated. The old principles were fine, but a new history was necessary." While it was indeed a "political rupture" Douglass desired to see engendered by the election of Lincoln over the Southern slavery bloc, as Blight says, it is perhaps more precise to say that what Douglass willed was a political *rapture* or realized theodicy.[25] From pacifist preacher to political dispensationalist intent upon that "program of complete disorder" that is, as Frantz Fanon put it, neither the consequence of "magical practices … natural shock, nor … friendly understanding" but is, rather, "a historical process," Douglass soon saw the South's doomsday unfolding.[26] Little by little, his angry disillusionment with the politics of partisan compromise in the period immediately following the election of 1860 was absorbed by the glad fervor of vindication from the heavens.

Preaching the "'fire and strength' of the prophets" which James Darcey has said was "as much a part of our cultural inheritance as … the [Arnoldian] 'sweetness and light' of the Greeks," Douglass raised the pitch of apocalyptic speech to a feverish intensity.[27] Two months before the battle at Fort Sumter, he proclaimed the "God in history everywhere pronouncing the doom of those nations which frame mischief by law." The South, he warned, would "be made to drink the wine-cup of wrath and fire, which her long career of cruelty, barbarism and blood shall call down upon her guilty head."[28] Whereas his prayer for "fire … thunder … storm … whirlwind, and the earthquake" ten years prior to rouse the nation from its somnambulism on the slavery question had been but a high-flown flourish, Douglass's marshalling of biblical imagery in 1861 was serious and predictive.[29] It was something slightly more than "apocalyptic language," to depart from Blight slightly. It expressed a political theology in striking, dispensational outline. The start of war encouraged Douglass's millennial faith, a faith not unique to Douglass – Lincoln's "Second Inaugural Address" (1865) and Julia Ward Howe's "The Battle Hymn of the Republic" (1862) are perhaps the most memorable distillations of it – but one to which he gave a most terrible cast. In June, he once again likened the war to "the apocalyptic vision" according to which "John describes a war in heaven" in Revelations (FDP 3:437). A year later, he imagined the judgment fully unfolded as a "rumbling … social

Earthquake" wrecks the country and "sorrow and sighing are heard" throughout, like so much weeping and gnashing of teeth. "Our country," Douglass announced, "is now on fire" (FDP 3:522).

It would be simple to lay Douglass's millennialist excitements at the feet of his own exceptionalist self-fashioning, but in large part his conversion to violent means through a millennialist hope reflected, as Blight has shown so deftly, in "a spiritual interpretation of the war that fits squarely into several intellectual and theological traditions: millennialism, apocalypticism, civil religion, the providential view of history, and the jeremiad."[30] Ever the *bricoleur*, Douglass combined them all. All for the sake of the manhood of the race. That is, as Douglass's fight with Covey, and the Christian salvation narrative it dramatized between the lines of its telling, rekindled in him the fire of freedom and "a sense of my own manhood" (N 65), so Douglass, heir to a doctrine of muscular moral struggle and holy violence bequeathed by John Brown, came to the conviction that the manhood of the slave, and, thus, his deeply gendered assimilability into the national body, rested in the slave's resistance under God to the emasculating power of slavery's racial terrorism. If Douglass became a man and Christian in the fight, in other words, then those still yet enslaved would find the salvation of a new Union and of a new manly nobility – tested, tried, and loyal – in the purifying fire of war when the first shall be last and the last blessedly vindicated.

NOTES

1. John Yoder, *For the Nations: Essays Evangelical and Public* (Eugene, OR: Wipf and Stock Publishers, 1997), 152, 134.
2. Quoted in Peter Brock, *Pacifism in Europe to 1914* (Princeton, NJ: Princeton University Press, 1972), 378.
3. T. T. Geer, *Fifty Years in Oregon: Experiences, Observations, and Commentaries upon Men, Measures, and Customs in Pioneer Days and Later Times* (New York: Neal Publishing Company, 1912), 42.
4. Unnamed Englishman quoted in "War," *Richmond Enquirer*, July 1, 1845, 3. See, too, nineteenth-century Irish nationalist Daniel O'Connell quoted in "O'Connells and America," *Richmond Enquirer* 31 (October 1845), 2.
5. See Eric Sundquist, *To Wake the Nations: Race in the Making of American Literature* (Cambridge, MA: Harvard University Press, 1993), 83–87.
6. I have in mind such notable scholars as Philip Foner, Waldo Martin, Benjamin Quarles, William McFeely, Robert Levine, John Blassingame, David Blight, and Nathan Huggins.
7. Bernard R. Boxill, "The Fight with Covey," in *Existence in Black: An Anthology of Black Existential Philosophy*, ed. Lewis R. Gordon (New York: Routledge, 1997), 273.
8. H. Richard Niebuhr, *Christ and Culture* (1951; New York: HarperCollins, 2001), xi.

9. Frederick Douglass, "Men of Color, To Arms!" in *The Oxford Frederick Douglass Reader*, ed. William L. Andrews (New York: Oxford University Press, 1996), 223–25.

10. Ronald T. Takaki, *Violence in the Black Imagination: Essays and Documents*, expanded edition (New York: Oxford University Press, 1993), 18, 28.

11. Richard Yarborough, "Race, Violence, and Manhood: The Masculine Ideal in Frederick Douglass's 'The Heroic Slave,'" in *Frederick Douglass: New Literary and Historical Essays*, ed. Eric Sundquist (Cambridge: Cambridge University Press, 1990), 176. As Yarborough's vital essay reminds us, even in his account of the fight with Covey, Douglass went to great lengths to portray himself on the defensive and, despite overcoming the overseer, parrying rather than assertively issuing the greater number of blows.

12. Boxill, "The Fight with Covey," 275. Emphasis mine.

13. J. Kameron Carter, "Race, Religion, and the Contradictions of Identity: A Theological Engagement with Douglass's 1845 *Narrative*," *Modern Theology* 21:1 (January 2005), 54, 38.

14. *Ibid.*, 48.

15. Importantly, Douglass is not the only one in whom the sufferings of Christ are to be seen in *Narrative*. Carter observes that it is Aunt Hester whom Douglass first insinuates into the passion mythos. Her body's naked helplessness and the unspeakable bloodiness of Anthony's sadistic assault upon her casts Hester's humiliation in a familiarly scriptural light. Working below the surface of parallel plots and imagery of what Carter calls "slavery's ontology" (46), the *Narrative* would seem to privilege the slave woman's suffering as the proper index of that ontology and the slave's chronic sacrifice in it. But Aunt Hester's beating is the counter-scene to Douglass's own would-be beating. Her suffering is a female suffering that is, in effect, overcome by Douglass's more manly inviolability.

16. Henry David Thoreau, "A Plea for Captain John Brown," in *The Heath Anthology of American Literature*, Vol. 1, ed. Paul Lauter et al. (Lexington, MA: D. C. Heath and Company, 1990), 2030–31.

17. Quoted in John Demos, "The Antislavery Movement and the Problem of Violent 'Means,'" *New England Quarterly* 37:4 (December, 1964), 505, 508.

18. Thomas Hughes, *The Manliness of Christ* (Boston: Houghton Mifflin Company, 1879), 6.

19. Douglass's April 1849 address to "the Colored Citizens of the City of New York" reflects Douglass's ambivalence forcefully:

> Some men go for the abolition of slavery by peaceable means. So do I; I am a peace man; but I recognize in the Southern States at this moment, as has been remarked here, *a state of war* ... I want [the country] to know that at least one colored man in the Union, peace man though he is, would greet with joy the glad news, should it come to-morrow, that an insurrection had broken out in the Southern States.

Here sentiments of war and peace commingle and clash. The "peace man" welcomes "insurrection" as the slaves' defense under "the state of war." Frederick Douglass, "Great Anti-Colonization Mass Meeting," *The Liberator*, May 11, 1849: 19. See, too, Robert Levine's analogous view of Douglass's "temperate revolutionism" in *Martin Delany, Frederick Douglass, and the Politics of Representative Identity* (Chapel Hill: University of North Carolina Press, 1997), 101.

20. William Gleason, "Volcanoes and Meteors: Douglass, Melville, and the Poetics of Insurrection," in *Frederick Douglass and Herman Melville: Essays in Relation*, ed. Robert Levine and Samuel Otter (Chapel Hill: University of North Carolina, 2008), 115.

21. David Blight, *Frederick Douglass' Civil War: Keeping Faith in Jubilee* (Baton Rouge: Louisiana State University Press, 1989), 61.

22. *Ibid.*, 64.

23. Elliot J. Gorn, *The Manly Art: Bare-Knuckle Prize Fighting in America* (Ithaca, NY: Cornell University Press, 1986), 163.

24. Quoted in Blight, *Frederick Douglass' Civil War*, 55.

25. *Ibid.*, 73, 61.

26. Frantz Fanon, "Concerning Violence," in *On Violence: A Reader*, ed. Bruce B. Lawrence and Aisha Karim (Durham, NC: Duke University Press, 2007), 79.

27. James Darcey, *The Prophetic Tradition and American Radical Rhetoric* (New York: NYU Press, 1997), 7.

28. Quoted in Blight, *Frederick Douglass' Civil War*, 62.

29. *Ibid.*, 76.

30. *Ibid.*, 101.

6

GREGG CRANE

Human Law and Higher Law

In setting the standards for what is or is not appropriate behavior, parents and children frequently confront an important distinction in the quality and nature of rulemaking. Certain acts are prohibited or required simply because the rulemaker decides it must be so and has the power to insist on obedience. When the child asks, "Why must I make my bed before breakfast?" the parent replies, "Because I say so." Other rules, however, seem weightier or more profound. Prohibitions on bullying other children or teasing one's pet often come with a conversation about values, such as kindness, reverence for life, or the golden rule.

Applying this commonplace distinction to the workings of a legal system often leads to confusion. In his famous essay, "The Path of the Law," Oliver Wendell Holmes, Jr. cautions us not to mistake law for morality. To understand the law, Holmes argues, "you must look at it as a bad man, who cares only for the material consequences which such knowledge enables him to predict, not as a good one, who finds his reasons for conduct, whether inside the law or outside of it, in the vaguer sanctions of conscience." Like the child responding to a command that carries no more profound justification than the will of the parental lawmaker, the "bad man" studies the law in order to predict what kinds of actions will get him into trouble (regardless of whether he finds such acts morally reprehensible or not). In Holmes's view, the language of law can sound like the language of morality, but one only has to recollect that "many laws ... enforced in the past" and "enforced now ... are condemned by the most enlightened opinion of the time" to see the necessity for distinguishing between legal and moral discourses.[1]

Like Holmes's "bad man," we probably obey most laws out of practical rather than moral considerations, and the bulk of the law's myriad provisions and requirements would seem to be fairly remote from transcendent moral principles. Yet there are moments when the question of a law's moral legitimacy becomes critically important, moments when we want the law to represent something more than the will of the rule maker. From an early age, Frederick Douglass intuited that slavery was authorized by nothing more profound than the will of one people to dominate another. Slavery was a man-made system not ordained by God or necessitated by nature, and to accept the law of slavery as legitimate was "simply to reduce mankind absolutely to the law of brute force" (FDP 2:285). Confronted with the criminalization of humanitarian aid to fugitive slaves by the Fugitive Slave Law of 1850, Theodore Parker, a minister and abolitionist, wrote that he was willing to "suffer much, sooner than violate a statute that was merely inexpedient," but "when the rulers have … enacted wickedness into a law which treads down the inalienable rights of man to such a degree as this, then I know no ruler but God, no law but natural justice." In "Resistance to Civil Government" (1849), Henry David Thoreau, thinking along similar lines, asks:

> Can there not be a government in which majorities do not virtually decide right and wrong, but conscience? – in which majorities decide only those questions to which the rule of expediency is applicable? Must the citizen ever for a moment, or in the least degree, resign his conscience to the legislator? Why has every man a conscience, then?

For Douglass, Parker, Thoreau, and many others considering the law of slavery, the political power of a democratic majority to write its will into law must, on occasion, be checked by a higher moral authority.[2]

The subordination of human law to "higher law" was one of many themes in William H. Seward's inaugural speech before the US Senate on March 11, 1850. His topic was Henry Clay's "Compromise of 1850," which included admission of California as a free state and a new, more potent Fugitive Slave Law. When it came to the latter provision, Seward threw down a gauntlet on the issue most sharply dividing the country. He flatly denied "that the Constitution recognizes property in man" and asserted that the nation's charter must heed "a higher law." If passed, the manifest evil of this law would inspire an expanding "public conscience," "transcending" party politics and sectional interests, to reassert (and more clearly define) the ethical basis of the American legal and political system.[3]

"No portion of [Seward's speech] met with a wider or more unsparing condemnation," observed the New York *Tribune*, than the notion that constitutional doctrine could be governed by the nation's changing moral notions. Many objected that Seward's argument licensed people to choose which laws they would obey. As the *Richmond Enquirer* put it, "The prominent idea set forth is, that the persons … can at any moment relieve themselves from the duty of obedience … by announcing that their conscience … forbids the compliance which the law demands."[4] Some contended that "higher law" sanctioned slavery. George Fitzhugh argued that benevolently authoritarian institutions, such as slavery and marriage, represented the only moral way of addressing pervasive and apparently natural human inequalities.[5] For proslavery novelist Caroline Lee Hentz, the "great commanding truth" of human society is that "wherever civilized man exists, there is the dividing line of the high and the low." If such inequality is permanent and ubiquitous (at least in "civilized" societies), then the only relevant "higher law" question in Hentz's view is not how to erase what is indelible but what is the best and most compassionate form of regulation for an unavoidably hierarchical society. Hentz would replace the Northern society torn apart by capitalism's ceaseless competition and selfishness with the Southerner's "affectionate community" of slaves and slaveholders.[6]

While the prevailing reaction to Seward's speech was critical, his comments did find a sympathetic audience. Harriet Beecher Stowe wrote "The Freeman's Dream" (August 1850), which proved to be a trial run for the fugitive slave scenes in *Uncle Tom's Cabin* (1852). In "The Freeman's Dream," Stowe imagines the Northern farmer who, faced with fugitive slaves, obeys the law and refuses to help. He subsequently dies and must face an adverse divine judgment: "Depart from me ye accursed! for I was an hungered, and ye gave me no meat." The farmer is condemned for choosing the lower law of men instead of the higher law of God. Explicitly weighing in on Seward's side of the argument, Stowe's story censures those "who seem to think that there is no standard of right and wrong higher than an act of Congress, or an interpretation of the United States Constitution."[7] When he heard higher law reckoned a kind of joke by lawyers and politicians, Ralph Waldo Emerson began taking notes on what he thought would become a treatise in defense of higher law jurisprudence. Ainsworth Rand Spofford, future Librarian of Congress, wrote a pamphlet laying out the rationale and authorities for a higher law approach to the Constitution, and William Hosmer wrote a book defending higher law jurisprudence.[8]

Frederick Douglass frequently cited Seward's invocation of higher law and, throughout his long career of public advocacy, insisted that American law must be founded on universal ethical norms to be legitimate. He came to view human law as an on-going attempt to put moral inspiration into practice through political dialogue and public consensus. For Douglass, "Perfection is an object to be aimed at by all, but it is not an attribute of any form of government. Mutability is the law for all" ("Our Composite Nationality," FDP 4:244). Instead of a static legal code and set of social customs that simply and clearly mirror moral absolutes, Douglass conceived of the quest to give life meaning and to imbue our doings with ethical value as a continuing process of discovery, invention, and transformation:

> Men talk much of a new birth. The fact is fundamental. But the mistake is in treating it as an incident which can only happen to a man once in a life time;

whereas, the whole journey of life is a succession of them. A new life springs up in the soul, with the discovery of every new agency by which the soul is raised to a higher level of wisdom, goodness and joy. The poor savage, accustomed only to the stunning war whoop of his tribe, and to the wild and startling sounds in nature, of winds, waterfalls, and thunder, meets with a change of heart the first time he hears the Divine harmonies, of scientific[?] music: and the child experiences one with every new object, by means of which it is brought into a nearer and fuller acquaintance with its own subjective nature. With every step he attains a larger, fuller and freer range of vision.   ("Pictures and Progress," FDP 2:460)

In his oratory and autobiographical writing, Douglass presents his own protean self-transformations as an analogue for a fluid Constitution continually being rewritten by new participants and in light of their diverse perspectives.

While he consistently asserted that a valid legal system is grounded in ethical principles, Douglass's speeches reveal a substantial shift in how he approached the topic of law and ethics. Douglass's early speeches routinely invoke religious concepts and scripture to conjure a shared recognition of the iniquity of slavery. In "My Slave Experience in Maryland" (May 6, 1845), he contrasts God's law, which stands for the fundamental truth "that shalt not oppress," and "the Constitution," which "says oppress" (FDP 2:33). Given the contrast, the choice is clear. Morality, sympathetic feeling, and religious teaching – higher law – should trump the lower law of men. The stated aim in these early addresses is not to force change on the slaveholder but to "awaken" him "to a sense of the iniquity of his position" (FDP 2:42). Douglass wants to bring about a conversion in the slaveholder and his allies. He points to the example of James Birney, a former slaveholder, who was awakened to the evils of slavery and changed his ways ("Baptists, Congregationalists, the Free Church, and Slavery," FDP 1:107). The emphasis in Douglass's early speeches on religious themes and figures reveals the influence of Garrisonian abolitionism. For William Lloyd Garrison and his followers, the clearest arguments against slavery were religious rather than legal or political in nature.[9] Arguing for God-directed self-control as the true source of public order and dispensing with the messy and uncertain processes of political argument and compromise, Garrison's conception of government stressed the unambiguous dictates of conscience not political process.

In his early oratory, Douglass does not analyze slavery. Instead, he presents its most horrible aspects and features (e.g., the separation of parents and children or the torture of slaves), assuming that his listeners will automatically "see" the iniquity of the institution. This strategy opens Douglass to the challenge that he has not proven the wrongness of slavery but merely assumed it by reference to abuses of the system. While Douglass would likely respond that abuse is the very essence of slavery, he might also claim that he does not have to *prove* that slavery is wrong:

> Truth needs but little argument, and no long metaphysical detail to establish a position. There is something in the heart which instantly responds to its voice. You feel differently when even the term slavery is mentioned, from the way you feel when the word freedom salutes your ears! Freedom! the word produces a thrill of joy even in the bosom of the slave-holder himself – in the absence of his slaves ... Oh, yes – our hearts leap up to the very name of freedom, while we recoil with horror at the sound of slavery. We feel, then, that the slave-holder is a wrong-doer, and we know that wrong-doers can have no fellowship with the meek and lowly Jesus.
>
> ("Baptists, Congregationalists, the Free Church, and Slavery," FDP 1:108)

Here, Douglass seems utterly confident that proof of the evil of slavery is unnecessary because the tide of human thought on this issue is moving irresistibly in an antislavery direction. Eventually, all will have to admit this truth. For Douglass, as for Harriet Beecher Stowe and many other antislavery advocates, the apparently innate human capacity for sympathy warrants one's faith in a universal moral intuition. And, substituting descriptions of how we feel about words such as "freedom" and "slavery" for a more analytic treatment of the subject, Douglass's early oratory seeks to draw forth and engender the very conclusion he posits as inevitable.

The fact that Douglass was not initially inclined to undertake a detailed analysis of the transcendental values he invoked may simply flow from the fact that he was neither a philosopher nor a mystic, but it may also reflect an understanding that such ultimate or noumenal values are finally unprovable and that what matters for the social reformer is the changing public consensus about what these values entail and require. Lacking direct access to these ideals, one can, as Douglass well understood, both assert the permanence and absoluteness of such values and acknowledge that our sense of them is evolving. The conversion moment or moral epiphany rests on this paradox: one learns that a practice enduring over millennia is "at war with the best feelings of the human heart," but this radical shift does not lead one to doubt the permanence of ethical ideals ("American Prejudice against Color," FDP 1:60).

In the early 1850s, Douglass experienced a conversion or radical shift of his own in regard to the US Constitution. Like his mentor Garrison, Douglass initially rejected the Constitution and the American legal system as fatally tainted by their recognition and protection of slavery. Garrison urged his followers not to vote or otherwise participate in a legal and political system corrupted by slavery, and he advocated a secessionist view that the North should spurn continued union with the slaveholding South. In a bit of political theater, Garrison would burn a copy of the Constitution as a symbolic condemnation of the pact with Hell. For much of the first decade of his work as a public antislavery speaker and advocate, Douglass stuck to the Garrisonian line, often arguing that the Constitution should be condemned as a proslavery document. Then, with little warning, Douglass broke with the Garrisonians, arguing that the nation's charter should be interpreted as antislavery; henceforth, his invocations of higher law became less religious, more political, and more analytic.

To position this transformation in Douglass's career, it is helpful to distinguish between the three antislavery positions prominent in the years leading to the Civil War. In addition to the Garrisonian position, there were two antislavery points of view that argued against rejecting the Constitution. Moderate antislavery constitutionalists, such as Seward, Charles Sumner, Thaddeus Stevens, and Salmon Chase, hoped slavery would die without federal support. They conceded that the bifurcation of state and federal governments may have reserved a space for slavery as a matter of local law in the Southern states, but they contended that the Constitution required the federal government to protect the essential liberties and rights of all persons within its jurisdiction. The moderates worked to bar the extension of slavery into the territories (where the federal government had exclusive jurisdiction), to eradicate slavery in the District of Columbia, and used federal patronage and appointments in the states to work against slavery. Radical antislavery constitutionalists, such as Alvan Stewart, William Goodell, Lysander Spooner, Gerrit Smith, James McCune Smith, Jermain W. Loguen, and Amos Dresser, read the Constitution as making slavery everywhere illegitimate. Radicals critiqued the racist limitations of the Republican mainstream while remaining in correspondence with and lending support to the more radical of the Republican leaders, such as Sumner and Stevens. Founded in 1854 by former Whigs, Free-Soilers, and Northern Democrats, the Republican Party coalesced around an opposition to the expansion of slavery, but there was considerable diversity in its members' notions as to what this opposition entailed or implied. Radical antislavery constitutionalists eschewed major-party politics in order to push the higher law critique further than the moderates could do within those party structures. The radicals' approach to the Constitution boiled down to a hermeneutic imperative to read the nation's charter as enacting justice, not oppression, which entailed reading the document against its grain at times in order to square it with basic moral norms.[10]

Eventually, Douglass began to chafe at his role within the Garrisonian antislavery movement and to balk at certain aspects of the Garrisonian position.

For example, Garrison valued Douglass's eloquence as a witness against slavery more than his canny analysis of the peculiar institution. Garrison's desire that Douglass avoid such analysis and simply "[t]ell his story" may have derived in part from some trace of racial prejudice or envy, but it certainly derived as well from the apolitical, even anarchic aspect of Garrison's religious higher law approach, which sought to replace a flawed human law not with a better human law but with God's law. One does not have to figure out, construct, negotiate, plan, or structure God's law – one simply bears witness to and obeys it. The denial of human agency in and static quality of this absolutist approach provoked Douglass as much as the objectification involved in being displayed as a victim of slavery.

When Douglass returned from his first trip to Britain, his Garrisonian allies (and handlers) found him full of heterodox ambitions and ideas that could not be contained. From the perspective of "a denizen of the world," Douglass came to realize that, for individual moral inspiration to have effect it must enter public discourse in such a way as to create a new moral consensus – as Emerson put it, "although the commands of the Conscience are *essentially* absolute, they are *historically* limitary."[11] In attempting to achieve justice, we act on a moral impulse deriving, we believe, from eternal moral principles, but acknowledge at the same time that the implementation of that moral impulse in consensual politics and law is temporal and experimental. The eternal truths of the higher law, as Douglass put it, unfold within the "constant evolution of moral ideas" for which we are responsible, not God:

> The idea that man cannot hold property in man, that all men are free, that human rights are inalienable, that the rights of one man are equal to those of another, that governments are ordained to secure human rights did not come all at once to the moral conscience of men, but have all come very slowly in the thoughts of the world.[12]

Meeting with considerably less racism in Britain, Douglass could see that racism was a piece of human manufacture and the key impediment to a revised social and legal order. Conceived while Douglass was abroad, the project of his paper, *The North Star*, was to unmake this majority racism and to replace it with a cosmopolitan discourse of ethics and law. In the pages of *The North Star* and elsewhere, Douglass would portray the continued existence of slavery as not just an American problem but an impediment to global progress. And he saluted the influence of foreign reformers whose outsider's perspective could help to illuminate the provincial biases limiting American justice.

As an editor, Douglass was drawn into conversation with a broader range of antislavery views. He engaged radical and moderate antislavery constitutionalists who argued, contrary to the Garrisonians, that the Constitution should be embraced as an egalitarian, antislavery charter. Gerrit Smith confronted Douglass with William Goodell's contention that a straightforward reading of the Preamble justified the eradication of slavery: "To promote the general welfare" could not be consonant with "crushing the laboring, the producing class, in half the States of the Republic," and securing "the blessings of Liberty" had to require the "overthrow" of "the deadly antagonist to liberty, to wit, slavery."[13] Encounters with Smith and others compelled Douglass "to re-think the whole subject, and to study, with some care, not only the just and proper rules of legal interpretation, but the origin, design, nature, rights, powers, and duties of civil government" (MB 392).

On May 7, 1851, at the Syracuse meeting of the American Anti-Slavery Society convention, Douglass shocked the meeting and the ranks of antislavery by summarily announcing his adoption of a radical reading of the Constitution. Douglass described his new point of view to Gerrit Smith: "I am only in reason and conscience bound to learn the intentions of those who framed the Constitution *in the Constitution itself*" (LW 2:157). We should not let the seeming transparency of this statement obscure the aggressively creative interpretive approach Douglass is taking here. Strictly remaining within its four corners, one cannot produce coherent interpretations of the Constitution's many ambiguities. By focusing on its express but abstract wording (which does not include the terms "slave" or "slavery") *and* presuming that it favors justice, Douglass can exclude from the Constitution extrinsic historical evidence that does not comport with present conceptions of justice (e.g., that many of the Framers owned slaves or that the Constitution's slavery clauses were part of a deal with the Southern states to ensure ratification). And excluding such negative extrinsic evidence, in turn, enables Douglass – an ex-slave and disfranchised black American – to read the document's abstract terms as comporting with present conceptions of justice and to rewrite its history as endorsing a more just vision of American society. By presuming "that the Constitution" favors "liberty" (a reasonable position given the express wording of the Preamble), one can dismiss evidence that some Framers, contrary to the principle of liberty, "desired compromises [favoring] slavery" ("Antislavery Principles and Antislavery Acts," FDP 2:349). With such evidence out of the way, the conclusion becomes inescapable that the Framers intended the Constitution to be capable of expansion so as to "secure the equality of *all* the people." In Douglass's new radical view of the nation's charter, the Framers had anticipated that changes in the national moral consensus would redirect readings of the nation's highest law.

It is important to note how Douglass distinguishes between the document's past and its future:

No doubt there were men in the Convention who desired compromises that would favor the interests of slavery – they may have thought they obtained them. But it is more certain that a large body – among them a large number of slaveholders – were earnest anti-slavery men, and intended to frame a Constitution that would *finally* secure the equality of *all* the people – all the persons if you please – in these States. What I contend is, that if the Constitution shall be *presumed* to favor liberty, and to be consistent with its noble preamble, its language will inevitably secure the extinction of human slavery, and forever, in this Republic. (FDP 2:349; emphasis added)

Douglass's reading of the antislavery intent of the document is driven by a future-oriented sense that the document can be made to be antislavery in aim and effect if we effectively will it to be so. Douglass's reading of constitutional history admits that there were proslavery interests represented at the Convention but sees those interests as marginal to the better aims of the Convention. On this view, the Civil War amendments would explicitly recognize what was already potential in the document.

Douglass's higher law vision of the Constitution is most provocatively advanced in his famous address "What to the Slave Is the Fourth of July?" (July 5, 1852). To help us see how radical Douglass's speech is in its direful figuration of the nation's moral condition and its hopeful vision of a mutable Constitution, we should briefly observe the contrast offered by the speeches of Senators Henry Clay, John Calhoun, and Daniel Webster on the Compromise of 1850, speeches that became the touchstone for proslavery versions of the Constitution in the 1850s. In debating the best way to save the Union, Clay, Calhoun, and Webster self-consciously drew authority to speak from the notion that they were representative of the constituent elements of the country (Calhoun speaks as a Southerner, Clay claims the insight of a border state citizen [Kentucky], and Webster speaks "not as a Massachusetts man, nor as a Northern man, but as an American").[14]

By contrast, Douglass's outsider status gives him a different vantage on the significance of the Fourth of July. Telling his listeners, "It is the birthday of *your* National Independence, and of *your* political freedom," Douglass claims authority to speak on this occasion by virtue of "the distance" he has traveled to get to "this platform" from "the slave plantation, from which I escaped" and "the difficulties" he surmounted "in getting from the latter to the former" ("What to the Slave," FDP 2:360). This journey allows Douglass to perceive and credibly announce both the nation's failure and its promise, making him representative not of the Union as it has been, but of what it can become. Where Calhoun, Clay, and Webster seek to arrest the forces of change, calling for the restoration of a prior equilibrium between the sections ("harmony and fraternal feelings," "brotherly love and affection," and the preservation of "the great American family"), Douglass flatly announces that change is inevitable.[15] The republic, according to Douglass, is like a river. Until it dries up, it is in continual motion. The only question is what its course will be. Douglass finds hope in the fact that the nation's relative youth ("she is still in the *impressionable* stage of her existence") may enable a necessary transformation made more radical by virtue of the guilt that must be confronted (FDP 2:361). Where Calhoun condemns the North for violating the fixed terms of a sacred deal between the sections, Douglass praises the deal struck by "the fathers of this republic" as intentionally left open: "With them, nothing was 'settled' that was not right" (FDP 2:365).

But the most thunderous contrast can be heard in Webster's and Douglass's characterizations of the United States. Webster's peroration pleads for the sake of a great and just nation:

> It is a great, popular, constitutional government, guarded by legislation, law, and judicature, defended by the holy affections of the people. No monarchical throne presses these States together; no iron chain of despotic power encircles them; they live and stand upon a government, popular in its form, representative in its character, founded on principles of equality, calculated to last, we hope, forever. In all its history it has been beneficent. It has trodden down no man's liberty; it has crushed no State; is has been in all its influences benevolent and beneficent – promotive of the general prosperity, the general glory, and the general renown.[16]

The irony of Webster's touting of American beneficence in a speech urging that there is no conceivable moral ground on which to deny the return of fugitive slaves could hardly have been lost on Douglass. Douglass crushes this exceptionalist, self-satisfied illusion with a blistering summation of the hypocrisy entailed in this vision of the Union:

> What, to the American slave, is your 4th of July? I answer: a day that reveals to him, more than all other days in the year, the gross injustice and cruelty to which he is the constant victim. To him, your celebration is a sham; your boasted liberty, an unholy license; your national greatness, swelling vanity; your sounds of rejoicing are empty and heartless; your denunciations of tyrants, brass fronted impudence; your shouts of liberty and equality, hollow mockery; your prayers and hymns, your sermons and thanksgivings, with all your religious parade, and solemnity, are, to him, mere bombast, fraud, deception, impiety, and hypocrisy – a thin veil to cover up crimes which would disgrace a nation of savages. There is not a nation on the earth guilty of practices, more shocking and bloody, than are the people of these United States, at this very hour.   (FDP 2:371)

To illustrate these charges, Douglass offers the "fiendish and shocking" "spectacle" of the internal slave trade, "the sound of the slave-whip," the separation of families, the brutal exposure of the women to be sold (FDP 2:373). The Fugitive Slave Law epitomizes the vile direction the nation has taken in substituting power for notions of morality and consent: "[Slavery] is now an institution of the whole United States. The slave power is co-extensive with the star-spangled banner and American Christianity" (FDP 2:375).

Where Webster's oration closes with the dulcet tones of justice and equanimity in an attempt to retune the national harmony and restore the status quo, Douglass's speech shatters the complacencies of the nation's self-image with the discord of slavery. The aim of Douglass's jeremiad is to precipitate a transformation of the nation's self-conception and its interpretation of the Constitution. To spur such self-transformation, Douglass must decisively interrupt the tendency of Americans to remember only the "facts which make in their own favor." One of the most powerful and insidious of these tendencies is the attempt by Webster and others to avoid the crisis of constitutional conscience by retreating into fantasies of a shared ancestry's heroic past. To drain the affective power of such images, Douglass contrasts proud claims of revolutionary era ancestry (so often invoked by Webster and other politicians) with recognition that revolutionary ideas have no genealogy: "It was fashionable, hundreds of years ago, for the children of Jacob to boast, we have 'Abraham to our father,' when they had long lost Abraham's faith and spirit. That people contented themselves under the shadow of Abraham's great name, while they repudiated the deeds which made his name great" (FDP 2:366–68). The ideas and actions of each generation of citizens, not blood, make a republic's development worthy of celebration.

By abruptly pivoting from his withering condemnation of the nation's hypocrisy to praise the Constitution as "a GLORIOUS LIBERTY DOCUMENT," Douglass pushes his audience into an acrobatic recognition of the coexistence of slavery and freedom, power and consent: "In *that* instrument I hold there is neither warrant, license, nor sanction of the hateful thing; but, interpreted as it *ought* to be interpreted, the Constitution is a GLORIOUS LIBERTY DOCUMENT. Read its preamble, consider its purposes. Is slavery among them? Is it at the gateway? or is it in the temple? It is neither." Against the heinous particularities of American slavery, Douglass juxtaposes his and his audience's always present ability to reread the nation's charter in the interests of justice. Thanks to the abstractness and openness of the Constitution, we can continue to author the Union and its organizing principles through our reinterpretation of the national charter:

Now, there are certain rules of interpretation, for the proper understanding of all legal instruments. These rules are well established. They are plain, common-sense rules, such as you and I, and all of us, can understand and apply, without having passed years in the study of law. I scout the idea that the question of the constitutionality or unconstitutionality of slavery is not a question for the people. I hold that every American citizen has a right to form an opinion of the constitution, and to propagate that opinion, and to use all honorable means to make his opinion the prevailing one.

Amateurism is as central to Douglass's jurisprudence as it was to the founding fathers. The average citizen, in Douglass's view, has the ability and the responsibility to revise the basic charter by reading it to conform to what he or she sees as "the evolution of moral ideas." In stating that "I hold that every American citizen has a right to form an opinion of the constitution, and to propagate that opinion, and to use all honorable means to make his opinion the prevailing one," Douglass champions the agency of the citizen-jurist who forms an opinion of the Constitution and garners the public support necessary to render his/her interpretation effective (FDP 2:385).[17]

Douglass's vision of amateur constitutional interpretation implies an ongoing negotiation of the governing moral consensus animating and directing the national charter. As only justice is "final" and the human agents creating that justice are imperfect, a society's civic virtue lies in the continuing revision of this consensus not in fictions of arrival like that touted by Webster in which the Framers' consensus as to the Constitution's meaning is held up as forever definitive. If based on moral agency, not race, Douglass and the disfranchised people he represents clearly qualify for citizenship and participation in revising the nation's charter.

The constitutional transformation Douglass hopes his speech will help to engender, however, is not simply a matter of changing slaves into citizens. One could say that that is almost a happy by-product of another transformation Douglass is more directly concerned with in "What to the Slave Is the Fourth of July?" The aim of his speech's vitriol is to convert the self-satisfied members of a mythic Anglo-Saxon clan into citizens: political beings who define their political and legal association not by consanguinity but through consent and moral agency. Douglass powerfully recasts the national narrative as a continuing confrontation of the challenge to read justice into the terms of the national charter despite our history of injustice. In rising to this challenge, we confront the grievous failures of our history as well as the promise of our express dedication to justice, liberty, and equality.

While the brutal conflagration of the Civil War did not eradicate racism in the vanquished South or the victorious North, as Bruce Ackerman has forcefully argued, the Civil War amendments depended for their enactment on a shift in the nation's higher law consensus.[18] The extent of this shift is suggested in an 1864 *North American Review* article, "The Constitution and its

Defects." The article notes that during the first decades of the nineteenth century "the work of testing the morality of national legislation by the application of fundamental principles was abandoned by the leading minds of the country." But looking back from 1864, one felt ashamed by "the general contempt and ridicule excited ... by appeals to the 'higher law,'" which only represented the simple truth that

> government is after all a conventional arrangement, entitled, no doubt, to the utmost respect, and not to be disturbed unless it plainly fails to answer the purpose for which it was instituted; but that cases may arise, not calling for revolution, in which justice and truth are so outraged, under color of law, that it becomes the duty of good citizens to be guided rather by the principles of morality, on which the law ultimately rests all its claims to obedience, than by the law itself.[19]

Even after their post-Reconstruction retrenchment, the Thirteenth (barring slavery), Fourteenth (establishing the fundamental citizenship rights of black Americans), and Fifteenth (setting forth the right of black American men to vote) amendments continued to give African Americans the right to argue for their rights. These amendments, in Douglass's view, put "the supreme law of the land on the side of justice and liberty," giving discrete political minorities a powerful tool with which to advocate for full citizenship and justice (LT 932). As he put it in a post-war address, "Sources of Danger to the Republic," February 7, 1867, the best thing about the Constitution is that it is capable of "embrac[ing] man as man": "In the eye of that great instrument we are neither Jews, Greeks, Barbarians or Cythians, but fellow-citizens of a common country, embracing men of all colors" (FDP 4:153). But, Douglass reminds us, as good as that document is,

> it is simply a human contrivance. It is the work of man and men struggling with many of the prejudices and infirmities common to man, and it is not strange that we should find in their constitution some evidences of their infirmities and prejudices. Time and experience and the ever increasing light of reason are constantly making manifest those defects and those imperfections, and it is for us ... to remove those defects. (FDP 4:153–54)

NOTES

1. "The Path of the Law" (1897), in *The Essential Holmes*, ed. Richard Posner (Chicago, IL: University of Chicago Press, 1992), 161–62.
2. Theodore Parker, "The Function of Conscience" (1850), in *The Slave Power* (New York: Arno, 1969), 340; Henry David Thoreau, "Resistance to Civil Government" (1849), in *Walden and Civil Disobedience* (New York: Signet, 1960), 223.
3. "Freedom in the New Territories," in *The Works of William H. Seward*, ed. George E. Baker, 5 vols. (New York: Redfield Press, 1853), 1:51, 1:66, 1:71, 1:74.

4. New York *Tribune*, March 20, 1850; *Richmond Enquirer*, March 27, 1857.

5. See, e.g., George Fitzhugh, *Sociology for the South; or the Failure of Free Society* (Richmond, VA: A. Morris, 1854), 25–26, 89, and *Cannibals All!, or Slaves Without Masters* (1857; Cambridge, MA: Belknap Press of Harvard University Press, 1988), 243, 218–19, 134–35.

6. Caroline Lee Hentz, *The Planter's Northern Bride* (1854; Chapel Hill: University of North Carolina Press, 1970), 32, 149.

7. Harriet Beecher Stowe, "The Freeman's Dream," *National Era*, August 1, 1850.

8. Ralph Waldo Emerson, "WO Liberty," in *The Journals and Miscellaneous Notebooks of Ralph Waldo Emerson*, 16 vols., ed. William H. Gilman (Cambridge, MA: Harvard University Press, 1960–82), 14:373–430; Ainsworth Rand Spofford, *The Higher Law Tried by Reason and Authority* (New York: S. W. Benedict, 1851); William Hosmer, *The Higher Law in its Relations to Civil Government* (Auburn, NY: Derby & Miller, 1852).

9. Lewis Perry, *Radical Abolitionism: Anarchy and the Government of God in Antislavery Thought* (Ithaca, NY: Cornell University Press, 1973), 18, 52, 53; Bertram Wyatt-Brown, *Lewis Tappan and the Evangelical War against Slavery* (Cleveland, OH: Case Western Reserve University, 1969), 270–71.

10. William Wiecek, *The Origins of Antislavery Constitutionalism in America* (Ithaca, NY: Cornell University Press, 1977), 16, 17, 19, 202; Eric Foner, *Free Soil, Free Labor, Free Men: The Ideology of the Republican Party Before The Civil War* (New York: Oxford University Press, 1970), 116–17.

11. Ralph Waldo Emerson, "The Conservative" (1841), in *The Portable Emerson*, ed. Mark Van Doren (New York: Viking, 1946), 94.

12. Quoted in Waldo Martin, Jr., *The Mind of Frederick Douglass* (Chapel Hill: University of North Carolina Press, 1984), 172.

13. William Goodell, *American Constitutional Law* (1844; Freeport, NY: Books for Libraries, 1971), 41.

14. John C. Cahoun, "Speech on the Admission of California – and the General State of the Union," March 4, 1850, in *Union and Liberty: the Political Philosophy of John C. Calhoun*, ed. Ross M. Lence (Indianapolis, IN: Liberty Press, 1992), 590; Henry Clay, *Speech of the Hon. Henry Clay, of Kentucky, on taking up his Compromise Resolutions on the Subject of Slavery* (New York: Stringer & Townsend, 1850), 21–22; Daniel Webster, "The Constitution and the Union," March 7, 1850, in *The Papers of Daniel Webster: Speeches and Formal Writings*, 7 vols., ed. Charles M. Wiltse (Hanover, NH: University Press of New England, 1988), 2:515.

15. Calhoun, "Admission of California," 600; Clay, *Compromise Resolutions*, 13; Webster, "Constitution and Union," 2:548.

16. Webster, "Constitution and Union," 2:550–51, 2:541.

17. Perry Miller has observed how, in sharp distinction to the founders' amateurism, law and politics increasingly in the nineteenth century became the province of a specialized class of professionals. Antislavery did much to reclaim the more participatory political model of the founders. Perry Miller, *The Life of the Mind in America* (New York: Harcourt Brace, 1965), 104.

18. Bruce Ackerman, *We the People: Transformations* (Cambridge, MA: Harvard University Press, 1998), 99–252.

19. "The Constitution and its Defects," *North American Review* 99 (1864): 119–21.

7

ARTHUR RISS

Sentimental Douglass

In his 1845 *Narrative*, Frederick Douglass recalls how, as a small child, he had "often been awakened at the dawn of day by the most heart-rending shrieks of an own aunt of mine" (N 18). In particular, he recollects that the first time he witnessed his Aunt Hester being whipped possessed an especially "awful force," declaring that he "shall never forget it whilst I remember any thing." Living with his grandmother on the "outskirts of the plantation," Douglass had been sheltered from "the bloody scenes" of slavery, and thus this "horrible exhibition" marks – both literally and figuratively – the mythic moment that the child comes into consciousness about slavery (N 19, 20). Or as Douglass states, it was the "blood-stained gate" through which he entered into the "hell of slavery" (N 18). Teaching Douglass what it means to be a slave ("I had never seen any thing like it before"), this event is, as scholars have often noted, a primal scene, the moment that launches what Douglass later calls his "career as a slave" (N 18, 19, 65).

Given that Douglass represents his observation of the brutalization of his aunt as his compulsory invitation to the system of slavery, it is not surprising that this "terrible spectacle" has become one of the most analyzed episodes in the *Narrative*.[1] In particular, questions have been consistently raised about the scene's ultimate significance because its narrative focus is directed neither on Douglass nor his aunt but on Douglass's master, Captain Anthony. Douglass details Anthony's preparation, whipping, and words, expressing horror at the convergence of sadism and lust that drives Anthony to half strip and ferociously beat the extremely attractive slave woman for being "in company" of another slave (N 19). Despite the fear and horror that Douglass explicitly expresses at Anthony's sensational cruelty, his intense interest in Anthony's actions has led some critics to explore "Douglass' potential identification" with his master rather than with his Aunt Hester, to ask whether a latent fascination, a libidinously charged voyeurism, or perhaps even a dangerous complicity with the agent of brutality threaten both a reader's and Douglass's sympathy with the "victims" of slavery.[2]

Douglass himself seems to anticipate such a critique; in later versions of his autobiography he carefully revises his account of this event, shifting the focus more clearly away from Anthony onto Aunt Hester – now orthographically rendered as Esther. He more clearly subordinates the agent of violence to the object of violence and more forcefully highlights the experience of the "suffering victim" (MB 177). For example, in *My Bondage and My Freedom* (1855) Esther, rather than Anthony, is given a voice, and in *Life and Times of Frederick Douglass* (1881; 1892), Douglass recounts how Esther resists Anthony and continues seeing her lover.[3] But perhaps the most telling revision is that in subsequent autobiographies the torture of Aunt Hester – an event so central to the 1845 *Narrative* – no longer announces the moment that he discovers himself as a slave. Indeed, in both *My Bondage and My Freedom* and in *Life and Times* Douglass identifies as the originary moment of his subjectification as a slave not his witnessing of the sensationalized torture of his aunt but his abrupt, irrevocable, and quintessentially sentimental separation from his grandmother: "My grandmother! My grandmother! And the little hut, and the joyous circle – under her care, but especially *she*, who made us sorry when she left us but for an hour, and glad on her return, – how could I leave her and the good old home" (MB 143–44).

Douglass becomes a slave, in these later accounts, at the moment when this separation – the anticipation of which "haunted" his childhood – finally does arrive:

> Grandmammy had indeed gone, and was now far away, "clean" out of sight. I need not tell all that happened now. Almost heart-broken at the discovery, I fell upon the ground, and wept a boy's bitter tears, refusing to be comforted. My brother and sisters came around me, and said, "Don't cry," and gave me peaches and pears, but I flung them away, and refused all their kindly advances … I knew not how or where, but I suppose I sobbed myself to sleep. There is a healing in the angel wing of sleep, even for the slave-boy; and its balm was never more welcome to any wounded soul than it was to mine, the first night I spent at the domicile of old master. The reader may be surprised that I narrate so minutely an incident apparently so trivial, and which must have occurred when I was not more than seven years old; but as I wish to give a faithful history of my experience in slavery, I cannot withhold a circumstance which, at the time, affected me so deeply. *Besides, this was, in fact, my first introduction to the realities of slavery.*   (MB 150; emphasis added)

In 1855, it appears, the "realities of slavery" are the "realities" of sentimental discourse, his initiation into slavery inseparable from an initiation into sentimentality. Previously, Douglass may have been told he "was A SLAVE – born a slave" but this "fact was incomprehensible" (MB 147). His separation from his grandmother makes this fact comprehensible. And, it makes it comprehensible in an unambiguously sentimental register: slavery violates the principles of sympathy and love; it separates families, disrupts the home, and victimizes children. Indeed, it is precisely such affective language that creates the sympathetic bond between Douglass and his readers central to sentimentality. Here, there is no longer any question of whom to sympathize with or any danger of an uncontrolled identification. In fact, one suspects that Douglass introduces his account by stating he "need not tell" his reader "all that happened" because he presumes that his readers will be already be deeply familiar with such a scene: they had, after all, already read Stowe's *Uncle Tom's Cabin* (1852).

Such a revision is emblematic of Douglass's turn towards the sentimental.[4] This is not to say that there are no sentimental moments in the 1845 *Narrative*. There certainly are. One thinks immediately of Douglass's famous apostrophe to the synecdochic "white sails" on Chesapeake Bay – a passage about which Garrison asked "[w]ho can read" and be "insensible to its pathos and sublimity" or ignore that it contains a "whole Alexandrian library of thought, feeling, and sentiment?" (N 8). Or one thinks of Douglass's imagining of his grandmother, who having grown too old to be of use to her master, is left to die alone in the woods, groping her way in the dark for a "drink of water": "She stands – she sits – she staggers – she falls – she groans – she dies – and there are none of her children or grandchildren present, to wipe from her wrinkled brow the cold sweat of death, or to place beneath the sod her fallen remains" (N 48–49). Such moments, however, seem simultaneously marginal and conspicuous in the context of the text's distinctively "plain" style.[5] In 1855 things change. Having witnessed the spectacular success of *Uncle Tom's Cabin*, Douglass, it appears, deliberately revises his autobiography to make his story more conventionally sentimental, altering in particular the mythological ur-moment that crystallizes what it means to be a slave.[6] As Eric Sundquist has noted, Douglass seems to be writing *Uncle Tom's Cabin* into the very "fabric" of *My Bondage and My Freedom*, or, as P. Gabrielle Foreman has phrased it, "While the Douglass of the *Narrative* ... does not engage in consistent sentimental renderings of domesticity; the 1855 narrator does."[7]

In this essay I want to explore Douglass's sentimental turn. What is one to make of the fact that *My Bondage and My Freedom* – a text that Douglass identifies with his political, philosophical, and literary independence – is marked by such an enthusiastic embrace of the sentimental that the life it presents often looks as if it could have been written by Stowe?[8] I will argue that Douglass can be seen as engaged in a sustained meditation on the power of the sentimental and that we – despite the significant scholarly work dedicated to recognizing how the sentimental crucially structured antebellum discourse and despite the substantial critical re-examinations of the literary value and political force of the sentimental – are still not taking the sentimental as seriously as Douglass did.

The most obvious explanation of Douglass's shift towards sentimentality is, as I have suggested, that Douglass wants to replicate the success of *Uncle Tom's Cabin*, to convert his audience to the antislavery cause as powerfully, if not more powerfully, than Stowe did. As Douglass dramatically declares in his 1855 lecture "The Anti-Slavery Movement," extracts of which are reprinted in *My Bondage and My Freedom*, the inspirational force of *Uncle Tom's Cabin* offers the most powerful evidence that the antislavery movement will eventually triumph: "One flash from the heart-supplied intellect of Harriet Beecher Stowe could light a million camp fires in front of the embattled host of slavery, which not all the waters of the Mississippi, mingled as they are with blood, could extinguish" (MB 449). Or as he recollects in the *Life and Times of Frederick Douglass*, the effect *Uncle Tom's Cabin* had on the "American heart" was "amazing, instantaneous, and universal … More than to reason or religion are we indebted to the influence which this wonderful delineation of American chattel slavery produced on the public mind" (LT 726, 905–6). Such praise for Stowe in particular and, by extension, the sentimental in general is not surprising. Indeed, given that the most influential religious, scientific, and legal texts of the period supported the institution of slavery, it often seems as if the sentimental stood not simply as the primary but as the only effective strategy with which to challenge the ostensibly rational and fact-based argument for slavery.[9] As Philip Fisher elegantly observes, during the antebellum period the sentimental stood as "the primary radical methodology" because it "experimented" with offering "full and complete humanity to classes of figures from whom it has been socially withheld."[10]

Such an account characterizes the sentimental as an instrumental rhetoric: sentimentality proved itself a remarkably effective weapon in the war against race-based slavery and thus Douglass pragmatically uses it to inspire in his (white) reader a seemingly irresistible sympathetic identification with the plight of the slave, an identification that, he imagines, is needed to incite the social change necessary to abolish slavery.[11] This line of thought understands Douglass's sentimentality as fundamentally "ironic," a "rhetorical strategy," a "literary performance," a "calculated appeal" that "manipulates" the "literal or referential" for specific political ends.[12] This reading of Douglass's sentimentality as essentially a staged performance makes a lot of sense, for, as Henry Louis Gates has noted, anyone "who writes more than one autobiography must be acutely aware of the ironies implicit in the re-creation of successive fictive selves, subject to manipulation and revision."[13]

A corollary of this account of Douglass's sentimentality as a purely literary effect, stylized persona, or self-conscious political tactic is the claim that while Douglass does appreciate the tremendous value of the sentimental, he remains deeply suspicious of and perhaps even indicts the premises of sentimentality – at least, as such sentimentality is expressed by the popular middle-class white female writers of the time such as Stowe, Maria Cummins, and Susan Warner. According to this argument, Douglass "rejects sentimental abolitionist misconceptions regarding sympathy" because he sees dominant conceptions of sympathy as "insufficient at best and politically regressive at worst." That is, Douglass appropriates the rhetoric of sentimentality only in order to "challeng[e]" Stowe's "representational strategies," to subvert sentimentality's too easy positing of affective and intersubjective connections between those safely outside and those terribly inside race-based slavery.[14]

To posit such an antagonistic relationship between Douglass and the sentimentality of the dominant culture places Douglass alongside authors such as Harriet Wilson and Harriet Jacobs who set out to identify sentimental sympathy as a form of white privilege.[15] Jacobs, for example, analyzes the problem of sentimental affect when she confronts her concern about discussing her decision to take a white lover in order to avoid being raped by her master. Jacobs fears that her readers (imagined as predominantly female and white) will no longer sympathize with her or her fellow female slaves if they discover that she voluntarily violated the moral imperative of female purity. Anticipating the charge of complicity, Jacobs directly addresses her audience:

> But, O, ye happy women, whose purity has been sheltered from childhood, who have been free to choose the objects of your affection, whose homes are protected by law, do not judge the poor desolate slave girl too severely! If slavery had been abolished, I, also, could have married the man of my choice; I could have had a home shielded by the laws; and I should have been spared the painful task of confessing what I am now about to relate; but all my prospects had been blighted.[16]

A female slave, according to Jacobs, is not supported by the social and legal apparatus required for sexual purity and thus does not have the opportunity to behave as those protected by the state do. For Jacobs, the belief that to be an appropriate object of sympathy one must be "pure" is a luxury she cannot afford and a privilege her audience has been given rather than earned. Jacobs, in short, is questioning the extent to which the sentimental impulse to universalize too quickly discounts significant differences of race, class, and social position.[17]

What both the celebratory and the suspicious accounts of the sentimental share is the assumption that Douglass is fundamentally alienated from the sentimental, either using it strategically to establish effective antislavery propaganda or examining it skeptically to recover the particular "bodily experience" of the slave, the recalcitrant fact of difference that the sentimental threatens to erase. According to each argument, Douglass never merely *is* sentimental. Douglass's mastery of his text and life is assumed to be synonymous with his mastery of the sentimental, his voice emerging only to the extent that he deliberately manipulates or indicts the sentimental, always maintaining a safe and certain distance from it.

Such readings of Douglass's sentimentality seem to be informed by an abiding suspicion of the sentimental as intrinsically false, to express a lingering sense that the sentimental is too subjective, excessively emotional, self-indulgent, inauthentic, anti-intellectual, propagandistic, or metaphysically suspect to be an end in itself. Thus even though the sentimental is no longer identified as a derogatory code name for the female or domestic (the form has been identified as pervading all forms of antebellum discourse) and is no longer dismissed as a mark of non-literary writing (a determination that tenaciously brackets the question of what standard is being used to judge quality writing), a powerful stigma, nonetheless, remains.[18] The sentimental still seems to be defined in terms of its relationship to some truth outside itself, by the way it pulls us from (or, more rarely, to) something obviously straightforward, real, or unequivocally authentic.

One sees this critique of the sentimental as inevitably distorting the world and failing to reflect some self-sufficient or disinterested fact expressed in perhaps its most sophisticated form by Lauren Berlant. Troubled by the "contradictions" that either "deliberately" or "inevitably" animate "politically motivated deployments of sentimental rhetoric," Berlant proposes that sentimentality

> uses personal stories to tell of structural effects, but in so doing it risks thwarting its very attempt to perform rhetorically a scene of pain that must be soothed politically. Because the ideology of true feeling cannot admit the nonuniversality of pain, its cases *become all jumbled together* and the ethical imperative toward social transformation is replaced by a civic-minded but passive ideal of empathy. The political as a place of acts oriented toward publicness becomes replaced by a world of private thoughts, leanings, and gestures.[19]

Berlant suggests that by casting politics in terms of an "affective identification and empathy" that crosses "fields of social difference," we mistakenly personalize a structural problem and thus attend to an effect (personal pain) rather than the impersonal historical and institutional causes of such pain. The sentimental incites us to mistake the alleviating of an individual's suffering with the bringing about of real social justice, substituting a concern with excessive feeling for the worldly space in which politics matter.[20]

If Berlant offers a theoretical account of how the sentimental is antithetical to the complexity of the real and insubordinate of history, Douglass's oft-cited

"Letter to His Old Master" (1848), a text included in the Appendix to *My Bondage and My Freedom*, offers a concrete example of how Douglass's sentimentality has been axiomatically framed as opposed to an unvarnished representation of reality. Such readings are symptomatic of the way that the substance of the sentimental seems to be systematically discounted.

In this public letter to Thomas Auld, written on the tenth anniversary of his escape from slavery, an indignant Douglass attacks Auld for holding Douglass's siblings in bondage and repeats the charge from the 1845 *Narrative* that Auld turned his beloved grandmother "out to die" alone, far from her family, in some desolate cabin:

> And my dear old grandmother, whom you turned out like an old horse, to die in the woods – is she still alive? … If my grandmother be still alive, she is of no service to you, for by this time she must be nearly eighty years old – too old to be cared for by one to whom she has ceased to be of service, send her to me at Rochester, or bring her to Philadelphia, and it shall be the crowning happiness of my life to take care of her in her old age. Oh! she was to me a mother, and a father, so far as hard toil for my comfort could make her such. Send me my grandmother! that I may watch over and take care of her in her old age. (MB 417)

Critics have been particularly struck by the fact that in 1849 (and perhaps earlier) Douglass knew that these accusations about Auld's heartless treatment of his siblings and his grandmother were not true. Despite this knowledge, Douglass decides to reprint this letter and the 1845 passage about his grandmother in 1855 in *My Bondage and My Freedom*.[21] Moreover, he does not include a second public letter to Auld that he writes on the eleventh anniversary of his escape (dated September 3, 1849) in which he calls his earlier attacks on Auld "unjust and unkind" and acknowledges having learned from a reliable source that Auld has emancipated all his slaves "except my poor old grandmother, who is now too old to sustain herself in freedom." Indeed, according to Douglass, Auld is "now providing for her in a manner becoming a man and a Christian."[22]

The critical reaction to Douglass's foregrounding of Auld's cold indifference to Betsey Bailey and his cruelty towards Douglass's siblings is quite revealing. The specific "charges of brutality against Thomas Auld," at least when reiterated in the 1855 text, are, in the words of one critic, "deliberately inaccurate" and "grossly inaccurate."[23] But somewhat surprisingly this historical inaccuracy is deemed trivial. Critics simultaneously acknowledge that the "charges" against Auld are without "evidence" and assert that this falsehood is "not very important" because the "calculated appeal" of such sentimentality "is *not* to a historical fact."[24] The sentimental, apparently, is not expected to be faithful to history because it is assumed to be uninterested in history, unsatisfied by the literal or referential. Indeed, it often appears that the letter has been privileged precisely to the extent that its sentimental rhetoric is not tethered to historical fact: it has been called a "prime example of confrontational slavery propaganda," "an extraordinary example of self-presentational strategy ... a study in manipulated wrath," and a "bizarre, moving, and unforgettable document of the tensions within Douglass's identity."[25]

It is, however, this seemingly axiomatic opposition between the brute, objective, unmanipulated, irrefutable fact and the emotional, subjective, and highly artificial register of the sentimental that Douglass calls into question. To understand Douglass's account of his family in terms of whether or not Auld literally did treat Douglass's siblings poorly or really did abandon his "dear old grandmother" "like an old horse" is to see Douglass's family as a simple, self-evident fact, one whose history Douglass (perhaps excusably) misrepresents. But, as Douglass explains, he had "no family" while a slave:

> I had never seen my brother nor my sisters before; and, though I had sometimes heard of them, and felt a curious interest in them, *I really did not understand what they were to me, or I to them. We were brothers and sisters, but what of that?* Why should they be attached to me, or I to them? Brothers and sister were by blood; but slavery had made us strangers. *I heard the words brother and sister, and knew they must mean something; but slavery had robbed these terms of their true meaning.* (MB 149, emphasis added)

This passage appears to distinguish a "true" and a "false" meaning of the words "brother" and "sister." Douglass laments that as a slave he could not grasp the "true meaning" of these words. But, as he also makes clear, these words only possess such a "true meaning" because he is no longer a slave. In other words, Douglass is not discussing what "brother" and "sister" mean in and of themselves, rather he is offering an account of how these terms come to signify: their "true meaning" is fundamentally contingent, dependent upon whether he is inside or outside the slave system. As a slave, the "true" meaning of "brother" and "sister" is that these words mean nothing. His claim that he did not understand what these words mean is retroactive, existing only because he is no longer a slave. And, similarly, the anger he feels over Auld's treatment of his siblings is itself a symptom of his freedom. For Douglass, the crucial fact is not whether Auld really treated his family well or poorly, but that he has the experience of having a family at all.

Strikingly, Douglass imagines that he acquires the siblings he now loves because he has learned to be sentimental:

> Think it not strange, dear reader, that so little sympathy of feeling existed between us ... we had never nestled and played together ... The domestic hearth,

with its holy lessons and precious endearments, is abolished in the case of a slave-mother and her children. "Little children, love one another," are words seldom heard in a slave cabin.   (MB 149)

Douglass's dependence upon classic sentimental images (the hearth, in particular) testifies to how his now seemingly natural feelings for his brother and sister are a consequence of his learning the classic sentimental narrative. His claim that he always loved his brother and sisters but simply was not allowed to express this love is itself wholly dependent upon his having learned the protocols of sentimental narrative ("Little children, love one another"). Such a moment is not a sign of how Douglass is manipulating feelings but evidence of how he imagines sentimentality as that which produces these seemingly natural human feelings in the first place. Familial love, he suggests, is never inevitable. Since there is nothing in the words "brother" or "sister" that intrinsically imposes a particular feeling, sentimental sympathy must be learned before anyone can have a family. The difference between slavery and freedom is simply that slavery systematically refuses to teach such lessons.

Sentimentality, in other words, is not an excessive representation of feeling or something that Douglass simply deploys rhetorically, it is what creates feeling. It produces not simply Douglass's but everyone's sense of the seemingly intrinsic affective force of the words "brother" and "sister" and thus allows us the experience of having an actual, referential brother and sister. It is sentimentality itself that produces the family that Douglass, once outside slavery, sets out to defend in his "Letter to His Old Master." To understand Douglass's sentimentality as a distortion of reality is to ignore the extent to which Douglass represents sentimentality as an enabling condition rather than merely a representational mode. That is, Douglass aligns a difference in sentimental feeling to a difference in his circumstance, designating the sentimental as that which simultaneously expresses and enacts this difference. Having become free, Douglass becomes sentimental and now experiences what those who have never been slaves unreflectively take to be reality.

Douglass's account of his changing relationship to his mother (a figure who, along with the child, is central to any sentimental lexicon) and in particular his shifting understanding of her death (the moment most mythologized in sentimental literature), stand as the clearest expression of how Douglass represents becoming sentimental as synonymous with not being a slave. As Douglass explains, since slavery separates slave mothers from their infants, it systematically thwarts the development of any bond between a mother and her child. Because of this institutionalized practice, Douglass states that his "tenderest affection" was "diverted from its true and natural object" (MB 152), and as a consequence, he confesses, he received news of his mother's death with "no strong emotions of sorrow for her" (MB 157). Perhaps in deference to his increasing sentimentality, in *My Bondage and My Freedom* Douglass softens the cold detachment that slavery produces, no longer stating as baldly as he did in the *Narrative* that he "received the tidings of her death with much the same emotions I should have probably felt at the death of a stranger" (N 16).

But the story of Douglass's relationship with his mother does not end with such an ostensibly unnatural estrangement. Once free, Douglass can begin to apprehend what it means to have a mother: "I had to learn the value of my mother long after her death, and by witnessing the devotion of other mothers to their children" (MB 157). He discovers what his mother "naturally" is only by imagining his mother imitating the ritualized devotion he observes in other mothers. It is, in short, a fundamentally sentimental and abstract notion of the way "a mother acts" that grounds Douglass's particular knowledge of how his mother acted. Indeed, since this imaginary sentimental mother is precisely what allows Douglass to appreciate his mother, it should not be surprising that the mother he discovers he always already had tallies with sentimentality's cult of motherhood – "soothing ... tender ... watchful," deeply protective and self-sacrificing. Douglass's mother is a citation, a representational effect, an image of an image. Or to put this another way, Douglass never mourned for his mother while a slave but he comes to posit her as the object that his mourning precisely incites when he has learned to be sentimental and thus can mourn an object he both never had yet always did. His *real* mother is not the cause of his sense of loss or of his mourning; rather she is the consequence of his sentimental education.[26] This is not a paradox, but a consequence of the fact that Douglass sees sentimentality as an expression of human feelings that are themselves only possible because one has learned to be sentimental. And, having established a sentimental relation to another, one then imagines that such a relationship always already existed.

Given the fundamentally performative nature of sentimentality, it does not seem accidental that it is in a book that Douglass finds the mother whom slavery has taken away. As Douglass explains:

> There is in *"Prichard's Natural History of Man,"* the head of a figure – on page 157 – the features of which so resemble those of my mother, that I often recur to it with something of the feeling which I suppose others experience when looking upon the pictures of dear departed ones. (MB 152)

Here Douglass replaces the sentimental locket with an ethnographic text and again it is the image that precedes that which it ostensibly represents. Indeed, Douglass makes clear that what he is talking about is not any literal likeness between this figure and his mother since the picture he claims resembles his mother is male (an etching of Ramses II copied from statuary) and Egyptian (a figure who for Prichard represents the racial type he calls "Indian") and without the "deep, black, glossy complexion" Douglass says his mother possessed (MB 152).[27] But rather than, as some critics have done, question Douglass's "selection" of such a figure to "impersonate" his mother, one must ask exactly who is impersonating whom and what exactly is being impersonated.[28] For ultimately it appears that what motivates Douglass is not any manifest physical similarity but a hidden and interior correspondence: Douglass portrays his mother "as remarkably sedate in her manners" (MB 152), and Prichard describes the image of Ramses II as possessing a "general expression [that] is calm and dignified."[29] The slave Harriet Bailey and Ramses the Great share text more than image, an interiority more than an appearance. Douglass *knows* that his mother "among other slaves, was remarkably sedate in her manners" because he read Prichard's text. He has not found a picture that resembles his mother; he has found a mother that resembles a description of a king. And having found his "true" mother, he then sees this portrait as a faithful representation.

If Douglass establishes a sentimental relationship to his mother only retroactively, this is not to say that Douglass's sentimentalized mother is in some sense not real or that his real mother remains fundamentally mysterious or unknown. Rather it is to describe the sentimental as that which incites Douglass to make his mother real in a very particular way. His mother intrinsically demands a particular kind of attention only after the fact, only after freedom has installed a sentimental relation. If slavery creates one kind of mother, freedom creates another. There remains no absolute or innocent mother for him to recover, no impersonal or absolute reality to which he must submit and conform. There are simply two competing mothers, one Douglass knows when a slave, the other he knows when free. And the difference between these two mothers is fundamentally sentimental and political rather than natural and given.

Douglass, in short, is interested in denaturalizing the sense that the feelings one expresses are ever natural. Indeed, since sentimentality lies at the origin of one's feelings and one's sense of sympathetic identification, Douglass challenges any critique of the sentimental premised on the claim that the sentimental distorts or fails to appreciate authentic feelings or true differences. Not only does no object in and of itself demand a particular feeling, but no subject inevitably feels. Sentimental attachments emanate neither from an object nor a subject but from a context. Douglass, in short, reverses the traditional argument against the sentimental's epistemological, ethical, and social deficiencies. He questions the notion of there being some objective, absolute, or self-evident quality in anything or anyone against which the sentimental inevitably crashes.

Douglass's celebrated discussion of slave songs foregrounds what is at stake in his sentimental turn. In a passage from the 1845 *Narrative* that he quotes in subsequent versions, Douglass explains:

> I did not, when a slave, understand the deep meanings of those rude, and apparently incoherent songs. *I was myself within the circle, so that I neither saw or heard as those without might see and hear.* They told a tale which was then altogether beyond my feeble comprehension; they were tones, loud, long and deep, breathing the prayer and complaint of souls boiling over with the bitterest anguish. Every tone was a testimony against slavery, and a prayer to God for deliverance from chains. The hearing of those wild notes always depressed my spirits, and filled my heart with ineffable sadness. The mere recurrence, even now, afflicts my spirit, and *while I am writing these lines, my tears are falling. To those songs I trace my first glimmering conceptions of the dehumanizing character of slavery.* I can never get rid of that conception.   (N 24, emphasis added)

Having experienced a sentimental education, Douglass claims he no longer has a "feeble comprehension" of these songs, but it would be more accurate to say that once outside the "circle" of slavery he hears a completely different song, one no longer "incoherent" but possessing a "deep meaning," the "complaint of souls boiling over with the bitterest anguish." In this passage, however, Douglass does more than foreground how any claim about the "true meaning" of these songs depends upon whether one is inside or outside slavery. He links sentimentality to the notion of humanity itself. These songs allow Douglass to chart his transition from being subject to slavery's "dehumanizing" effect to becoming free as a difference between having and not having sentimental feelings. By expressing his sentimental feeling (here marked by the ultimate measure of sentimentality – tears) Douglass demonstrates his humanity. And although Douglass yearns for such feelings to be intrinsic to the songs or in the slaves or in himself, what most pains him is precisely that this is not the case. These songs possess no self-evident meaning, and are comprehended neither by slaves (such as himself) nor perhaps even by the singers (all are inside the circle). Indeed, if tears are taken as a sign of one's humanity and if Douglass cries only because he learns to be sentimental, then sentimental feelings can be seen not as expressing but as producing one's essential humanity. Being sentimental thus is not merely a reaction to how slavery dehumanizes human beings but that which makes us into human beings in the first place.

Douglass's sentimental turn, in other words, is not simply telling us that "how we read determines what we read" – what Henry Louis Gates has elegantly designated as the "black hermeneutic circle" – nor is he arguing for some radically skeptical position, asserting that all meaning is illusory, that no meaning is stable, or that the relation between the signifier and signified, the sign and the referent is essentially arbitrary.[30] Rather, Douglass is positing the sentimental as that which determines who we are. For Douglass, it is the foundation of the personal itself, the source of what we feel and know as well as its effect. One might therefore say that Douglass is a representative man precisely to the degree that he is a sentimental one.

NOTES

1. See, for example, Jenny Franchot, "The Punishment of Esther: Frederick Douglass and the Construction of the Feminine," in *Frederick Douglass: New Literary and Historical Essays*, ed. Eric J. Sundquist (Cambridge: Cambridge University Press, 1990): 141–65; David Van Leer, "Reading Slavery: The Anxiety of Ethnicity in Douglass's *Narrative*," in Sundquist, *Frederick Douglass*, 118–40; Stephanie A. Smith, *Conceived by Liberty: Maternal Figures and Nineteenth-Century American Literature* (Ithaca, NY: Cornell University Press, 1994), 111–33; Gwen Bergner, "Myths of Masculinity: The Oedipus Complex and Douglass's 1845 *Narrative*," in *The Psychoanalysis of Race*, ed. Christopher Lane (New York: Columbia University Press, 1998), 241–60; Saidiya V. Hartman, *Scenes of Subjection: Terror, Slavery, and Self-Making in Nineteenth-Century America* (New York: Oxford University Press, 1997), 3–7; Fred Moten, *In the Break: The Aesthetics of the Black Radical Tradition* (Minneapolis: University of Minnesota Press, 2003), 3–23.

2. For the prime source of this line of discussion, see Deborah E. McDowell, "In the First Place: Making Frederick Douglass and the Afro-American Narrative Tradition" (1991), reprinted in *Narrative of the Life of Frederick Douglass, An American Slave, Written by Himself*, ed. William L. Andrews and William S. McFeely (New York: Norton, 1997), 172–83.

3. On revisions of this scene see Franchot, "The Punishment of Esther," 155–57; Smith, *Conceived by Liberty*, 119–24; Priscilla Wald, *Constituting Americans: Cultural Anxiety and Narrative Form* (Durham, NC: Duke University Press, 1995), 80–85; P. Gabrielle Foreman, "Sentimental Abolition in Douglass's Decade: Revision, Erotic Conversion, and the Politics of Witnessing in 'The Heroic Slave' and *My Bondage and My Freedom*," in *Sentimental Men: Masculinity and the Politics of Affect in American Culture*, ed. Mary Chapman and Glenn Hendler (Berkeley: University of California Press, 1999), 149–62.

4. This sentimental turn can be seen as part of what William Andrews has called Douglass's progressive "novelization" of his life. See William Andrews, *To Tell a Free Story: The First Century of Afro-American Autobiography, 1700–1865* (Urbana: University of Illinois Press, 1986), 281–91.

5. See, for example, Michael Meyer, "Introduction" to Frederick Douglass, *The Narrative and Selected Writings* (New York: Random House, 1984); and John Carlos Rowe's anti-sentimental reading of the 1845 *Narrative* in *At Emerson's Tomb: The Politics of Classic American Literature* (New York: Columbia University Press, 1997), 96–123.

6. For a detailed account of Douglass's complex relationship with and defense of Stowe, see Robert S. Levine, *Martin Delany, Frederick Douglass, and the Politics of Representative Identity* (Chapel Hill: University of North Carolina Press, 1997).

7. Eric J. Sundquist, *To Wake the Nations: Race in the Making of American Literature* (Cambridge, MA: Harvard University Press, 1993), 102; Foreman, "Sentimental Abolition," 150.

8. As many have noted, in *My Bondage and My Freedom*, Douglass foregrounds how the Garrisonians treated him as a commodity or "thing" and thus represents his break with them as marking his freedom from a form of bondage, albeit one quite different from chattel slavery (MB 361–62). Thus, it is not by accident that *My Bondage and My Freedom* ends at the moment Douglass breaks with Garrison.

9. See Arthur Riss, *Race, Slavery, and Liberalism in Nineteenth-Century American Literature* (Cambridge: Cambridge University Press, 2006).

10. Philip Fisher, *Hard Facts: Setting and Form in the American Novel* (New York: Oxford University Press, 1987), 92, 99.

11. For the most significant study of how the sentimental was deployed during the antebellum period to advance arguments both for and against slavery, see Cindy Weinstein, *Family, Kinship, and Sympathy in Nineteenth-Century American Literature* (Cambridge: Cambridge University Press, 2004).

12. Quotations are from Sundquist, *To Wake the Nations*, 101–2; Foreman, "Sentimental Abolition," 150; Jeffrey Steele, "Douglass and Sentimental Rhetoric," in *Approaches to Teaching: Narrative of the Life of Frederick Douglass*, ed. James C. Hall (New York: Modern Language Association of America, 1999), 72; Gregory S. Jay, *America the Scrivener: Deconstruction and the Subject of Literary History* (Ithaca, NY: Cornell University Press, 1990), 267, 268.

13. Henry Louis Gates, Jr., *Figures in Black: Words, Signs, and the "Racial" Self* (New York: Oxford University Press, 1987), 116.

14. Marianne Noble, "Sympathetic Listening in Frederick Douglass's 'The Heroic Slave' and *My Bondage and My Freedom*," *Studies in American Fiction* 34:1 (Spring 2006), 54–55.

15. See Hazel Carby, *Reconstructing Womanhood: The Emergence of the Afro-American Woman Novelist* (New York: Oxford University Press, 1987); and Karen Sanchez-Eppler, *Touching Liberty: Abolition, Feminism, and the Politics of the Body* (Berkeley: University of California Press, 1993).

16. Harriet A. Jacobs, *Incidents in the Life of a Slave Girl*, ed. Jean Fagan Yellin (Cambridge, MA: Harvard University Press, 1987), 54.

17. For a sense of the prevalence and influence of this suspicion of the sentimental's drive towards an identitarian sameness, see Laura Wexler, "Tender Violence: Literary Eavesdropping, Domestic Fiction, and Educational Reform," in *The Culture of Sentiment: Race, Gender, and Sentimentality in Nineteenth-Century America*, ed. Shirley Samuels (New York: Oxford University Press, 1992), 9–38; Sanchez-Eppler, *Touching Liberty*; Glenn Hendler, *Public Sentiments: Structures of Feeling in Nineteenth-Century American Literature* (Chapel Hill: University of North Carolina Press, 2001).

18. For two quite different defenses of the "authenticity" of the sentimental, see Joanne Dobson, "Reclaiming Sentimental Literature," *American Literature* 69:2 (1997): 263–88; and Eve Kosofsky Sedgwick, *Epistemology of the Closet* (Berkeley: University of California Press, 1990).

19. Lauren Berlant, "Poor Eliza," in *No More Separate Spheres: A Next Wave American Studies Reader*, ed. Cathy N. Davidson and Jessamyn Hatchers (Durham, NC: Duke University Press, 2002), 297.

20. Lauren Berlant, "The Subject of True Feeling: Pain, Privacy, and Politics," in *Cultural Pluralism, Identity Politics, and the Law*, ed. Austin Sarat and Thomas R. Kearns (Ann Arbor: University of Michigan Press, 1999), 53.

21. Douglass's Letter was published in *The North Star* on September 3, 1848 and *The Liberator* on September 22, 1848. In the Appendix to *My Bondage and My Freedom*, Douglass states he wrote this letter while in England in exile.

22. *The Liberator*, September 14, 1849. Reprinted in *Frederick Douglass: Selected Speeches and Writings*, ed. Philip S. Foner, abridged and adapted by Yuval Taylor (Chicago, IL: Lawrence Hill Books, 1999), 143–44.

23. Eric J. Sundquist, "Introduction" to *Frederick Douglass: New Literary and Historical Essays*, 6; Sundquist, *To Wake the Nations*, 97.

24. Sundquist, *To Wake the Nations*, 99; Jay, *America the Scrivener*, 268.

25. David W. Blight in *Narrative of the Life of Frederick Douglass*, ed. David W. Blight (Boston: Bedford Books, 1993), 134; William M. Ramsey, "Frederick Douglass, Southerner," *Southern Literary Journal*, 40:1 (Fall 2007), 121; Waldo E. Martin, Jr., *The Mind of Frederick Douglass* (Chapel Hill: University of North Carolina Press, 1984), 6.

26. I borrow the term "sentimental education" from Richard Rorty, "Human Rights, Rationality, and Sentimentality," in *Truth and Progress, Philosophical Papers*, Vol. 3 (Cambridge: Cambridge University Press, 1998), 167–85.

27. See Peter F. Walker, *Moral Choices: Memory, Desire, and Imagination in Nineteenth-Century American Abolition* (Baton Rouge: Louisiana State University Press, 1978); and Michael A. Chaney, "Picturing the Mother, Claiming Egypt: *My Bondage and My Freedom* as Auto(bio)ethnography," *African American Review* 35: 3 (Fall 2001): 391–409.

28. Franchot, "The Punishment of Esther," 159.

29. James Cowles Prichard, *The Natural History of Man: Comprising Inquiries into the Modifying Influence of Physical and Moral Agencies on the Different Tribes of the Human Family* (London: N. Bailliere, 1848), 157.

30. Gates, *Figures in Black*, 96–97.

8

Douglass among the Romantics

The years in Frederick Douglass's life between 1838 and 1860 represent a period of intellectual and personal growth. Having escaped from slavery in 1838, Douglass over the next two decades became one of the most renowned black abolitionists of the nineteenth century. His oratory and writing skills were so great that audiences who read his works or heard him speak did not believe that he had been a slave. Douglass's 1845 *Narrative of the Life of Frederick Douglass, An American Slave* was meant to verify his life in slavery. When audiences at abolition rallies doubted his former slave status, Douglass would remove his jacket and expose his whip-scarred back. His narrative and his scars removed any doubts about his authenticity.

In order to fully appreciate Douglass's intellectual growth between 1838 and 1860, it is necessary to look at the rise of an American literary tradition and the development of a unique strand or aspect of American social and political thought during these years. Douglass's intellectual growth emerges during what has been called the American Romantic period or sometimes known as the American Renaissance. American Romanticism, though unique, also draws on British and German influences, especially the idealism of Immanuel Kant, who is particularly helpful in understanding Douglass.

Romanticism and Transcendentalism

It is the focus on the primacy of the individual that gives American Romanticism its particular ideological bent. Individual intuitive moral consciousness constitutes what it means to be human. Each individual is a rational thinking being with innate moral knowledge. Each individual is to be respected as a human being. The individual should be allowed to develop to the fullest of his or her ability. The individual is a part of nature and connected to all other individuals by this relationship. The development of the individual was best fostered in a communion with nature, which is the setting for the development of selfhood. Romanticism also rejects forms of association that tend to block or hinder the intellectual or spiritual development of the individual. Slavery and the oppression of women in this reading of human existence were social and moral wrongs. It should be remembered that Thoreau wrote "Resistance to Civil Government" (1854) and later gave his abolitionist lecture, "A Plea for John Brown" (1859), as a replacement for Douglass, who had been scheduled to speak but left the country after being implicated in Brown's plot to start a slave rebellion. As this suggests, the political and literary writings of the period expressed an American sense of morality and selfhood.

The literary works of this period have become classics of American literature. Emerson's great essays beginning with "Nature" (1836) along with Hawthorne's *The Scarlet Letter* (1850), Thoreau's *Walden* (1854), Whitman's *Leaves of Grass* (1855), and Melville's *Moby-Dick* (1851) and "Benito Cereno" (1855) draw on the themes of Romanticism.

It should be remembered that during this period we also get the following writings by black male and female writers.[1] Douglass's "The Heroic Slave" (1853), William Wells Brown's *Clotel: Or, The President's Daughter* (1853), Frank J. Webb's *The Garies and Their Friends* (1857), Martin R. Delany's *Blake: Or, The Huts of America* (1859), Harriet E. Wilson's *Our Nig: Or, Sketches from the Life of a Free Black* (1859), and Hannah Crafts's *The Bondwoman's Narrative* (c. 1853–61) added the perspective of individuals denied their humanity to the literature of the Romantic period. It is a period in American history when black and white writers ideologically argued about what it meant to be human.

In New England, thinkers and writers like Emerson, Thoreau, and Margaret Fuller were instrumental in the development of the Transcendentalist movement. Emerson writes:

> It is well known to most of my audience, that the Idealism of the present day acquired the name of Transcendental, from the use of that term by Immanuel Kant, of Konigsberg, who replied to the skeptical philosophy of Locke, which insisted that there was nothing in the intellect which was not previously in the experience of the senses, by showing that there was a very important class of ideas, or imperative forms, which did not come by experience, but through which experience was acquired; that these were intuitions of the mind itself; and he denominated them Transcendental forms. The extraordinary profoundness and precision of that man's thinking have given vogue to his nomenclature, in Europe and America, to that extent, that whatever belongs to the class of intuitive thought, is popularly called at the present day Transcendental.[2]

American Transcendentalists got much of their German Romanticism through British Romantics (especially Coleridge and Carlyle). Drawing on the writings of Kant and other German Romantics and the writings of non-Western thinkers, the Transcendentalists saw man as a spiritual being. Each person was endowed with a natural intuitive sense of self. Human beings have a soul that is infused with a desire for divine inspiration and a love of freedom. The Transcendentalists were idealists and rejected the materialist conception of understanding the world. In essence, they chose Kant's ideals about the nature of human understanding over those of John Locke. The term Transcendentalism became the name of the school of thought that was not a unified system but a way of thinking about the world that put emphasis on individuality and the person's place in nature. In 1836, the Transcendental Club was formed and Emerson's essay "Nature" was published. The movement set a tone for what became an American philosophical tradition that had a great impact on both the social and intellectual growth of the United States in the nineteenth century.

The writings and speeches of the members of this intellectual group were part of a major shift in the social and political climate of the country. The writers and thinkers of this period began to break away from both the religious hold of Calvinism and the political conservatism of the times. There was a push for religious liberalism and individual freedom that was instrumental in both the abolitionist movement and the women's rights movement.

The Transcendentalists were advocates of abolition, women's rights, and religious tolerance. One of the most important aspects of Transcendental thought was its focus on the role of the individual as both an agent of change and the embodiment of the nature of personhood. Indeed, major works of the period highlighted the role and often the struggles of the individual as she or he attempted to negotiate the problems of life that often befell them. The works of Hawthorne, Melville, Wilson, Delany, and Douglass exhibit the impact of the Transcendentalists. Romanticism and Transcendentalism impacted both the literary and the political life of the United States and made this period intellectually exciting for Douglass.

Douglass as Romantic

A large part of Douglass's prominence during this period can be attributed to his autobiographical writings. In these writings, he makes use of the major themes of literary Romanticism: individualism, power, and heroism. The theme of individualism appears in the first narrative when he gives us some hint of his distancing himself from Garrison. Clearly the *Narrative* goes against the Garrison doctrine of non-resistance in that Douglass describes his fight with Covey as being an important part of his psychological rebirth.

Douglass's departure from non-resistance is especially clear when he describes the battle in *My Bondage and My Freedom* (1855):

> Well, my dear reader, this battle with Mr. Covey, – undignified as it was, and as I fear my narration of it is – was the turning point in my *"life as a slave."* It rekindled in my breast the smouldering embers of liberty; it brought up my Baltimore dreams, and revived a sense of my own manhood. I was a changed being after that fight. I was *nothing* before; I WAS A MAN NOW. It recalled to life my crushed self-respect and my self-confidence, and inspired me with a renewed determination to be A FREEMAN. A man, without force, is without the essential dignity of humanity. Human nature is so constituted, that it cannot *honor* a helpless man, although it can *pity* him; and even this it cannot do long, if the signs of power do not arise. (MB 286)

Douglass, here, expresses his individualism and his understanding that he was a man before he was a slave. As a man, he had the right to defend himself from injustice and abuse. This is a far cry from the moral doctrine of Garrison.

It was the contention of Garrison that non-resistance and pacifism were one and the same. One should not resist even in cases of self-defense. Douglass believed in the use of force in cases of self-defense. There are numerous stories of his protecting himself and going to the aid of friends who were threatened by physical violence or involved in altercations. Douglass thinks that the individual can both be an agent of moral suasion and still defend him or her self. This position agrees with the Transcendentalist view of following one's own moral intuitions, a point that is especially important in Douglass's only known work of fiction.

In 1853, Douglass published "The Heroic Slave," a work that can also be seen as his contribution and his connection to the literature of American Romanticism.[3] It was first published as chapters in Douglass's newspaper. It was next published as part of a collection of antislavery writings in the anthology, *Autographs for Freedom*, edited by Julia Griffiths. This anthology was used to raise money for *Frederick Douglass' Paper* by the Rochester Ladies' Anti-slavery Society of which Griffiths was secretary.

In "The Heroic Slave," Douglass takes as the impetus for his story the historical event of the November 1841 slave mutiny aboard the US brigantine *Creole*.[4] The ship carrying 134 captives was bound for New Orleans from Virginia. Along the way, Madison Washington, an escaped slave, led a takeover of the ship and sailed it to the free British port of Nassau in the Bahamas. The British refused to return the captives to their slave-owners and the mutineers were allowed to stay in the Bahamas. While the revolt did not receive as much attention as the *Amistad* takeover, the leader of the mutiny, Madison Washington, became a hero to many of the black abolitionists, particularly Douglass.[5] Douglass used Madison as an example of the bravery and heroic nature of black men in at least three speeches. Most notable is his reference to Madison Washington in his 1847 "Farewell Speech to the British People" and the 1857 "West Indian Emancipation Speech." Douglass's use of Madison in "The Heroic Slave" is provocative in that it powerfully conjoins Romanticism and abolitionism.

At this point, I want to briefly discuss moral suasion in Douglass's "The Heroic Slave." According to the philosopher Frank Kirkland:

> [M]oral suasion is *prima facie* the use of rhetoric to persuade others about the moral wrongness of slavery and the moral rightness of abolition. What is here operative in moral suasion, however, is the presupposition that the language of morality directly influences conduct. That is to say, moral suasion requires the belief that it can awaken through rhetoric moral sensibility and, as a consequence, motivate us to do what is good.[6]

Kirkland argues that we must see that moral suasion can be understood in at least two ways – one that rests on moral sentimentalism and whose advancement of reason is rhetorically saturated; the other that hinges on natural law and whose advancement of reason is discursively amplified. In this manner, we can understand both the obligation and the motivational aspects of moral suasion. Kirkland discusses the role that rhetoric plays in Douglass's thought. Moral suasion is seen in this context as an interchange between persons, either spoken or written meant to change their views about a moral issue. In the case of Douglass it is the wrong of slavery. In the "The Heroic Slave," Douglass, however, gives us another way to think about how attitudes towards blacks can be changed.

Douglass gives us two examples of a change in attitude about slavery or about blacks that is not caused by a written or verbal interchange between two persons. The act of moral suasion can take place just by the hearing of a soliloquy. Here is the scene: Madison Washington is in the woods lamenting his condition as a slave. A northern traveler (Mr. Listwell) stops to water his horse and hears the sound of a human voice and is drawn to its source. Listwell does not disturb Madison but feels compelled to listen. Madison bemoans his condition of servitude and what it has done to him and his family. Madison vows to be free and departs. Listwell is moved by the soliloquy and vows, from that hour on, to be an abolitionist. Listwell says: "I have seen enough and heard enough, and I shall go to my home in Ohio resolved to atone for my past indifference to this ill-starred race, by making such exertions as I shall be able to do, for the speedy emancipation of every slave in the land."[7] Listwell is moved to abolitionism by Madison's speech.

Two aspects of this scene should be noted. First, Douglass describes the manner in which Madison speaks. Madison is an excellent speaker, his voice is commanding, and his use of language is equal to that of any white man. Second, his appearance is striking:

> Madison was of manly form. Tall, symmetrical, round, and strong. In his movements he seemed to combine, with the strength of the lion, a lion's elasticity ... His face was "black, but comely." His eyes, lit with emotion, kept guard under a brow as dark and as glossy as the raven's wing. His whole appearance betokened Herculean strength yet there was nothing savage or forbidding in his aspect.   (HS 134)

Douglass thus suggests a theme that is present in his other speeches that whites can come to respect blacks by the behavior blacks exhibit. It is often not color but behavior that causes some of the problems that black people face. Douglass seems to think that self-presentation can be a way in which to change the minds of persons predisposed to have negative ideas about blacks. It is by manly behavior that attitudes about blacks can be changed. This notion is repeated at the end of the story. Sometime after the takeover of the ship, a white sailor is describing what he remembers about the mutiny. The sailor had been knocked unconscious. He does not remember the violence that took place during the takeover, but is impressed with Madison's demeanor when he regains consciousness: "I confess, gentleman, I felt myself in the presence of a superior man; one who, had he been white, I would have followed willingly and gladly in any honorable enterprise. Our difference of color was the only ground for difference of action" (HS 134). The sheer strength of Madison's character and demeanor was enough to make the sailor realize that Madison, although black, was a man. Here we have Douglass drawing on the Romantic themes of individualism, power, and heroism. It is the power of the person exhibited through his or her demeanor or speech that has the ability to motivate a positive moral response.[8] The power of self-presentation is the key.

However, it is at this point that the issue of self-presentation becomes unclear. Douglass's use of what Jane Hathaway calls the mid-nineteenth-century American manhood model may be seen to be white, conventional, conservative, and conforming.[9] One might think that Douglass's use of manhood here places him outside of the Romantic tradition, that his conception of self sets blacks apart from whites in a significant manner.

However, Douglass's affinity with Transcendentalism and his understanding of racism in the United States make his conception of manhood a wise choice. As Maurice Lee notes:

> Scholars have not been slow to note Transcendental aspects of Douglass's thought, even if only limited evidence supports a sustained relationship ...

Douglass did cross paths with various transcendentalists, and his newspaper occasionally reprinted selections from antislavery transcendentalist texts.[10]

Douglass's first narrative was praised by Transcendentalists like Theodore Parker and Margaret Fuller in their reviews of his book.[11] Douglass's work was also widely known, and he knew many of the best thinkers of his period.

One of the more interesting aspects of Douglass's writing is that he drew upon the works of many diverse scholars. It is therefore not surprising that one finds Kantian attributes in Douglass's work. Gregg Crane argues that both Emerson and Douglass can be read as pushing for a cosmopolitan constitutionalism.[12] Crane explores the impact of Kant's writings on the thinking of both Emerson and Douglass:

> A Kantian kinship between Emerson and Douglass can be felt in the prominence each gives to the fluid quality of and the interrelation between aesthetic and ethical judgment. For example, Emerson declares in "Circles" that "There is no virtue which is final" and in a later antislavery address criticizes Americans for "ador[ing] the forms of law, instead of making them the vehicles of wisdom and justice." Douglass similarly avows that "Perfection is an object to be aimed at by all, but it is not an attribute of any form of government. Mutability is the law for all." Both men laud literary or aesthetic experience for illuminating the ceaseless process of revision involved in evaluative judgments.[13]

Douglass understands the power of literary works to change the morality of people. During the period in which Douglass was writing, many whites thought of blacks as morally and intellectually inferior. Douglass's self-presentation in the narratives and the novella, he thought, would force whites to rethink their views of the humanity of blacks. Crane, I should note, is interested in Douglass's thought and contribution to the constitutional debates during this period. My concern is with Douglass's writings as a way to force whites to see blacks as humans and/or touch the moral sentiment that would move them to abolitionism.

I want to argue that Douglass's use of "manhood" places him squarely in the Romantic tradition with a deep connection to the Transcendentalists. The Transcendentalists, it should be remembered, reject the empiricism of Locke for the idealism of Kant. Their use of Kant puts their understanding of what it means to be human in a very different light from that of the empiricist. To the credit of some of them, they did not adhere to Kant's social anthropology and racist attitudes.[14] What they draw from Kant is the contention that humans are thinking, rational moral beings. Writing from within this ideological framework, Douglass has to describe himself and Madison in a manner consistent with the view that he was a man and more importantly a freethinking human from birth.

Two brief points here. First, Kant, it should be remembered, was one of the more important thinkers of the eighteenth century. Indeed the age of enlightenment gets its name from his 1784 essay, "What is Enlightenment?" Kant is concerned with our understanding of the use of the sciences as a way to attain knowledge of the external world. He thought that those philosophers who adhered to either the rationalism of Descartes or the empiricism of Locke had reasoned wrongly about human knowledge acquisition. Kant thought Descartes, as the representative rationalist, failed to appreciate that science is both rational and empirical and empiricists were guilty of discounting reason in knowledge acquisition. The mind, for Kant, is active in the production of knowledge in that the information attained through the senses is shaped by the mind. Knowledge is an interaction between the knower and the external world. This for Kant was a "Copernican Revolution" in our thinking about how humans obtained knowledge.

This new way of thinking about knowledge acquisition required a new understanding of what it meant to be a rational human being. Humans were no longer passive receivers of knowledge but active participants in its creation. Kant argued in the *Critique of Practical Reason* (1788) that the individual is a reasoning being and that moral rules and standards cannot be imposed on persons by external forces. The individual's own active reason is the source of his or her morality. Only by expressing one's own reasoning to determine one's interests can one be considered autonomous. Each person is seen as what Kant calls an end in his or her self. It is this *self* that must be respected, and the development of the *self* must be protected. This emphasis on the Kantian conception of the autonomous *self* becomes the focal point of much of Romantic individualism.

Second, Kirkland notes:

> Unlike Douglass, Kant is ensnared in the Enlightenment views on race. That is to say, Kant believes that race is grounded in (allegedly real) biological natures, which differentiate groups from one another, which are (supposedly) inherited and shared by members of a group, and which are used to define and explain the intellectual, moral, and aesthetic qualities and the cultural and social status of a group. So Kant believes that the character of individuals is wholly defined by their membership in a race. With skin color as the mark, race catalogues the kind of qualities and registers the caste naturally pertinent to the individual's group. Moreover, it becomes criterial for justifying why certain groups, say, blacks, and not others (1) cannot be in a political association with other groups, (2) can be subject to unequal treatment, and (3) can be enslaved, colonized, or exploited. Indeed it has been argued that Kant attributed the features of enlightenment to those whose race favorably assigned them in nature.[15]

Douglass walks a fine line between Kant's enlightenment conception of the person and the virulent racism of the age. He understands that he has to embody both the enlightenment conception of the individual while at the same time speaking for black people. Writing from within this ideological framework, Douglass has to describe himself and Madison in a manner consistent with the view that he was a man and more importantly a free-thinking human from birth. Remember his remarks about his fight with Covey.

Let me be clear here: none of this is meant to imply that Douglass was a Kantian. Like Kirkland, I am making the weaker case that Douglass's engagement with the thinkers of his time influenced his understanding of the need for a Kantian conception of the person to avoid the pitfalls of the empiricists. To this end, the Kantian position allows Douglass to correctly depict himself and Madison in the model of manhood that would best express his humanity to his readers. Douglass had to shape the persona of himself and Madison to appeal to the moral sentiments of his main readers – that is, whites who might support abolition. This would make his Kantian sensibilities compatible with both Kirkland's and Lee's position on the Scottish philosophical influences on Douglass. Douglass, indeed, wants to touch or reach the moral sentiments of his readers.

In his writings, Douglass has to present a person his reader would and could identify with as a person. Douglass had to create, as Henry Louis Gates, Jr. notes, a fictive self:

> I do not mean to suggest any sense of falsity or ill-intent; rather, I mean by fictive the act of crafting or making by design, in this instance a process that unfolds in language, through the very discourse that Douglass employs to narrate his autobiographies.[16]

William Andrews has a similar understanding of Douglass's creation of self:

> The narrator he fashioned for My Bondage and My Freedom brilliantly exemplifies Melville's contention that only "through the mouths of the dark characters" of a great writer do we find that which is "so terrifically true, that it were all but madness for any good man, in his proper character to utter, or even hint of them."[17]

Douglass must speak both for blacks and to whites in a manner that exemplifies the humanity of blacks. In this regard, Douglass has to write as if the institution of slavery cannot or did not wholly shape blacks. I would add that this creation of a fictive self is employed in the "The Heroic Slave" and that this self appears fully moral and intelligent in spite of the horrors of slavery. This is more than a question of literary style. It is in his writings of this period that Douglass is involved in philosophical debates about human nature and the humanity of the Negro.[18] The issue is: "Are Negroes Human?"

The question of racial diversity and what it meant for understanding the status of raced people was at the center stage of scientific and philosophical debates.[19] When we add to this debate the moral consequences of the positions of the idealist and empiricist, we can understand why Douglass shapes both his narratives and his fiction in the style he did. The manner in which humans are conceived of as human differs greatly from the materialist and idealist conception of self. For the materialist, in this case, the empiricist, the person is the total of his or her experiences. Persons are shaped by their experiences. The idealists or Transcendentalists understand persons as ends in themselves. Persons as such have a moral worth that cannot justly be violated and slavery is such a violation.

William Andrews asks about nineteenth-century African Americans: "Could the Afro-American still discover and develop himself according to his own ideals while living in racist America in the middle of the nineteenth century?"[20] Andrews thinks that *My Bondage and My Freedom* suggests that this question can be answered with a qualified yes. It would take the efforts of both blacks and whites working together to continue the struggle for independence and self-determination. I would contend that for Douglass this only makes sense if blacks are not entirely shaped intellectually and morally by their slave experience.

The empiricists argued that morality and intellect are not innate, but they are learned by experience. For both Locke and Hume, persons are either their memories or they are just memories of their perceptions. Two points here: if the slave is incapable of understanding morality through sense perception, then slavery does him or her no harm. Thus slaves cannot understand the wrongness of their plight, for their inferior intellect and morality are not touched by the hardships of slavery. But if the slave's mind is a *tabula rasa*, then the slavery experience is the principal intellectual and moral shaping factor. It will make the slave both child-like and ignorant. If morality is learned, then the slave's moral life and his understanding of his or her place are contingent on the type of master they had. Slavery is wrong because it creates slaves. But Douglass works from the position that slavery is wrong because men and women are made slaves. It is a rejection of the empiricist understanding of intellectual and moral development. Douglass in his autobiographies and in "The Heroic Slave" posits himself and Madison as men who understand the wrongness of slavery *as men*, not through some strange manner of sense acquisition. It is this understanding of human worth and intelligence that seems to underlie the thinking of the Transcendentalists. It is an understanding of the person that transcends race. It is because this moral understanding is in all persons that Listwell and the sailor could be moved to appreciate the wrongness of slavery and the manhood of Madison.

We also see Douglass drawing on Emerson's "Uses of Great Men" (1850) in "The Heroic Slave."[21] If Douglass thinks of Madison or himself, in his writings, as representative men, it is because they both are representative of the humanity that blacks and whites possess as human beings. In the preface to *My Bondage and My Freedom*, Douglass writes:

> I see, too, that there are special reasons why I should write my own biography, in preference to employing another to do it. Not only is slavery on trial, but unfortunately, the enslaved people are also on trial. It is alleged, that they are, naturally, inferior; that they are *so low* in the scale of humanity, and so utterly stupid, that they are unconscious of their wrongs, and do not apprehend their rights. Looking, then, at your request, from this stand-point, and wishing everything of which you think me capable to go to the benefit of my afflicted people, I part with my doubts and hesitation, and proceed to furnish you the desired manuscript; hoping that you may be able to make such arrangements for its publication as shall be best adapted to accomplish that good which you so enthusiastically anticipate. (MB 106)

Douglass is clear that this work speaks to all humanity. It is not meant to applaud his accomplishments but to speak for and to his fellow humans. As Andrews notes, discussing James McCune Smith's use of representative man in his introduction to *My Bondage and My Freedom*, it is in a "distinctly Emersonian sense, as denoting a kind of epitome or standard by which others might measure themselves."[22]

In his personal narratives and his work of fiction, Douglass and Madison are not totally self-made men but men. This is an important factor for Douglass. These works would reach a larger audience than his speaking tours where he could be seen and explain the nature of his accomplishments. In print, he has to be careful not to cast blacks as anything but human. He has to draw on a conception of human behavior that would not allow whites to see blacks as anything but human. This understanding of Douglass's view of his writing as an instrument of social change and moral suasion would explain why the use of the Coleridge quote at the beginning of *My Bondage and My Freedom* is essential for Douglass. "By a principle essential to Christianity, a PERSON is eternally differenced from a THING; so that the idea of a HUMAN BEING, necessarily excludes the idea of PROPERTY IN THAT BEING." This quote is foundational for Douglass. He puts himself clearly in a philosophical camp that espouses the humanity of blacks from birth. Blacks are not animals and cannot be made animals. As Lee correctly notes, Douglass in *My Bondage and My Freedom* is "constructing a sophisticated argument grounded in a theory of the mind."[23]

Douglass is astute enough to know that how people come to understand the world and the humanity of the people who populate it is an essential aspect of the argument of the supporters of slavery. His understanding of this point can be seen in his speech, "The Claims of the Negro Ethnologically Considered" (1854). Douglass starts his speech by referring to an article in the *Richmond Examiner* that asks the question: "Is the negro a Man?" The writer of the article concludes that the abuses heaped upon the negro are not wrongs because they are not men. Douglass takes this opportunity to refute the arguments against the humanity of blacks. After giving what he takes to be sufficient counter-arguments, Douglass asks:

> What, if we grant the case, on our part is not made out? Does it follow that the negro should be held in contempt? Does it follow, that to enslave him and imbrute him is either *just* or *wise*? I think not. Human rights stand upon a common basis; and by all reason they are supported, maintained and defended, for one variety of the human family, they are supported, maintained and defended for *all* the human family; because all mankind have the same wants, arising out of a common nature. A diverse origin does not disprove a common nature, nor does it disprove a united destiny. The essential characteristics of humanity are everywhere the same. (FDP 2: 523–24)

This speech shows that Douglass is well aware of the philosophical importance of the debates about the humanity of blacks. He also understands that there is a moral issue at stake: the belief that all humans are of one blood and thus should be accorded equal and just treatment as humans.

He addresses these concerns in his autobiographical and fictional writings. In *My Bondage and My Freedom* and "The Heroic Slave," Douglass has to show that slavery had not shaped blacks so as to deform them morally or intellectually, nor are blacks so unlike whites to be a permanent other. To this end, even though one's father was not known, one's date of birth was not known, and after the cruel treatment of the slaveholders, Douglass and Madison were still humans who think, who understand, and who long for freedom. It is this conception of the person that drives both the narrative and the novella.

The Kantian conception of the person, as taught by Transcendentalism, provides us with a focal point to assess Douglass's narrative and his work of fiction. These works are written as a representation of human ability. This was indeed Fuller's assessment of the *Narrative*.[24] Douglass's writings show that blacks are humans with the same wants and wishes as other humans. Blacks want their individualism acknowledged and their status as humans respected. These are positions that Douglass hoped his readers would appreciate. In this regard, Douglass's writings show that he reflected deeply on the problems of individualism and power, particularly how these problems impacted on the lives and minds of both black and white Americans.

When we situate Douglass's life among the great writers of the nineteenth century, we are able to experience the best and worst of life in the United

States. Douglass, born in slavery, writes one of the classics of American literature. Douglass was a statesman, abolitionist, confidant of presidents, publisher, women's rights advocate, and philosopher.[25] This is the best of America. That he had to accomplish these feats coming out of slavery represents the worst of America. The problems of individualism, power, and heroism are still issues facing the black community. Frederick Douglass's life is a testament to the struggle to make sense of these problems. His writings show the influence of the Romantic literary writers, the Transcendentalists, and the blacks thinkers like Smith, Henry Highland Garnet, Samuel Ringgold Ward, and Martin Delany. Douglass, in his autobiographical works and his fictional work, is indeed of, and among, the American Romantics.

NOTES

1. William L. Andrews, "The 1850s: The First Afro-American Literary Renaissance," in *Literary Romanticism in America*, ed. William L. Andrews (Baton Rouge: Louisiana State University Press, 1981), 38–61.
2. Ralph Waldo Emerson, *Essays and Lectures* (New York: Library of America, 1983), 198.
3. Robert K. Wallace, *Douglass and Melville: Anchored Together in a Neighborly Style* (New Bedford, MA: Spinner Publications, 2005); William S. McFeely, *Frederick Douglass* (New York: W. W. Norton, 1995), 115. See also *Frederick Douglass and Herman Melville: Essays in Relation*, ed. Robert S. Levine and Samuel Otter (Chapel Hill: University of North Carolina Press, 2008).
4. George Hendrick and Willene Hendrick, *The* Creole *Mutiny: A Tale of Revolt Aboard a Slave Ship* (Chicago, IL: Ivan R. Dee, 2003).
5. Jane Hathaway, *Rebellion, Repression, Reinvention: Mutiny in Comparative Perspective* (Westport, CT: Praeger, 2001), 244.
6. Frank M. Kirkland, "Enslavement, Moral Suasion, and Struggles for Recognition: Frederick Douglass's Answer to the Question – 'What is Enlightenment?'" in *Frederick Douglass: A Critical Reader*, ed. Bill E. Lawson and Frank Kirkland (Malden, MA: Blackwell, 1999), 244.
7. Frederick Douglass, "The Heroic Slave," in William L. Andrews, *The Oxford Frederick Douglass Reader* (New York: Oxford University Press, 1996), 131–63 at 135. Subsequent references to this text are cited "HS" in the text.
8. McFeely, *Frederick Douglass*, 22.
9. Hathaway, *Rebellion, Repression, Reinvention*, 246.
10. Maurice S. Lee, *Slavery, Philosophy, and American Literature, 1830–1860* (Cambridge: Cambridge University Press, 2005), 100–1.
11. Andrews, *The Oxford Frederick Douglass Reader*, xv.
12. Gregg Crane, *Race, Citizenship and Law in American Literature* (Cambridge: Cambridge University Press, 2002), 87.
13. *Ibid.*, 90.
14. See, for example, Robert Bernasconi, "Who Invented the Concept of Race? Kant's Role in the Enlightenment Construction of Race," in *Race*, ed. R. Bernasconi (Oxford: Blackwell, 2001), 11–36; Laurence Thomas, "Moral Equality and

Natural Inferiority," *Social Theory and Practice* 31:3 (July 2005), 379–404; Bernard Boxill and Thomas Hill, "Kant and Race," in *Race and Racism*, ed. Bernard Boxill (Oxford: Oxford University Press, 2001), 448–71.

15. Kirkland, "Enslavement," 255.

16. Henry L. Gates, Jr., *Figures in Black: Words, Signs, and the "Racial" Self* (Oxford: Oxford University Press, 1987), 103.

17. Andrews, *The Oxford Frederick Douglass Reader*, xiv.

18. See especially Douglass's "The Claims of the Negro Ethnologically Considered" (1854).

19. See, for example, *Race, Hybridity, and Miscegenation: Josiah Nott and the Question of Hybridity*, ed. with introduction by Robert Bernasconi and Kristie Dotson (Bristol: Thoemmes Continuum, 2005).

20. Andrews, "The 1850s: The First Afro-American Literary Renaissance," 55.

21. Waldo E. Martin, Jr., *The Mind of Frederick Douglass* (Chapel Hill: University of North Carolina Press, 1984), 264.

22. Andrews, *The Oxford Frederick Douglass Reader*, xii.

23. Lee, *Slavery, Philosophy, and American Literature*, 100.

24. Margaret Fuller, review of *Narrative of the Life of Frederick Douglass, An American Slave, Written by Himself*, *New York Tribune* (June 10, 1845), in *The Portable Margaret Fuller*, ed. Mary Kelley (New York: Penguin, 1994), 379.

25. Roderick Stewart, "The Claims of Frederick Douglass Philosophically Considered," in *Frederick Douglass: A Critical Reader*, ed. Bill E. Lawson and Frank Kirkland (Malden, MA: Blackwell, 1999), 145–72.

9

PAUL GILES

Douglass's Black Atlantic: Britain, Europe, Egypt

The Dialogue with Garrison

The initial impetus to institutionalize Frederick Douglass in the American literary canon in the 1970s was linked primarily to the renewed visibility and popularity of his first autobiography, *Narrative of the Life of Frederick Douglass* (1845). For critics in the Civil Rights era still working within the academic framework established by F. O. Matthiessen's *American Renaissance* (1941), it became relatively easy to establish Douglass as the missing racial element within the orbit of an American literary nationalism thought to be centered on the masculine genius of a heroic Transcendentalism. We know that Douglass read and admired Emerson, and there are indeed many structural parallels between the writings of Emerson (and Thoreau) and Douglass's 1845 *Narrative*.[1] There is a similar stress on self-reliance, on a quest for personal freedom; there is an emphasis on oratorical power and emotional authenticity, generated in part by Douglass's performances on the abolitionist lecture circuit in the early 1840s under the patronage of William Lloyd Garrison; there is a philosophical temper of Idealism, whereby, in dramatically dualistic terms, the "dark night" of slavery is contrasted with an image of unfettered freedom, sailing ships "robed in purest white, so delightful to the eye of free-men" (N 58–59). Although the *Narrative* of course inflects racial politics differently than Transcendentalism, its underlying rhetorical strategies involving a passage from bondage to freedom are curiously similar, and, not surprisingly, various critics have commented on ways in which this work appropriates familiar tropes of the American literary tradition. Joseph Fichtelberg has compared it to a "Christian conversion" narrative, whereby the narrator's physical battle with his slave-breaker, Covey, is presented as "the turning-point in my career as a slave" (N 65), while Henry Louis Gates, Jr. has associated Douglass's depiction of his flight and passage to self-realization with US black literature's seemingly "great, unique theme" of escape from bondage.[2]

It is, then, easy to see why Douglass's first autobiography should have been quickly canonized as the most representative of the slave narratives, an African American version of a literary declaration of independence that, as James Olney commented, "points the course for black American writers from Booker T. Washington and W. E. B. Du Bois and James Weldon Johnson down to Richard Wright and Malcolm X and Ralph Ellison and beyond."[3] The fact that the *Narrative* also sold very well – 11,000 copies between 1845 and 1847, with nine editions in Britain during these first two years of its publication – also helped to consolidate the text's representative status, since it could be said to bridge the more abstract, philosophical discourses characteristic of Transcendentalism with the broader appeal of a more sentimental literary tradition that, thanks in no small part to changes in modes of production and a dramatic increase in the number of mass-market paperbacks, was beginning to flourish during the 1840s. Douglass, like Susan Warner and Fanny Fern a few years later, skilfully manipulated his rhetoric so as to engender emotional pathos and affect, and these melodramatic aspects helped to ensure the general accessibility and popularity of the 1845 *Narrative*, its appeal to a wide range of readers, including of course those who enjoyed tales of plantation life for prurient rather than purely political purposes. Douglass had been since 1841 a paid lecturer for Garrison's American Anti-Slavery Society, which financed the publication of his first autobiography; however, the AASS expressed a fear that the publicity generated by this work might imperil Douglass's own personal safety, since, as an escaped slave, he was still liable to be legally reclaimed by his master in Maryland. The AASS consequently decided to send Douglass on a lecture tour to Britain, and it was there that, away from the immediate influence of the New England abolitionists, Douglass came to realize how tired he was of his enforced role as a theatrical performer tied to Garrison's bidding. "Instead of the bright, blue sky of America," Douglass wrote to Garrison on January 1, 1846, "I am covered with the soft, grey fog of the Emerald Isle. I breathe, and lo! The chattel becomes a man" (MB 374). Douglass had moved from being the property of a plantation owner to the property of abolitionists, and, despite his representative status within the American literary tradition, it was in fact Europe that first gave him the taste of a different kind of freedom.

Douglass left Boston on August 16, 1845 for Ireland, where he spent five months before beginning a lecture tour of Scotland in January 1846. He then toured England, joined for part of the time by Garrison, before returning to America in April 1847. During his travels, Douglass encountered a whole range of political scenarios that impelled him to think through issues of freedom and oppression within a more expansive transnational framework. Garrison saw his mission as fundamentally to change people's hearts on the slavery question, and he therefore opposed any attempt to vitiate what he perceived as the horrific impact of the slave experience by any confusion of the politics of abolition with wider issues. For Douglass, however, such forms of moral purity seemed increasingly narrow and difficult intellectually to sustain. His first lecture on foreign soil, in Dublin on August 31, 1845, was on the evils of alcohol rather than slavery, and while in Ireland he visited the jail where Daniel O'Connell had been held a couple of years earlier, as a gesture of solidarity with the Irish patriot leader who had campaigned openly against slavery. Douglass also profited financially from a second edition of his *Narrative*, published in Dublin by Webb and Chapman in 1846, with a new preface and appendix. In the latter, the author took delight in publicly ridiculing letters by A. C. C. Thompson, a native of Delaware, who had insisted that Douglass's *Narrative* was so well written it must be fraudulent, since the escaped slave with whom he was acquainted in that vicinity was called "Frederick Baily" and was "unlearned": only an "educated man," averred Thompson solemnly, "one who had some knowledge of the rules of grammar, could write so correctly."[4] This mordant irony, which of course served to validate the authenticity of Douglass's story, helped further to boost his sense of autonomy, and he became particularly irked to learn in Dublin that Maria Weston Chapman, a doyenne of the Boston Anti-Slavery Society, had written to Dublin publisher Richard D. Webb asking that he "keep an eye" on Douglass to make sure he would not be won over by those in the English antislavery movement who did not support Garrison. Douglass wrote Chapman a sharp reply, saying that he would not "tolerate any efforts to supervise and control" his activities.[5]

When Douglass moved on to Scotland, he found himself engaged in controversy with the Free Church of Scotland, which had the previous year sent representatives to the American South on a fund-raising mission. Since the American Presbyterian Church was one of the most popular congregations in the slave states, they managed to collect for their friends and allies in the Free Church some £3,000. At a meeting in Arbroath in February 1846, however, Douglass chastised the Free Church for "wallowing in the filth and mire of slavery," and he skilfully presented the argument so that "SEND BACK THE MONEY" became a familiar slogan in every town he visited in Scotland, one daubed on city walls and chanted at meetings (FDP 1:156). For Douglass, this episode was an insight into the transnational tentacles of slavery, the way in which, like apartheid a hundred years later, it could be implicitly sanctioned and financially supported by those who were not directly involved in its practice. While Douglass flattered his audience in

Paisley, Scotland, on March 18, 1846 by asserting that "[l]iberty is commensurate with and inseparable from British soil," he also acknowledged in the same address how "slavery is such a gigantic system that one nation is not fit to cope with it," thereby suggesting again his recognition of the politics of slavery as a complicated transnational business (LW 5:29). Indeed, as he moved through Britain on his speaking tour Douglass became increasingly aware of the complex, interlocking nature of social and economic power, the ways in which slavery could not always be reduced simply to a question of what Garrison liked to call "moral suasion." In Ireland Douglass associated slavery with the murderous poverty he witnessed there, and he also spoke at Bristol in 1846 of "political slavery in England," using the term metaphorically in association with practices in the army and navy: "Why does not England set the example by doing away with these forms of slavery at home," Douglass asked, "before it called upon the United States to do so?"[6]

All of this further alienated Douglass from Garrison, for whom the evils of racial slavery transcended everything else. Garrison was similarly hostile to the friendship Douglass struck up with the white English woman Julia Griffiths, whom he first met at a speaking engagement at her home town of Newcastle-upon-Tyne, and who, under the spell of Douglass's not inconsiderable personal charm, subsequently moved to Rochester, New York to assist him with his work. Griffiths remained in Rochester for seven years, staying at first in the Douglass household, and there has been much (inconclusive) speculation about the exact nature of the relationship between them. What is clear, though, is that Griffiths was extremely efficient on a practical level, assuming responsibility for the financial management of Douglass's journal *The North Star*, whose first issue appeared in December 1847. The launch of *The North Star* was itself financed by Douglass's British abolitionist friends, who between them raised $2,175 to enable him to purchase a printing press, with the journal's title deliberately evoking Feargus O'Connor's *Northern Star*, the leading paper of the Chartist movement. Again, the Chartists were a group Douglass had encountered while in England, and he collaborated with Chartist leaders William Lovett and Henry Vincent in 1846 to launch publicly the new Anti-Slavery League. Garrison was also present on that occasion, but he objected to the practical assistance offered by British abolitionist sympathizers, led by Ellen and Anna Richardson of Newcastle, who raised the funds in 1847 to purchase Douglass's freedom from his owner, Hugh Auld of Maryland. For Garrison and other American radicals, this amounted to an implicit recognition of property rights in humans, something that was anathema to their Christian conscience.

On one level, this difference of approach exemplifies the division between Garrison's party, dedicated as it was to an eradication of slavery in accordance with higher law, and Douglass himself, who tended politically to take more pragmatic lines. For Douglass, the end tended to justify the means, and he had no compunction about manipulating the engines of publicity to achieve his goals. We see this in his great admiration for Charles Dickens's *American Notes* (1842), to whose antislavery sentiments Douglass referred during several of his speeches in England in 1846, and later on in his admiration for Harriet Beecher Stowe's *Uncle Tom's Cabin* (1852). As he grew older Douglass became above all a realist in politics, experienced at operating the levers of power, and his time in England and Ireland helped to hone these skills by alerting him to ways in which the ideologies of national romance – in this case, the Romantic myth of Britain as a cradle of liberty – tended to go hand in hand with a more coercive social system, within which forces of domination and control were played out on a more surreptitious basis. Although African Americans such as himself were legally free in Britain in a way they were then not in the United States, Douglass was all too aware of how British public intellectuals such as Thomas Carlyle were linking the maintenance of slave labour in the Caribbean to the preservation of established social order at home, so that Douglass became sharply aware of the rhetorical gap between words and action, between the myth of British "liberty" for all and the realities of the country's participation in the so-called "coolie" trade. Douglass himself was never averse to appropriating Romantic myths for useful purposes, and indeed in 1838 he had adopted his own name from that of a heroic warrior in Walter Scott's poem *The Lady of the Lake* (1810), apparently simply because he liked how it sounded. But whereas the 1845 *Narrative* is driven primarily by oratorical energy and sentimental affect, Douglass's writing from the 1850s onward correlates these emotional dynamics with a more critical and reflexive understanding of the multifaceted nature of social relations.

Politics of the 1850s

Toward the end of his second autobiography, *My Bondage and My Freedom* (1855), Douglass looks back to what he calls his "two years of semi-exile in Great Britain and Ireland" (MB 389). That notion of "semi-exile," betokening a condition half in and half out of the United States, is significant to the larger trajectory of his later works. *My Bondage and My Freedom*, which is nearly four times as long as the earlier *Narrative*, seeks deliberately to gain more distance and perspective upon Douglass's experiences as a slave, offsetting its initial binary opposition between bondage and freedom against a much broader sense of how both these terms permeate society in different ways. It is true that *My Bondage* goes over much of the same ground as the 1845 *Narrative*, but it tends to treat its material in a more analytical and less directly personal fashion. Thus, for example, Douglass writes of how "[t]he slaveholder, as well as the slave, is the victim of the slave system" (MB 171), even if "[t]he slave is a subject subjected by others," while "the slaveholder is a subject, but he is the author of his own subjection" (MB 189). There is more political consciousness in this later autobiography – the narrator says he is not just the slave of Master Thomas, but "the slave of society at large" (MB 247) – and also more recognition of how notions of legitimacy depend upon the establishment of particular points of view: "Every slaveholder," he writes, "seeks to impress his slave with a belief in the boundlessness of slave territory, and of his own almost illimitable power" (MB 310). There is also a conceptual link between this 1855 work and what Carla Peterson has described as a general shift from first-person to third-person narrators in African American prose works written during the 1850s, when authors such as Delany and William Wells Brown sought to describe a wider social canvas by moving away from the sometimes claustrophobic confines of an autobiographical aesthetic form.[7] All of this signaled a further move away in Douglass's writings of the 1850s from the position of Garrison and the New England radicals, who placed less emphasis on slavery as a social or institutional problem, preferring to present it in more direct personal terms as a question of individual moral choice.

Despite, then, frequent critical attempts to find points of overlap between Douglass and the Transcendentalists, after the mid-1840s there were increasing points of divergence between their respective positions and projects. It is no surprise to find that when James Russell Lowell proposed Douglass as a member of Boston's Town and Country Club in 1849, he found Emerson among those reluctant to support him, since Douglass's penchant for increasingly flashy forms of self-publicity, no less than his skepticism about the ethical dimensions of politics, would have alienated him from many in the Boston intellectual firmament.[8] Conversely, Douglass became an increasingly visible and recognized leader of the African American community in the years leading up to the Civil War, and when the conflict began he kept President Lincoln under pressure to issue the Emancipation Proclamation, which finally arrived in September 1862 (to be effective from January 1, 1863). Lincoln met with Douglass three times in the White House, lauding him as "one of the most meritorious men, if not the most meritorious man, in the United States," and, in one of the last eras before the advent of the telegraph, both leaders shared a canny proclivity and expertise in polishing their public images to ensure the widest possible exposure (LW 3:45). Like Lincoln, Douglass had by this time grown into a sophisticated political thinker, perhaps less akin in style to Emerson than to John Stuart Mill, whose seminal work *On Liberty* (1859) addressed the problem of individual freedom and social coercion within a different but parallel context. Many American slaves had fled to England after the passage of the Fugitive Slave Act in 1850, so the whole question of personal liberty and how it related to the authority of state power was a burning issue at this time on both sides of the Atlantic.

Douglass's second trip eastward across the Atlantic came in November 1859, when a visit to England for six months had the beneficial effect of enabling him to avoid extradition to Virginia for his alleged involvement in John Brown's attack on Harpers Ferry. Like other African Americans of his time, Douglass always looked on Britain as a safe haven in legal terms, even if he believed that country's forms of social and racial oppression to be more insidious than some of those holding a candle to the memory of William Wilberforce would have cared to admit. Paul Gilroy, whose seminal work *The Black Atlantic* (1993) has strongly influenced the reconsideration of Douglass within a transatlantic context, argues that he "played a neglected role in English anti-slavery activity"; but it is important to recognize how Douglass used Britain primarily to gain an alternative perspective on US society, rather than seeking to identify with British culture itself.[9] In "The Heroic Slave," a fictional account written in 1853 of a mutiny that had taken place twelve years earlier on the *Creole* slave ship, Douglass's hero Madison Washington chronicles his escape to Canada by writing of how he "nestle[s] in the mane of the British lion, protected by his mighty paw from the talons and the beak of the American eagle."[10] The *Creole* subsequently sails into the British port of Nassau in the Bahamas, where all of the slaves are set free, an episode which refers back pointedly to the Slavery Abolition Act of 1833, which made slavery illegal throughout the British empire. And yet, as Ivy G. Wilson has observed, the implicit analogies in "The Heroic Slave" between Madison Washington and George Washington, and the ways in which the author clearly links his hero with other American patriots such as James Madison, ensure a more complex series of crosscurrents whereby this narrative suggests how "permitting slavery to exist amounts to returning the United States to the status of a colony of the British empire."[11] Douglass thus idealizes Britain here for the paradoxical purpose of encouraging African Americans to recapitulate their country's revolutionary gesture: he wants slaves to liberate themselves in the same way as Americans in the 1770s and 1780s threw off the British yoke. Just as Wilson Moses has shown how African Americans have simultaneously identified with the children of Israel in Egyptian bondage and with an Afrocentric mythology of pharaonic Egypt, so Douglass here exploits the contradiction whereby his African American fictional hero both idealizes and rejects Britain simultaneously.[12]

During the second half of his career, Douglass became adept at appropriating nationalist iconography for specific political purposes. This rhetorical manipulation began with his famous "change of opinion" on the US Constitution, which Douglass announced in May 1851, and it reverberated through his speech in Rochester a year later, "What to the Slave Is the Fourth of July?" (1852). In both of these instances, Douglass was seeking not simply to take an oppositional stance toward the United States, but to rotate the axis of its master narratives so as to bring patriotic narratives into alignment with African American interests. Just as Douglass was quick in the 1860s to recognize the symbolic potential of Abraham Lincoln, so in his later career he became an astute operator in the fluid world of public rhetoric.[13] These chameleonic aspects to Douglass's life and work, however, also ensure that his specific positions on particular issues are often hard to pin down. On the question of Ireland, most notoriously, he shifted his line of argument throughout his career. During his own trip to Ireland he expressed considerable sympathy with Daniel O'Connell and the Fenians, a group campaigning for Irish national independence, and in 1871 he remarked approvingly on the way the British Royal Family had been hissed on a visit to Dublin. The following year, he even went so far as to describe himself as "something of an Irishman as well as a negro."[14] But such equations between "Irishman" and "negro" are held firmly in check in Douglass's final autobiography, *Life and Times* (1881, 1892), where he insists on dissociating civil equality (which he supported) from social equality (which he did not). Although Douglass continues here to indict British policy toward Ireland for the "injustice and oppression" which has reaped "bitter consequences," he also declares that any notion of an "aggrieved" underclass, what he calls a "black Ireland in America," would be disastrous for the US (LT 973). While continuing to honour the memory of O'Connell – a true "transatlantic statesman" (LT 683) – Douglass is critical of a later generation of Irish leaders who, he says, tended more chauvinistically to campaign for liberty for the Irish, but not for other races. In particular, he sharply criticizes John Mitchell, an Irish emigrant who expressed proslavery sentiments on his arrival in America, while he also describes as one of the darkest chapters in the Civil War the riots by an Irish mob in New York in July 1863 against enlistment in the Union army, a reaction which also manifested itself here in the lynching of African Americans. Douglass always maintained an interest in Irish affairs, hearing Prime Minister William Gladstone discuss the Irish question in Parliament during his final visit to England in 1887, and subsequently speaking himself at a meeting in Washington in support of Irish Home Rule. But, opposed as he generally was to ideas of racial essentialism, Douglass recognized how the Irish in Ireland and the Irish in America were two quite different phenomena, working within a quite different set of social circumstances and expectations.

The Republican Intellectual

While in principle Douglass was sympathetic to the idea of solidarity between oppressed ethnic groups, in practice he found himself forced to recognize the mutual antagonism and hostility between the Irish-American and African American communities. For Douglass, different circumstances brought different political challenges, and such openness to contradiction, to a recognition of the disjunction between theory and practice, testifies to the way Douglass increasingly became a political pragmatist, with affinities in temperament and tone to Booker T. Washington. Indeed, Douglass, like Washington, became a stalwart of the Republican Party in his later years, being appointed by President Rutherford Hayes as US Marshall for the District of Columbia, where his primary task was to enforce federal court orders within the nation's capital. Douglass later held government posts in Haiti and Santo Domingo, and, although of course in the nineteenth century the Republican party was the more progressive on racial issues, it is nevertheless an oddity of cultural history that such a die-hard Republican politician was to become so closely associated with the academic agendas of multiculturalism at the end of the twentieth century. This anomaly has been generated partly by the excessive concentration on Douglass's earlier rather than his later work: *Life and Times*, in particular, is in general a philosophically conservative book, where the narrator recounts his feeling that he "had on my side all the invisible forces of the moral government of the universe" (LT 896), but where he also associates such "moral government" with a spirit of desperate struggle. Gilroy has floated the name of Nietzsche in conjunction with the later work of Douglass, and its edgy ambience would certainly appear to have more in common with the harsh world of the naturalist philosophers – Charles Darwin is mentioned in this text (LT 939) – than with the evangelical Christian faith of a Sojourner Truth. *Life and Times* is nearly twice as long as *My Bondage and My Freedom*, and six times as long as the 1845 *Narrative*, but that is not the only reason it has not been so frequently assigned in the American college classroom.

In the latter part of his career, then, Douglass moved further away from recycling the pieties of freedom, and more toward a recognition of race as an element within a brutal *realpolitik*, something derived in part from European cultural influences. Although there is no direct evidence that Douglass was familiar with Nietzsche or Hegel, we know that he had been introduced to the world of German philosophy by Ottilie Assing. Assing, who, according to her biographer, regarded herself as Douglass's "natural" wife, came upon Douglass by reading *My Bondage and My Freedom*. She probably began an affair with him in the 1850s, though details of this are now difficult to establish because most of Assing's letters were burnt in a fire at Douglass's house in Rochester in 1872, while his letters to her were destroyed under the terms of Douglass's will.[15] Assing, born in Hamburg, began working as an American correspondent for the German newspaper *Morgenblatt* in 1851, sending back articles on American art and culture to be published in Germany. It was she who introduced Douglass to Ludwig Feuerbach, David Friedrich Strauss, and other German advocates of "Higher Criticism," which treated Biblical narratives as myth. After reading Feuerbach's *Essence of Christianity* (1841) with Douglass, Assing wrote to the German philosopher about "the satisfaction ... of seeing a superior man won over for atheism."[16] Douglass subsequently kept busts of Feuerbach and Strauss in his study, doubtless gifts from Assing, along with portraits of abolitionist friends and heroes such as Wendell Phillips, John Brown, Abraham Lincoln, and Toussaint L'Ouverture. Assing herself translated *My Bondage and My Freedom* into German, publishing it in 1860 as *Sklaverei und Freiheit*. She and Douglass remained close friends until the 1870s, and the significance of her influence as what Christoph Lohmann calls "an atheist and freethinker" on Douglass has probably been underestimated.[17] In his later writings, Douglass, despite his religious skepticism, follows Feuerbach and Strauss in continuing to manipulate and exploit the residual power of religious metaphors, even while emptying out their metaphysical connotations. "Men have their choice in this world," he declared in a lecture delivered at the Zion Church in Rochester on June 16, 1861: "They can be angels, or they may be demons ... The slaveholders had rather reign in hell than serve in heaven" (LW 3:119–20). Douglass's refurbishment here of Milton's language in *Paradise Lost* (1667), like the way he held up the language in the Declaration of Independence and the US Constitution, suggests again ways in which he exploits the cultural force of symbolic capital without himself having any specific commitment to it as a form of positive truth. Although over the past forty years there has been a massive critical sentimentalization of Douglass within the US academy, an appropriation of him as a spokesperson for liberal versions of identity politics, he remains in many ways a much more enigmatic and elusive figure.

The interest of Douglass's later writing, then, lies in its increasingly complicated and problematic relation to US national narratives. Whereas in the 1845 autobiography liberty is presented as antithetical to slavery, from the 1855 *My Bondage and My Freedom* onward, it is more the capacity to switch positions, to show ways in which "legally sanctioned bondage emerges as the undeniable twin of freedom," as Russ Castronovo puts it, that forms the nexus of Douglass's bifocal vision.[18] There are, of course, many conceptual corollaries for this kind of irony, including Douglass's own mixed race provenance, along with those institutional forms of repression that remained blind for so long to ways in which the American mythology of a self-made man not only was racially inflected but depended crucially upon the systematic exclusion of African Americans.[19] In this sense, some of the power of Douglass's rhetoric derives from something like parody, from the way he sets up familiar American icons and images and forces his audience to reimagine them from an unfamiliar perspective. We see this in his famous address where he asks, "What to the American slave is your Fourth of July?" (MB 434), and also in a speech delivered in New York on August 4, 1857 to commemorate the twenty-third anniversary of emancipation in the British West Indies, where he travesties John Winthrop's famous sermon of 1630 by relocating the Biblical city on a hill from New England to Old England: "The day and the deed are both greatly distinguished. They are a city set upon a hill ... It has made the name of England known and loved in every Slave Cabin, from the Potomac to the Rio Grande" (LW 2:426).

Although Douglass himself was famous for his parodic imitations of slave masters and proslavery preachers, he probably would not have been very happy with this notion of parody as a structural component of his work, since it might seem to imply a form of negativity, an undermining of conventional value, which he as a staunch American patriot would have wished to avoid. Nevertheless, it is clear that the power of Douglass's oratory depends upon an aesthetic of defamiliarization, a reassignment of established ideas so that they are recast in a parallel but alien light. This is the classic type of parody as Linda Hutcheon has described it, a form of "repetition" and "authorized transgression" involving "difference rather than similarity ... a method of inscribing continuity while permitting critical distance."[20] This is also the basis for the significance of Britain within Douglass's imaginative world: not only did Britain furnish him with practical assistance for his manumission and publishing projects, it also provided the metaphorical "distance" that offered a symbolic example of how the Atlantic world might be organized differently. The politics of Chartism and the question of Irish emancipation were problematic issues in themselves for all kinds of reasons, but their central importance was the way they forced Douglass to assume a position of estrangement toward the plantation culture of the Old South. The viability of the plantation, as Douglass remarked in an 1853 essay on Stowe, depended on its power systematically to exclude the outside world, to imagine itself as "a little nation of its own." Slavery wants "just to be let alone," whereas the "exposure" of its ignominies depends upon a capacity to "drag slavery out of its natural darkness" into "the light" (LW 2:240–41). For Douglass, this process of enlightenment involved the inscription of an alternative conceptual space within which the antiquated customs of the plantation could be understood as contingent and, therefore, as reversible.

Douglass further explored this kind of relativity of perspective on his final trip to England in 1886–87, which included side trips to Paris, Rome, and Egypt. In Avignon, he ironically commends the old papal palace for its material rather than spiritual riches, its "large and beautiful grounds" and "very pleasant" aspect, all of which in his eyes exemplify "the German proverb, 'They who have the cross will bless themselves'" (LT 992). In Rome, Douglass talks of his "curiosity in seeing devout people going up to the black statue of St. Peter," adding wryly: "I was glad to find him black, I have no prejudice against his color" (LT 1004). Douglass's grim humor here involves another example of cultural transposition; as Robert S. Levine remarks, the anecdote "speaks to his effort to 'blacken' traditional accounts of European and Christian history by questioning assumptions of whiteness."[21] The kind of parodic transvaluation apparent in Douglass's invocation of a black St. Peter testifies to his proclivity for racial hybridity and mixing, and it also helps to explain his uneasiness in Egypt, where he finds acute poverty and degradation: "Egypt may have invented the plow," he observes sardonically, "but it has not improved upon the invention. The kind used there is perhaps as old as the time of Moses" (LT 1011). Constitutionally suspicious of the idea of origins, Douglass was uncomfortable with any notion of Egypt as a natural home or point of reference for African American civilization. As in his other travels, the landscapes of Africa provide a horizon of alterity against which Douglass's sense of himself as a patriotic American can be calibrated.

The alterity associated with such transnational perspectives can be correlated with Douglass's assumptions about hybridity within the African American cultural experience, which in turn might be associated with his discourse of hybridity in a stylistic sense. As Stephen Railton has argued, one of the characteristics of nineteenth-century American literature in general was the way in which, in its emphasis on the variegated skills of rhetorical "performance," it tended to draw eclectically upon the formal conventions of sermons, journals, and autobiography.[22] Douglass, like other American writers of his time, accommodated these various elements in a new generic mix. In a manuscript that John W. Blassingame dates to about 1865, Douglass discusses Emerson's comments on creative producers and poets, and he specifically asserts his interest in the "philosophy of art," refuting the claim that this is a subject "Negroes know nothing about" (FDP 3:620). In this sense, Douglass's art of estrangement, the way he recombines his own life story in relation to different social and philosophical dimensions, is no less consciously arranged than that of his literary contemporaries, both black and white. There is a similarity between Douglass's autobiographical idiom and William Wells Brown's novel *Clotel* (1853), published initially in London, which also follows a generically mixed style in the way it blends a personal slave narrative with a parallel account of American history, reinterpreting the *Mayflower* and the presidency of Thomas Jefferson in the light of stories about his illegitimate slave children. *Clotel* brings together lecture, fiction, and history in equal measure, and Douglass's writings from the same period have a similar kind of aesthetic momentum in the way they project the speaker's rhetorical voice into ever more complicated, self-alienating scenarios. Rather than simply repeating his life story, Douglass continued to experiment by situating his persona within a range of intellectual contexts, to explore different ways in which the African American subject might appear if slavery were to be represented in relation to violence, or eroticism, or politics, or (especially in *Life and Times*) questions of social power and naturalistic determinism. His writing depends upon a constantly shifting relationship between subject and object, between the articulation of a speaking position and the establishment of a more exigent social framework. In this sense, the trope of the black Atlantic becomes less a topographical element than a formal characteristic within Douglass's writing, since the imaginative rotation of his world upon a transatlantic axis manifests itself as a crucial element within his entire intellectual project.

NOTES

1. John Stauffer, "Frederick Douglass's Self-Fashioning and the Making of a Representative American Man," in *The Cambridge Companion to the African American Slave Narrative*, ed. Audrey Fisch (Cambridge: Cambridge University Press, 2007), 205.

2. Joseph Fichtelberg, *The Complex Image: Faith and Method in American Autobiography* (Philadelphia: University of Pennsylvania Press, 1989), 132; Henry Louis Gates, Jr., "Introduction: The Language of Slavery," in *The Slave's Narrative*, ed. Charles T. Davis and Henry Louis Gates, Jr. (New York: Oxford University Press, 1985), xviii.

3. James Olney, "The Founding Fathers – Frederick Douglass and Booker T. Washington," in *Slavery and the Literary Imagination*, ed. Deborah E. McDowell and Arnold Rampersad (Baltimore, MD: Johns Hopkins University Press, 1989), 3.

4. Frederick Douglass, *Narrative of the Life of Frederick Douglass*, 2nd edn. (Dublin: Webb and Chapman, 1846), cxxiv.

5. Patricia J. Ferreira, "Frederick Douglass in Ireland: The Dublin Edition of his *Narrative*," *New Hibernia Review/Iris Eireannach Nua* 5:1 (2001), 61.

6. William S. McFeely, *Frederick Douglass* (New York: W. W. Norton, 1991), 141.

7. Carla L. Peterson, "Capitalism, Black (Under)development, and the Production of the African American Novel in the 1850s," *American Literary History* 4:4 (1992), 562–63.

8. Thomas Wortham, "Did Emerson Blackball Frederick Douglass from Membership in the Town and Country Club?" *New England Quarterly* 65:2 (1992), 297–98.

9. Paul Gilroy, *The Black Atlantic: Modernity and Double Consciousness* (Cambridge, MA: Harvard University Press, 1993), 13.

10. Frederick Douglass, "The Heroic Slave," in *Violence in the Black Imagination: Essays and Documents*, ed. Ronald T. Takaki, 2nd edn. (New York: Oxford University Press, 1993), 56.

11. Ivy G. Wilson, "On Native Ground: Transnationalism, Frederick Douglass, and 'The Heroic Slave,'" *PMLA* 121:2 (2006), 458.

12. Wilson Jeremiah Moses, *Creative Conflict in African American Thought: Frederick Douglass, Alexander Crummell, Booker T. Washington, W. E. B. Du Bois, and Marcus Garvey* (Cambridge: Cambridge University Press, 2004), xiii.

13. Priscilla Wald, *Constituting Americans: Cultural Anxiety and Narrative Form* (Durham, NC: Duke University Press, 1995), 73.

14. McFeely, *Frederick Douglass*, 280.

15. Maria Diedrich, *Love Across Color Lines: Ottilie Assing and Frederick Douglass* (New York: Hill and Wang, 1999), 188.

16. *Ibid.*, 225.

17. *Radical Passion: Ottilie Assing's Reports from America and Letters to Frederick Douglass*, ed. Christoph Lohmann (New York: Peter Lang, 1999), xxix.

18. Russ Castronovo, *Fathering the Nation: Genealogies of Slavery and Freedom* (Berkeley: University of California Press, 1995), 213.

19. On this theme, see Toni Morrison, *Playing in the Dark: Whiteness and the Literary Imagination* (Cambridge, MA: Harvard University Press, 1992).

20. Linda Hutcheon, *A Theory of Parody: The Teachings of Twentieth-Century Art Forms* (New York: Methuen, 1985), 6, 26, 20.

21. Robert S. Levine, "Road to Africa: Frederick Douglass's Rome," *African American Review* 34:2 (2000), 223.

22. Stephen Railton, *Authorship and Audience: Literary Performance in the American Renaissance* (Princeton, NJ: Princeton University Press, 1991), 3–22.

10

IFEOMA C. K. NWANKWO

Douglass's Black Atlantic: The Caribbean

Frederick Douglass, over the course of his life, went from being a slave on US soil to being US consul in Haiti. That is to say, he went from being not even considered fully human according to US law to representing the US government in a foreign country. He is often thought of as the consummate exemplar of W. E. B. Du Bois's notion of "double consciousness."[1] Douglass strove throughout his life to reconcile his affinity for the United States with the pain of being rejected by that nation because of his race. Du Bois, in fact, echoed the language of Douglass, who characterized African Americans as "a nation, in the midst of a nation which disowns them," putting them in a position that is "anomalous, unequal, and extraordinary."[2] Douglass often spoke from both within and without America, insisting on his and his people's rights as Americans while simultaneously describing them as "aliens … in our native land" and referring to Americans as "them."[3] As these tropes signal, Douglass's internal conflicts manifest themselves strikingly in his writings about the world beyond the United States – especially about the African diaspora in the Caribbean. This population is crucial to examining the development of "Black" identities in the Americas in general, and to understanding Douglass's mindset in particular, because they constitute such a substantial proportion of the African-descended population of the "New World." Historians calculate that of Africans brought as slaves to the Americas, 95 percent were brought to South America and the Caribbean and only 5 percent to the United States.[4] Many African captives eventually transported to the United States were "seasoned" – meaning acclimated to enslavement – on Caribbean soil before they were taken to the United States for sale.

Douglass's "double consciousness" complicates and is complicated by another difficult dialectic – the tension between the struggle for acceptance as a US American on the one hand, and the claims of a racially based connection to people of African descent outside the United States on the other. The result is what might usefully be termed a "twice-doubled consciousness."[5] Douglass's material and ideological relationships with "foreign" people of African descent are a crucial part of his conceptualization, articulation, and representation of identity. His decisions about how to respond to the charge of being more a Haitian than an American, for example, yield insight into not only his ideas about the relationship between African Americans and Haitians in particular, but also the underpinnings of his conceptualization of African American identity. Consequently, a full understanding of his arguments about US African American identity in general, and US African Americans' relationship to the United States more specifically, cannot be gleaned without a consideration of the ways those arguments are created, bolstered, or undercut by his engagements with the Black world beyond the United States.[6]

The Americas

In his first two autobiographies, Douglass is virtually silent on the other Americas, including the Caribbean; in his essays, letters, speeches, and fiction, as well as Part Three of *The Life and Times of Frederick Douglass* (1881, 1892), he is more forthcoming. The silence in the autobiographies themselves is crucially related to their task of constructing a Black self in the United States. As Houston Baker has noted, Douglass's *Narrative* (1845) is an exemplar of the southern slave's use of autobiographical writing in his "quest for being," and a counterpoint to perceptions of the slave as a brute.[7] William Andrews similarly points out that autobiography allowed the free man to "declare himself a new man, a freeman, an American."[8] As autobiographies, Douglass's texts exhibit the crafting, silences, and conventions identified by numerous scholars in texts so defined.[9] And as a US Black, Douglass must work through his ambivalence toward the nation that has denied him full membership. How does the nation's negation of him affect his claim to citizenship, to his status as an American? Considered in this light, Douglass's ties (historical, racial, or otherwise) to non-US Black communities, especially those in the nearly contiguous Caribbean, threaten to complicate efforts to demonstrate his (US) Americanness. While the autobiographies overtly ignore the Black international, these silences in fact speak volumes.

For one thing, they evoke their historical contexts. The fear of national or transnational Black uprisings provoked by the Haitian Revolution (1791–1804) was still quite present in US society, as were individuals who had fled Haiti with their slaves to escape sure death.[10] The silence also arises out of the fact that the control of African Americans' movement, both physical and ideological, had always been and continued to be fundamental to the maintenance of the slave society. As Douglass's *Narrative* illustrates, slaves had to be prevented not only from running north, but even from moving freely between counties or plantations. Douglass's autobiographical writing tends to take the approach least likely to ignite White fear of the loss of this control of slave identity and ideology. He provides a glimpse of the underpinnings of his strategy when he notes in *Life and Times*:

> Slaveholders are known to have sent spies among their slaves to ascertain, if possible, their views and feelings in regard to their condition; hence the maxim established among them, that "a still tongue makes a wise head." They would suppress the truth rather than take the consequences of telling it, and in so doing they prove themselves a part of the human family. (LT 512)

The "still tongue" protects slaves' claim to humanity, and by extension, to freedom. The silences in the *Narrative* surrounding knowledge about non-US geography suggest that Douglass intentionally suppresses his own earlier self's knowledge of the international scene to advance his cause.[11] Douglass signals several times that he is leaving out the names of individuals or particular details in the service of "prudence," but factual inconsistencies indicate a more subtle crafting process (LT 663). In his "Cambria Riot" speech he narrates the development of the escape plot he hatched with his fellow slaves, insisting that they "knew nothing about Canada" and "could see no spot, this side of the ocean where we could be free" (FDP 1:50). Even the idea that a group of US slaves did not know about Canada seems questionable, especially when juxtaposed with his indication that they knew about England. The strategic nature of Douglass's represented ignorance of Canada becomes clearer when he undermines his own assertion. He recalls that after he had successfully run away and found an abolitionist friend in the North, his friend (David Ruggles) "wished to know of [me] where I wanted to go; ... I thought of going to Canada" (FDP 1:65). Nowhere in this conversation does Douglass indicate that Ruggles told him about Canada, so the logical conclusion is that Douglass, the slave, likely already knew of Canada's existence and that freedom could be found there.

In *My Bondage and My Freedom* (1855), Douglass himself provides a theory of his own silences on the world beyond the United States. He suggests that slaves are inherently resistant to thinking about "removal" or migration because of their history of forced placement and displacement: "[F]ree people generally ... have less attachment to the places where they are born and brought up, than have the slaves. Their freedom to go and come, to be here and there, as they list, prevents any extravagant attachment to any one particular place" (MB 238). He states further that "the slave is a fixture; he has no choice, no goal, no destination; but is pegged down to a single spot, and must take root here, or nowhere." The slave cannot move anywhere, and must therefore become bonded to the location in which he finds himself. Furthermore, Douglass notes:

The idea of removal elsewhere, comes, generally, in the shape of a threat, and in punishment of crime. It is, therefore attended with fear and dread. A slave seldom thinks of bettering his condition by being sold, and hence he looks upon separation from his native place, with none of the enthusiasm which animates the bosoms of young freemen, when they contemplate a life in the far west, or in some distant country where they intend to rise to wealth and distinction.

Slaves are forced to stay and forced to move, the latter generally as punishment. The result of this treatment is that slaves have a negative perception of any suggestion that they or anyone they love should move. As Douglass says, "Nor can those from whom they separate, give them up with that cheerfulness with which friends and relations yield each other up, when they feel that it is for the good of the departing one that he is removed from his native place." Moreover, for free people who move, "[T]here is, at least, the hope of reunion, because reunion is *possible*," but "with the slave ... [t]here is no improvement in his condition *probable*, – no correspondence *possible*, – no reunion attainable" (MB 239). Douglass actually equates a slave's "going out into the world" with "a living man going into the tomb." His silence on the other Black Americas can therefore usefully be read as reflecting his desire to represent both the slave's lack of knowledge and his own apprehensions (as a former slave) about going out into the world (physically or conceptually). Douglass's theory lays bare the relationship to place that grounded his own relationship with the world, and also the ways slavery encouraged, produced, and fed on the provincialism and parochialism of slaves. It stands to reason, then, that the ideology of slavery also feared, discouraged, and sought to destroy any hint of cosmopolitan knowledge or international solidarity in slaves and others of African descent.

In his fiction, essays, speeches, and newspapers, Douglass engages the Black world more frequently. In these texts he replicates the emphasis on African Americans' rights to Americanness evident in the *Narrative of the Life of Frederick Douglass, My Bondage and My Freedom*, and the bulk of *Life and Times*. For example, when he is asked by one of the readers of his newspaper, *Douglass' Monthly*, to publish his views on emigration to Haiti, he likens telling African Americans to emigrate to telling an Englishman or an Irishman to leave England or Ireland, again implicitly naming African Americans' ties to the United States: "[B]ut as we should not be in favor of saying to all the people of these countries, be off, so we are not in favor of saying to all the colored people here, *move off*" (LW 5:472). In these texts not explicitly marked as autobiographies, he also exhibits more openness to transnational notions of community. His engagement with the Black world beyond the United States is qualitatively different in these texts, in part because he is not required, by either genre or publisher, to focus on his own voice/story, to provide a narrative that is presumed to be purely a reflection of an experience, or to defend himself against specific personal accusations. That is not to say that this writing is wholly unfettered, but rather to say that the limitations and expectations differ significantly from those with which he had to contend as he wrote the autobiographies. The autobiographies were stories of Douglass's self, but of a particularly configured self that was expected to fall in line with what White abolitionist leaders wanted, especially in the case of the *Narrative*. Even though, as William Andrews notes in *To Tell a Free Story*, ex-slave narrators of the 1840s had more leeway, "the literary autonomy of men like Douglass ... was nevertheless restricted ... [for] the antislavery movement did not provide them a forum for their speaking and writing just so that they could express themselves."[12] The fiction, essays, speeches, and newspapers on the other hand, because they are written for disparate and wider ranging audiences and purposes, allow us to get a better sense of the depth and breadth of Douglass's thinking.

The British West Indies

Slavery in the British Caribbean bore a profound relationship to that in the United States in large part because of the ongoing trading relationships between the two (that between South Carolina and Barbados, for example, is almost legendary in historical circles). Needless to say, then, the push for emancipation in the British island colonies throughout the early decades of the nineteenth century struck fear in the hearts of US slave-owners and proslavery advocates. Conversely, it was a potential tool for antislavery activists in the United States. Douglass's choices about how and when to wield this tool are telling. In the *Narrative*, Douglass describes how he resolves to try to secure his liberty and that of his fellow slaves in 1834, the year the emancipation of West Indian slaves took effect – but makes absolutely no mention of the coincidence. The strangeness of this omission is more apparent if we compare Douglass's statement in the *Narrative* that "[i]n the early part of the year 1838, I became quite restless," with a letter to Douglass written by the abolitionist Wendell Phillips, and published as one of the introductions to the *Narrative* (N 85). Phillips's letter refers, in passing, to "the West India experiment," and its importance to the abolitionist movement in the 1830s (N 11). Phillips's introduction paves the way for Douglass to mention West Indian emancipation in the text of the *Narrative*, and might lead an alert reader to expect a parallel or connection to be made between events in the West Indies and either his foiled escape or his case of restlessness in 1838. And yet at the same time, it indicates a possible reason Douglass does not take that path. Emancipation had greatly reduced the profits of British landowners and merchants, and would probably not prove a persuasive example to Americans who were not already abolitionists. Douglass's expressed goal of speeding abolition in the United States was better served, then, by not bringing up West Indian emancipation.

The post-Civil War context seems to enable a different approach. In the Appendix to *Life and Times of Frederick Douglass*, Douglass reproduces a speech he gave at a West Indian Emancipation Day celebration in 1880, where he discusses the importance of the day for African Americans, both before and after the Civil War. Here Douglass explicitly articulates and celebrates the political, ideological, and identificatory links between people of African descent in the US and the Caribbean. He speaks of West Indian Emancipation Day as "preeminently the colored man's day" and of Black West Indians as "our brothers in the West Indies" (LT 926). "Emancipation in the West Indies," he pronounces, was "the first tangible fact demonstrating the possibility of a peaceable transition from slavery to freedom, of the Negro race."

He goes on, though, to emphasize the particularity of the American situation and, by extension, to name and claim the Americanness of the African Americans who are celebrating the freedom of West Indians: "Let no American, especially no colored American, withhold a generous recognition of this stupendous achievement" (LT 928). Douglass's relationship to the Black world beyond the United States shapes and is shaped by his relationship with Americanness, and his drive for full citizenship for African Americans. He spends half the speech speaking directly to the recent political history of the United States in general (the Civil War) and the condition and history of the African American in particular. He argues stridently that, although emancipation has taken place, conditions for the African American have changed little: "The citizenship granted in the fourteenth amendment is practically a mockery, and the right to vote, provided for in the fifteenth amendment, is literally stamped out in the face of government" (LT 932). In an implicitly comparative statement, he notes, "History does not furnish an example of emancipation under conditions less friendly to the emancipated class than this American example" (LT 933). His discussion of the West Indies serves as a point of departure for his discussion of the condition of African Americans, rather than as a focal point in itself.

While Douglass implicitly relies on the notion of a specific racial connection between Blacks in the United States and West Indies, he frequently dissolves it in a more general appeal to human brotherhood, which also includes the Whites who fought for emancipation and even those who owned slaves. "The emancipation of our brothers in the West Indies," Douglass writes, "comes home to us and stirs our hearts and fills our souls with those grateful sentiments which link mankind in a common brotherhood" (LT 926). He continues to privilege above all African Americans' claims to Americanness and shared humanity with Whites: "Human liberty excludes all idea of home and abroad. It is universal and spurns localization ... It is bounded by no geographical lines and knows no national limitations" (LT 927).

In its failure (or refusal) to mention the existence of other Black Americas, Douglass's *Narrative* parallels all extant nineteenth-century US and Caribbean slave narratives discovered to date. This trend, particularly when contrasted with the presence of the Black world in fiction and political essays of the same period, including those of Douglass, suggests that African American (as well as Afro-Caribbean) identity, as embodied in the autobiographical self, was intimately tied up with location and nation, and that any recognition of the possibility of other Black selves in the Americas would somehow conjure up the specter of an international Blackness inimical to nation-based projects. I want to suggest the term "binaristic Blackness" to describe this idea that only one group of Blacks can or should be the focus of a text, particularly a text concerned with uplift or amelioration of conditions. The concept is based on the image of a seesaw, in which if one is to be above, the other must be below. William Andrews rightly notes that "tensions, disjunctions, and silences can serve as an index to a struggle going on in a narrative."[13] The point implicit in Douglass's nonrepresentation of the other Black Americas in the *Narrative* and the bulk of the other autobiographies is that the furthering of the African American agenda within the United States, particularly while slavery continued, necessitated a textual distancing from the other Black Americas. The point rests on the presumption that the battle for rights or citizenship in a particularized national context must necessarily exclude the articulation of a transnational notion of community.

It is perhaps telling that it is fiction that provides the form most congenial to the coexistence of national and international Black selves. In his novella "The Heroic Slave" (1853), a fictionalized retelling of the mutiny undertaken by Madison Washington and the other slaves on the *Creole*, near the Bahamas, Douglass makes a point of writing of the presence of Bahamians on the shore cheering the rebels' accomplishments and welcoming them to their islands. By including the Bahamians, Douglass situates the rebels, previously figured as literal as well as spiritual descendants of the patriots of the American Revolution, as also part of a Black world. The rebels are both heirs to the American Revolution and brethren to the Black Bahamians.[14]

Haiti

In 1791 enslaved people in the French colony San Domingue rose up against their oppressors and enacted a revolution that changed the course of New

World history. With the founding of the republic of Haiti, the first Black republic in the New World, Atlantic governments, if they wanted to use any of the many resources (natural, political, economic) of the former colony, were forced to deal with Black Haitian leaders. Haiti was crucial to US government machinations in the Caribbean, including in its contentious relationship with the Spanish in neighboring Cuba, a relationship that ultimately led to war in 1898. As a result, US leaders struggled to find ways to endear themselves to Haiti's leaders to get the concessions that the United States wanted and needed. Frederick Douglass served as US consul to Haiti and chargé d'affaires of Santo Domingo from 1889 to 1891. From the moment his appointment was announced it met with resistance, particularly from powerful White US statesmen and businessmen who were opposed to Douglass on purely racial grounds.[15] They feared that a Black man would not strongly support or advance US interests, and would instead advocate for Haiti and plot with the Haitians against the United States. Douglass negotiates this negativity while also trying to express his sense of solidarity with Haiti:

> This clamor for a white minister for Haiti is based upon the idea that a white man is held in higher esteem by her than is a black man, and that he could get more out of her than can one of her own color. It is not so, and the whole free history of Haiti proves it not to be so. Even if it were true that a white man could, by reason of his alleged superiority, gain something extra from the servility of Haiti, it would be the height of meanness for a great nation like the United States to take advantage of such servility on the part of a weak nation. (LT 1028)

Even as Douglass asserts his connectedness to Haiti, implying that a Black man can "get more out" of Haiti than a White man, he adopts the language of US imperial/supremacist discourse, calling Haiti a "weak nation" and the United States a "great nation." As he attacks the "alleged superiority" of the White man, he positions Haiti as an infant to be pitied and protected, rather than taken advantage of. So, we clearly see how the double consciousness of race and nation, being both American and Negro, leads to a twice-doubled consciousness (a struggle to balance affinities), and a hierarchy that subordinates the non-US Black to the United States. His representation of his handling of this position recalls those moments in the autobiographies in which he refers to his fellow African Americans as "they." The hierarchy evident in this statement about Haiti also positions the non-US Black as a child in relation to the African American, through its simultaneously paternal and patronizing tone. This approach recalls Douglass's statement that, once he had learned to read and began to understand the nuances of slavery, he came to envy his fellow slaves' "stupidity" (N 42). The implication is that Haiti is to be protected from US meanness, and the African American is the protector. On the one hand, Douglass is squeezed between national and pan-Black affinities, but on the other he situates himself above the non-US Black. So while he is being crushed, he is engaging in creating some destructive torque of his own, just as he did at times in his representation of his own countrymen. Binaristic Blackness, as it appears in his troubled engagements with Haiti, is an unintended consequence of his striving for recognition of his humanity, equality, and US citizenship.

Annexationist sentiment in the United States was extremely high during the latter half of the nineteenth century. Rayford Logan's seminal text, *The Diplomatic Relations of the United States with Haiti, 1776–1891* (1941), explicates the methods by which the US government engaged Haiti in the service of its "manifest destiny" objectives. During Douglass's tenure in Haiti, the US government was endeavoring to expand its imperial power by building a military base on the Haitian island of Môle St. Nicholas.[16] As the US consul, Douglass's job involved him in negotiations for access to the island. He thus found himself caught between the imperialist designs of his country and his desire to help maintain the independence of a country replete with large numbers of his racial kin. In going from a solely US context to one that is not only foreign, but also Black and laden with significance for the pan-Black collective because of its status as the first Black nation in the Americas and as the location of the most successful Black slave revolution, Douglass's twice-doubled consciousness comes to the fore. Not only must Douglass struggle to be both American and Negro, but now he must struggle to be both a "good" US citizen and a good "brother" to the Haitians.

This duty places him squarely between national and pan-Black affinities, between double consciousnesses. The way in which he chooses to defend himself speaks volumes about the evolution of the worldview that was initially foreshadowed in the *Narrative*. The twice-doubled consciousness hinted at by the absence of the Caribbean from the *Narrative* now appears full-blown in Douglass's final autobiography. In his own defense he states:

> I am charged with sympathy for Haiti. I am not ashamed of that charge; but no man can say with truth that my sympathy with Haiti stood between me and my honorable duty that I owed to the United States or to any citizen of the United States ... The attempt has been made to prove me indifferent to the acquisition of a naval station in Haiti, and unable to grasp the importance to American commerce and to American influence of such a station in the Caribbean Sea ... I said then that it was a shame to American statesmanship that, while almost every other great nation in the world had secured a foothold and had power in the Caribbean Sea, where it could anchor in its own bays and moor in its own harbors, we, who stood at the very gate of that sea, had there no anchoring ground anywhere. I was for the acquisition of Samana, and of Santo Domingo herself, if she wished to

come to us. While slavery existed, I was opposed to all schemes for the extension of American power and influence. But since its abolition, I have gone with him who goes farthest for such extension.   (LT 1029)

Here we see Douglass even more explicitly trying to walk the fine line between asserting his right to Americanness, his loyalty to the United States, and not wholly disregarding his racial bond with the Haitians. He is fighting against the presumption that US Blacks, not really "American," either do not grasp or oppose outright the imperatives of manifest destiny that drive the attempt to acquire the Môle. He evinces not only a general concern with US prestige, but a specific desire that the United States should use its power to secure its dominance. He speaks of other nations and the United States needing to have "power in the Caribbean Sea." He almost explicitly embraces manifest destiny in his invocation of that discourse's geopolitical language (the United States standing at the "gate of the [Caribbean] Sea").

However, he ties his support of manifest destiny to the issue of slavery. Since the United States has now freed African Americans he is fully supportive of US attempts to take over the lands of others. At the same time, though, his statements also suggest a concern for his Caribbean brethren. He does not want his brothers to be re-enslaved, particularly by way of US imperialism. He makes a point of referring to Santo Domingo's part in the determination of whether the United States would acquire "her." He "was for the acquisition" only "if she wished to come to us." In his concern for his brothers in the Caribbean, Douglass reiterates the embrace of condition and race as grounds for "we-ness" evident in the previous autobiographies, while also adding a transnational dimension to that conception. This addition reveals a notion of community not bound by geography. He is willing to see the people of the Caribbean as part of his community. This expansive notion of community, however, coexists uneasily in Douglass's mind with a notion of expanding community.

In the process of defending himself against the charge of allowing his loyalty to the Haitians to overtake his loyalty to the United States, Douglass in his Appendix makes a point of calling attention to Haitian agency in the negotiations over the Môle St. Nicholas. He notes:

One fundamental element in our non-success was found, not in any aversion to the United States or in any indifference on my part, as has often been charged, but in the government of Haiti itself ... Nothing is more repugnant to the thoughts and feelings of the masses of that country than the alienation of a single rood of their territory to a foreign power.   (LT 1038–39)

The United States, Douglass is arguing, is not the only player in the game of expansion. Douglass's emphasis on Haitian agency is not untroubled, however.

He notes that the Haitian government "was evidently timid," recalling his characterization of Haiti as a "weak nation" earlier in the Appendix (LT 1028). He does historicize the Haitian fear of foreign occupation, noting that it was a natural result of "the circumstances in which Haiti began her national existence," when "the whole Christian world was," in his words, "against her" (LT 1039). He goes on to remind his fellow Americans that another cause of the Haitian rejection of their offer for the Môle was that "our peculiar and intense prejudice against the colored race" had "not been forgotten." Here, Douglass is claiming his Americanness and speaking as an American ("our"), defending his Haitian brethren, and othering them at the same time.

Douglass's textual treatment of differences between himself and Haitians in Part Three of *Life and Times* echoes his approach to dealing with differences within the African American community at points. As he did in his discussion of the betrayal of the escape plot he hatched with his fellow slaves, he exhibits a hesitance about calling attention to intra-community tensions. Douglass never explicitly shows himself to be in conflict with the Haitian leadership. He speaks abstractly about the government's timidity (a sentiment he goes on to represent as logical) and notes that he "thought that it would be in many ways a good thing for Haiti to have the proposed line of steamers." He never indexes any fissures in the relationship between himself and the Haitian leadership. In fact, he discloses that he refused his superior's demand that he go to speak directly to the Haitian Foreign Minister to encourage him to grant the desired concessions.

His approach to engaging the Haitians textually differs from his method of presenting differences between himself and other members of the African American community in one significant way – whereas he allows readers of the autobiographies to know the "characters" in his life, he does not do so with the Haitians. He focuses on the Haitian leaders' actions rather than on their personalities, political views, or culture. He calls attention to the Haitians' agency, but generally does not have them speak. William Andrews argues, "[D]ialogue in slave narratives tells us something about the negotiation of power that goes on in discourse, whether between a master and slave or a black autobiographer and a reader."[17] In *Life and Times*, Douglass includes no dialogue between himself and the Haitians or between the Haitians and anyone else. The result is that his voice is the only Black voice in the text. The battle, as he constructs it through his use, or in this case non-use, of dialogue is between himself and his White accusers in the United States.

Fundamentally, Douglass's relationship to the black world beyond the United States, as he represents it in his autobiographies, is the result of his conception of the way in which he needs to represent himself in order to answer his critics, to stake his claim to Americanness, and to improve the conditions of African Americans. Two approaches to conceptualizing the Black Caribbean result from the intertwining of these struggles to define a self and a collective. The first is an implicit othering of the non-US Black that, in Douglass's case, is manifested in the silence on and of the non-US Black in the bulk of the autobiographies and in his characterizations of Haiti as a nation that needs the help of the great and mighty nation that is the United States. The goal of the autobiographies, in addition to presenting Douglass himself, is to improve the situation of African Americans.

Another element of this implicit othering inheres in Douglass's complex embrace and rejection of the underpinnings of manifest destiny. He accepts the premise that the United States is the mightier nation, but argues that it must aim to use that power to help the weaker nations rather than to exploit them. His statement on his supporting annexation only after slavery was abolished in the United States evinces this belief in a benevolent manifest destiny. The point here is not that Douglass differs from his fellow African American leaders or from other progressives in this belief – even African American leaders like Martin Delany who were politically at odds with Douglass also embraced Black versions of the civilizing mission – but rather to point out specifically how it is a factor in the relationship between this African American and the Black world beyond the United States.[18] His embrace of this notion necessarily determines the conditions of possibility for his simultaneous claiming of Americanness and his envisioning of a connection to the non-US members of his race.

Douglass's second approach, primarily evident in his discussion of West Indian emancipation, is the incorporation of the non-US Black into a broad Black collectivism, while also using the non-US Black as a jumping off point for addressing the condition of African Americans, and for talking back to the dominant forces within the US context. In this, Douglass recalls David Walker who in his *Appeal to the Coloured Citizens of the World* (1829) invoked the Haitian Revolution to remind African Americans to have faith that God will ultimately deliver them from their "wretched condition under the Christians of America."[19] This approach, while an offshoot of binaristic Blackness in that there is clearly a prioritization of voice at work, deserves its own category because the prioritization takes place in the context through mentioning rather than through silence.

Douglass's autobiographies make clear that both double consciousness (of being Black and trying to be recognized as American) and the "twice-doubled consciousness" (of being African American and trying to articulate a sense of connection to non-US Blacks) are difficult if not impossible for him to escape. I submit that twice-doubled consciousness and binaristic Blackness are two of the most enduring legacies of slavery's denial of citizenship and humanity to people of African descent, and further that they are legacies that make the overturning of the transnational and national conditions of oppression that created and fed them especially challenging. They seem, in Douglass's writing, to always already determine relationships between people of African descent across national boundaries.

Throughout his career, Douglass continued to fight for full recognition of African Americans' US citizenship. He employed a multitude of strategies in order to make his argument more convincing. Among those was textual engagement with the Black world beyond the United States. That is not to say that Douglass only engaged the Black world beyond the United States in the service of this goal, but rather to say that his engagements were shaped by his fundamental goal, whether he decided to be silent on the Black world as in the *Narrative, My Bondage and My Freedom*, and the bulk of the *Life and Times*, or to speak directly of and/or from the Black world as in his speeches at the Columbian Exposition (1893) where he essentially served as a spokesman for Haiti, arguing for the significance of Haiti's contributions to civilization. In Douglass's case, the connection to the nation, or the desire for that connection, overwhelms all other linkages, including racial ones.

NOTES

1. On Douglass and double consciousness, see Eric Sundquist, "Introduction" and Rafia Zafar, "Franklinian Douglass," both in *Frederick Douglass: New Literary and Historical Essays*, ed. Eric Sundquist (Cambridge: Cambridge University Press, 1990); William L. Andrews, *To Tell a Free Story: The First Century of Afro-American Autobiography, 1760–1865* (Urbana: University of Illinois Press, 1986), 114.

2. Quoted in Chris Dixon, *African Americans and Haiti: Emigration and Black Nationalism in the Nineteenth Century* (Westport, CT: Greenwood Press, 2000), 251.

3. Frederick Douglass, "The Present Condition and Future Prospects of the Negro People," speech at the annual meeting of the American and Foreign Anti-Slavery Society, New York, May 11, 1853, reprinted in *Frederick Douglass: Selected Speeches and Writings*, ed. Philip S. Foner (Chicago, IL: Lawrence Hill, 1999), 251.

4. David Eltis, Stephen Behrendt, David Richardson, and Herbert Klein, *The Atlantic Slave Trade: A Database on CD-ROM* (Cambridge: Cambridge University Press, 1999).

5. Thanks to Cathy N. Davidson for suggesting this phrasing in her comments on an earlier draft of this project.

6. In this chapter, I employ a range of terms to index non-US people of African descent, including the Black world, the Black world beyond the United States, the Black international, and the other Black Americas. I make no significant distinctions in meaning among these terms; their fundamental goal is to call attention to the reality or possibility of intraracial difference and hierarchy.

7. Houston Baker, *The Journey Back: Issues in Black Literature and Criticism* (Chicago, IL: University of Chicago Press, 1980), 34.

8. Andrews, *To Tell a Free Story*, 120.

9. James Olney's edited collection *Studies in Autobiography* (New York: Oxford University Press, 1988) is a useful starting point for surveying this discourse because it juxtaposes analyses of autobiographies from a range of cultural and historical perspectives.

10. See Alfred N. Hunt, *Haiti's Influence on Antebellum America: Slumbering Volcano in the Caribbean* (Baton Rouge: Louisiana State University Press, 1988).

11. Space does not allow me to delve further into it here, but I would argue that Douglass references the White world beyond the United States to advance this cause, particularly in the speeches during and just after his travel to the British Isles.

12. Andrews, *To Tell a Free Story*, 106.

13. *Ibid.*, 105–6.

14. "The Heroic Slave" has been analyzed by scholars in terms of both the way Douglass links the rebels to the American revolutionaries and the profoundly gendered notion of the Black hero that he puts forward. The analyses I have found particularly useful are those undertaken by Maggie Montesinos Sale, "To Make the Past Useful: Frederick Douglass' Politics of Solidarity," *Arizona Quarterly* 52: 3 (Autumn 1995): 25–60, and *The Slumbering Volcano* (Durham, NC: Duke University Press, 1997).

15. Merline Pitre's article on this topic provides several fascinating tidbits of information about the relationship between Douglass and Senator Charles Sumner, and the tension in that relationship caused by their opposing views on annexation. Merline Pitre, "Frederick Douglass and American Diplomacy in the Caribbean," *Journal of Black Studies* 13: 4 (June 1983): 457–75.

16. For a more detailed discussion of the US's pursuit of the Môle, see Rayford Logan, *The Diplomatic Relations of the United States with Haiti, 1776–1891* (Chapel Hill: University of North Carolina Press, 1941), 315–96, as well as Myra Himelhoch, "Frederick Douglass and Haiti's Môle St Nicholas," *Journal of Negro History* 56:3 (July 1971): 161–80.

17. William Andrews, "Dialogue in Antebellum Afro-American Autobiography," in *Studies in Autobiography*, ed. James Olney (New York: Oxford University Press, 1988), 91. Although the bulk of Andrews's essay addresses slave narratives, he does suggest that his theory is also applicable to nineteenth-century Black autobiography more generally.

18. Martin Delany, *Official Report of the Niger Valley Exploring Party* (New York: T. Hamilton, 1861); *The Condition, Elevation, Emigration, and Destiny of the Colored People of the United States* (1852; Baltimore, MD: Black Classic Press, 1993).

19. David Walker, *Appeal to the Coloured Citizens of the World, in Four Articles* (1829; University Park: Pennsylvania State University Press, 2000), 22.

11

GENE ANDREW JARRETT

Douglass, Ideological Slavery, and Postbellum Racial Politics

In his 1871 essay, "The New Party Movement," Frederick Douglass laments that blacks in the South must fear "not the written law, which cannot execute itself, but the unwritten law of a powerful [Democratic] party, perpetually executing itself in the daily practices of that party" (LW 4:256). They must fear not corporal slavery but what I call *ideological slavery*. In the public sphere, this latter form of slavery uses ideas and discourse to "render" blacks only a "little better than slaves to a community, by being proscribed, limited, oppressed, and doomed to poverty and ignorance as effectually as though laws were passed ordaining their degradation." A writer, critic, editor, orator, and political activist, Douglass was well authorized to communicate his frustration with the real-world, practical effects of "the unwritten law." That emotion corresponds to his mixed opinion, also expressed in the essay, on the political status and outlook of blacks in America. He believes that, since their constitutional emancipation from slavery in 1865, blacks have enjoyed unprecedented success in law and politics. Yet, during this same period, they have also grappled with the rollbacks of their civil rights and the rise of the Democratic Party, two circumstances that have together stripped them of legal and political power. Thus, Douglass suggests that the unwritten laws of racial injustice and chauvinism may be as socially immediate and palpable as the laws written in the US Constitution or elsewhere by Congress.

In a representative selection of his letters, speeches, and essays written or published after 1865 – an intellectual corpus not often examined by scholars – Douglass argues that postbellum racial politics, in which blacks sought to negotiate, secure, and share social power, must counteract the ideological exploits of anti-black racism, or the belief that blacks are inferior to whites.[1] My use of *ideology* refers to Michael C. Dawson's definitive 2001 study of African American political science and history. Dawson defines ideology as "a world view readily found in the population, including sets of ideas and values that cohere, that are used publicly to justify political stances, and that shape and are shaped by society."[2] Accordingly, in his postbellum writings,

Douglass contends that the "ideas and values" of racism undermine the ideological influence of Constitutional and Congressional egalitarianism. Although abolished by the Constitution's thirteenth amendment, US slavery was an institutional manifestation of Western racism, and thus, in Douglass's eyes, could persist after 1865 in ideological form.[3] During this period, racism informed the language, ideas, and representations of the "Race Problem"; the violent and prejudicial conduct of many whites toward blacks; and the actions of certain blacks, such as Booker T. Washington, who, ironically, shared the views of these whites.

For this reason, Douglass's work in racial politics neither assumed only the form of abolitionism nor ended with emancipation. Rather, it continued thereafter as a two-fold political action that continued until his death. On the one hand, the political action reacted to the *formal* vicissitudes of local, state, and federal government, which often compromised or denied the rights of blacks to vote, hold office, register an affiliation with a political party, have their delegates confirmed at conventions, and serve on juries. On the other hand, vanquishing ideological slavery entailed not only the tools of formal politics, but also those discovered and modified in *informal*, yet still highly effective, political realms. Here, various social, cultural, and intellectual strategies protected blacks from the unwritten laws that oppressed them. In the nineteenth century, the strategies included, according to Steven Hahn, the development of biological and social "kinship," "labor" practices, "circuits of communication and education," not to mention the black church, emigration and migration societies, and paramilitary organizations. Generally, blacks succeeded in employing these methods to conjoin both formal and informal types of political action.[4] Douglass, in particular, pointed to the public meetings, literacy and reading groups, the black press, conventions, monuments, schools, and literary societies as the key areas of informal political action where blacks could perform the ideological work that the legal and legislative mandates of the Constitution and Congress could not accomplish alone.

Let us not doubt, however, that Douglass prioritized government, law, and public policy in black political life. In the nineteenth century, black political agency, consciousness, and mobilization developed in four historical stages: during the eras of slavery, the Civil War, Reconstruction, and Redemption/ Nadir. According to Hahn, enslaved blacks were neither "nonpolitical, pre-political, [n]or protopolitical" as a consequence of their deprivation of the citizenship and elective franchise that Congress and the amended Constitution had given them shortly after emancipation.[5] Rather, despite the social strictures of the South and the North, black communities had marshaled the cultural and religious resources for political action.

Blacks turned a host of difficult circumstances into opportunities for political advancement. While slavery included as much as it precluded black social activism, later the Civil War stimulated the rebellion of blacks on plantations. Fleeing their masters in large numbers, they joined the Union Army, helped overthrow the opposing Confederate Army, and devastated the Confederate defense of slavery. After formal emancipation, blacks learned how to reconstitute their slave communities as freed communities that could anticipate and adjust to the country's changing legal and political landscapes. The ratifications of the Constitutional amendments that Congress passed during the radical reconstruction of the South – in 1865, 1868, and 1870 – granted blacks the exclusive rights that whites had long enjoyed. The thirteenth amendment emancipated blacks from slavery; the fourteenth protected not only their due process and human equality in a court of law, but also their entitlement to the immunities and privileges of citizenship; and the fifteenth established their right to vote. The Civil Rights Acts of 1866, 1871, and 1875 further protected the citizenship of blacks, guarded their civil rights from the Ku Klux Klan, and demanded their equality of treatment in public spaces. In addition, between the Civil War's end and the late 1870s, the Union army deployed troops in the South to uphold the legal and political enfranchisement of blacks, auguring a more racially equitable, "New" South.[6]

The subsequent period of Redemption, however, rolled back black civil rights. Led especially by whites who were born in the "Old" South, demanded black subservience, and reacted to Reconstruction with disgust and anger, Redemption coincided with the controversial presidential election of 1876. The Democratic candidate, Samuel J. Tilden, won the popular vote yet lost the Electoral College to the Republican candidate, Rutherford B. Hayes. The Congressional resolution of the constitutional crisis – because the writers of the Constitution had failed to foresee the electoral discrepancy that Tilden faced – was the Compromise of 1877. The Republican Party agreed to withdraw the federal army from the South in exchange for the Democratic Party's concession to Hayes of the nineteenth presidency of the country.

The consequences of the agreement were remarkable. Over four million former slaves were left vulnerable to violent white supremacists and the rise of Jim Crow intimidation; the rate of blacks being lynched, among other kinds of racial terror, skyrocketed; the Republicans scaled back their fight for black civil rights; and blacks lost their foothold in Congress and state government. For these reasons, Reconstruction's end through the turn of the twentieth century became known not only as Redemption from the perspective of white Southern racists, but also as the "Nadir," the "Dark Ages of Recent American History," and the "Decades of Disappointment" from the antithetical ideological perspective.[7] Adding insult to injury, the US Supreme Court ruled that the 1875 Civil Rights Act was unconstitutional. Yet, despite the alleged redemption of the South, blacks remained mobilized by creating paramilitary defense organizations, strategic alliances with whites in the Democratic Party, and policies of emigration to certain countries outside the United States or of migration to certain states within it. In any political way they could, blacks protected and advanced themselves.

Published in 1871, Douglass's essay, "Politics an Evil to the Negro," makes the case that politics is "one of the most important levers that can be employed to elevate his race," contrary to the racist claim, mimicked by the essay's title, that politics corrupts it (LW 4:273). Black enfranchisement is the goal, first and foremost. In 1865, Douglass received an invitation to celebrate, alongside the Colored People's Educational Monument Association, the memory of recently assassinated President Abraham Lincoln. In a letter responding to it, he stresses "the immediate, complete, and universal enfranchisement of the colored people of the whole country" (LW 4:169). He goes on to say that the "great want of the country is to be rid of the Negro question, and it can never be rid of that question until justice, right and sound policy are complied with" (LW 4:170). For Douglass, black men (and not women) deserved the right to "the ballot" (LW 4:167); "the right to keep and bear arms," as part of paramilitary self-defense (LW 4:168); and the right to intermingle with whites, "enjoying the same freedom, voting at the same ballot-box, using the same cartridge-box, going to the same schools, attending the same churches, traveling in the same street cars, in the same railroad cars, on the same steam-boats, proud of the same country, fighting the same foe, and enjoying the same peace and all its advantages" (LW 4:172–73). Legislation and the court of law could formally remedy many of these racial inequities and divisions.

Formal political action, however, could not always overcome the unwritten laws of racism. Sensing this, Douglass favored a flexible notion of politics in which representations and exercises of power could manifest themselves in both formal and informal ways. His best statement on this issue appears in essays he wrote in support of women's suffrage.[9] In one essay, "Woman Suffrage Movement" (1870), Douglass's argument for women's suffrage contains the concepts he needed ultimately to reaffirm the case for black suffrage:

> If woman is admitted to be a moral and intellectual being, possessing a sense of good and evil, and a power of choice between them, her case is already half-gained. Our natural powers are the foundation of our natural rights; and it is a consciousness of powers which suggests the exercise of rights ... The power that makes her a moral and an accountable being gives her a natural right to choose the legislators who are to frame the laws under which she is to live, and the

requirements of which she is bound to obey ... Unless it can be shown that woman is morally, physically, and intellectually incapable of performing the act of voting, there can be no natural prohibition of such action on her part. (LW 4:232–33)

Just as the rebuttal of the moral, physical, and intellectual inferiority of women was central to asserting that they deserved the elective franchise, the refutation of such inferiority in blacks was equally central to arguing that blacks deserved it, too.[10]

Douglass's theory of power applied as well to the informal political implications of women's suffrage. In another 1870 essay, "Woman and the Ballot," he translates the notion of power across a variety of social and material contexts:

> Power is the highest object of human respect. Wisdom, virtue, and all great moral qualities command respect only as powers. Knowledge and wealth are nought but powers. Take from money its purchasing power, and it ceases to be the same object of respect. We pity the impotent and respect the powerful everywhere. To deny woman her vote is to abridge her natural and social power, and deprive her of a certain measure of respect. (LW 4:237)

In abstract terms, the accumulation or distribution of power not only worked in dialectical relation to the elective franchise; it represented the ideological narratives of social, cultural, and intellectual life – in sum, "natural rights," "wisdom," "virtue," "all great moral qualities," "respect," "knowledge," and "wealth."

These ideological narratives underwrote Douglass's moral philosophy of political egalitarianism. His particular insistence that the pursuit of justice should be an ideological prerequisite to black political action embraced the Constitution. One year after emancipation, Douglass published an essay, "Reconstruction," supporting this point: the Constitution "knows no distinction between citizens on account of color. Neither does it know any difference between a citizen of a State and a citizen of the United States. Citizenship evidently includes all the rights of citizens, whether State or national" (LW 4:204). The egalitarianism of the Constitution – as broadened and strengthened through amendments – was the doctrine by which Douglass regarded the utility of black political action.

Corruption, however, devalued the transformative potential of black political action. In the postbellum years, Douglass not only bemoaned the murder and mayhem blacks suffered at the hands of whites; he lamented the material, real-world proof of socioeconomic inequities between the two groups. The lack of law and civil rights enforcement compelled him to argue, in "The Need for Continuing Anti-Slavery Work" (1865), that slavery had continued in the postbellum era as ideological phantasmagoria: "It has been called by a great many names, and it will call itself by yet another name; and you and I and all of us had better wait and see what new form this old monster will assume, *in what new skin this old snake will come forth next*" (LW 4:169; my emphasis). Five years later, in an essay aptly titled "Seeming and Real," Douglass characterizes the discrepancy between law and custom not only as the reason for racial injustice, but as a conundrum of legal and political theory: "[L]aw on the statute book and law in the practice of the nation are two very different things, and sometimes very opposite things" (LW 4:227). The discrepancy between egalitarianism and the inhumane practices of many whites impugned the "practical value" of government documents such as the Constitution. As Deak Nabers notes, the Constitution's reputation as the "supreme law of the land" obscured the extent that it "states" or "accounts" for laws, but does not automatically "enact" them.[11] The Constitutional progression from egalitarian theory, to written word, to social impact indeed followed a long, circuitous, ideological road, comprising several divisions and kinds of political labor on the parts of US leaders and their constituencies.

In addition to formal politics, Douglass recognized other ways for blacks to overcome the minimal enforcement of the Reconstruction mandates. One way included the development of certain social, cultural, and intellectual strategies that could circulate ideas to the benefit of black empowerment. Public meetings and reading groups were small-scale examples of mobilization in which illiterate and intellectual blacks alike could interact and discuss racial politics.[12] Larger-scale examples included conventions – namely, state constitutional conventions and labor conventions – in which blacks could reach consensus on how to communicate their interests to actual politicians. According to Dawson, "the antebellum Negro Convention movement of the first half of [the nineteenth] century can be viewed as the first major forum for black ideological debate." This movement continued into the age of Reconstruction, when "the first opportunity for African Americans [arose] to combine ideological debate with high levels of political activity and mobilization."[13] Ideological debate between and among blacks and whites provided a social and cultural complement to the formal laws of Reconstruction.

Douglass underscored the importance of conventions to black social empowerment. In "The Southern Convention" (1871), he criticizes a Republican journal in Macon, Georgia, *The Union*, for opposing the "fact of the wronged, outraged, and down-trodden colored people of the South calling a convention [of Colored Citizens in Columbia, South Carolina] for the purpose of consulting as to the best means of bringing themselves up from the degrading position they have been forced into by slavery" (LW 4:251). Twelve years later, at a convention for black men held in Louisville, Kentucky, he delivered an address that fleshes out the political meaning of conventions. Contrary to the multitude of critics denouncing black assembly, Douglass cherished it as one of the "safety-valves of the Republic":

> [F]irst, because there is a power in numbers and in union; because the many are more than the few; because the voice of a whole people, oppressed by a common injustice, is far more likely to command attention and exert an influence on the public mind than the voice of single individuals and isolated organizations; because, coming together from all parts of the country, the members of a National convention have the means of a more comprehensive knowledge of the general situation, and may, therefore, fairly be presumed to conceive more clearly and express more fully and wisely the policy it may be necessary for them to pursue in the premises. Because conventions of the people are in themselves harmless, and when made the means of setting forth grievances, whether real or fancied, they are the safety-valves of the Republic.   (LW 4:376–77)

In this address, Douglass provides one of his most sustained analyses of the labor, capitalism, education, banks, civil rights, human equality, and political ambition of African America. His case for black conventions belonged to his broader theory that the nation was "governed by ideas as well as by laws" (LW 4:358). Conventions optimized the expression, circulation, and critique of the egalitarian principle of social justice. They permitted the widest cross-section of black communities to congregate in one place for the express purpose of exchanging ideas. Thus, they were one of the most influential forums for black self-empowerment.

Other, less ostensibly political instances of black activity were relevant. They included the intellectual cultivation of literacy and the black press, as well as the cultural founding of monuments, institutions of higher education, reading groups, and literary societies. The communicative uses to which blacks put literacy have been well documented.[14] Worth stressing, instead, is the mid-nineteenth-century rise of the black press – or the periodicals edited or owned by blacks – that Douglass appreciated as an organ of black political action, and in which he had significant editorial experience in both the antebellum and postbellum periods. From 1870 to 1874, he owned and edited *The New National Era*, a weekly newspaper in which he routinely espoused the virtues of the black press, and critiqued the fallacies or improprieties of other newspapers on the race question. But Douglass shot across the bow of conventional thinking when he stressed in 1891 that "the colored Press [should] say less about race and claims to race recognition, and more about the principles of justice, liberty, and patriotism" (LW 4:469). This statement supports Eric Sundquist's observation that, over the course of Douglass's life, his rhetoric gravitated toward the principles of the so-called Founding Fathers (namely, the original Framers of the Constitution and Declaration of

Independence), and thus away from the specifically racial radicalism that characterized his abolitionist and early postbellum political work.[15] Yet his comments in "Reconstruction," mentioned earlier, show that the ideological seeds of such rhetoric were already discernible. Douglass was consistently egalitarian in his postbellum political ethos, and thus belonged to a tradition of black political ideology that later included Ida B. Wells, W. E. B. Du Bois, and Martin Luther King, Jr.[16] Douglass's ascription of "the principles of justice, liberty, and patriotism" to the black press demonstrated his commitment to attaining these goals, which benefit all of humanity.

For Douglass, cultural artifacts and institutions such as monuments further helped to mount the ideological attack on the "unwritten" laws that oppressed blacks. In an 1865 letter declining an invitation to submit his name as an officer of the Educational Monument Association, Douglass discloses his opinions on what it means for blacks to erect a memorial of Lincoln: "A monument of this kind, erected by the colored people – that is, by the voluntary offerings of the colored people – is a very different thing from a monument built by money contributed by white men to enable colored people to build a monument" (LW 4:172). Monuments captured the negotiation between blacks and whites over power that had been played out in other political arenas of American life. The ability of blacks to fund and create their own cultural institutions represented a claim to power that was crucial to the broader claim of blacks to national citizenship. Eleven years later, Douglass reiterates this point in his speech, "Oration in Memory of Abraham Lincoln," an introduction to the Freedmen's Monument, located in Washington, DC, in memory of Lincoln. He declares that "we, the colored people, newly emancipated and rejoicing in our blood-bought freedom ... have now and here unveiled, set apart, and dedicated a monument," whose traits capture "something of the exalted character and great works" of Lincoln (LW 4:311). Monument culture and political culture were one and the same.

Douglass also recognized the political implication of schools. In "Howard University" (1870), he venerates the DC-based university, which, though located in "the city which knew [colored] people only as property," had arisen as "an Institution of learning, vieing [sic] in attractiveness and elegance, with those of the most advanced civilization, devoted to the classical education of a people which, a few years ago, the phrenologist, archaeologists and ethnologists of the country, told us we were wholly incapable of acquiring even a knowledge of the English language" (LW 4:234). The sign of civilization extended from literature written by blacks, acknowledged by scholars of the late eighteenth and nineteenth centuries, to the monuments and schools established by them.[17] Douglass refused to mince words when he stated, at the 1865 inauguration of the Douglass Institute in Baltimore,

Maryland, that the edifice "is destined to play an important part in promoting the freedom and elevation of the colored people of this city and State, and I may say of the whole Union" (LW 4:175). Once again, we see that black cultural establishments can serve a political cause, as long as their ideological attack on racial injustice and chauvinism empowered blacks in the process.

Literary societies empowered blacks by promoting literacy, encouraging learning and intellectual exchange, spawning reading cultures, and attending to the racial-political concerns of the era. According to Elizabeth McHenry, the DC-based Bethel Historical and Literary Association was, since its founding in 1881, a "public or 'popular' forum that permitted a growing middle and upper class to mingle and converse and encouraged them to engage one another in healthy and productive debate on the political matters that affected them most directly." Bethel was "a prototype of the post-Reconstruction black public sphere, and, at the same time, a model for the development of African-American literary societies nationwide."[18] "The Race Problem," a scarcely examined 1890 speech Douglass delivered to Bethel and a full house of rapt listeners in DC's Metropolitan AME Church, deserves extended discussion here. More than any other postbellum speech, "The Race Problem" expounds on the political value of the literary society, and explains the political struggle over public ideas and discourse that had contributed to the ideological enslavement of blacks.

Bethel was an ideal occasion for Douglass's political rhetoric. In the speech, he opens by stating that it "is an institution well fitted to improve the minds and elevate the sentiments not only of its members, but of the general public. Nowhere else *outside* of the courts of law and the Congress of the United States have I heard vital public questions more seriously discussed" (my emphasis).[19] In this social context "outside" the formal realm of politics, Douglass explores a range of issues. The Christianity practiced by whites, to begin with, argued that humanity is equal before God, but then it theologized the inferiority of blacks. The US government's recruitment of men into the military, though urgent, assigned blacks subservient duties, if they were even enlisted at all. Marriage was a social and cultural cornerstone of the country, yet certain laws forbade blacks themselves (as well as affianced blacks and whites) to enter into it. Educational leaders and institutions touted the importance of literacy and learning, yet denied blacks access to them. Douglass portrayed these as examples of the unfailing hypocrisy of many whites and, to a lesser extent, blacks who shared their racist views.

More relevant to our purpose is Douglass's urging that Bethel must help in the ideological war against the race problem, a discourse that was circulating in both formal and informal contexts of political activity. His ideological emphasis stemmed from a moral philosophy that, as I alluded to earlier, held truth and justice sacred. "Truth is the fundamental, indispensable, and ever-lasting requirement in obtaining right results," he asserts in the speech. "No department of human life can afford to dispense with truth." For this reason, he despises the "advantage to error ... which is often employed with marked skill and effect in the presentation to the minds of men of what may be called half truths for whole truths."[20] History suggests that these words by Douglass were symptomatic of the larger concern, among black writers and intellectuals in the late nineteenth century, with the racist information that popular culture was circulating through all levels of US society. The hybrid amalgam of truths and falsehoods in this information heightened the political anxieties of high black society over its public representations. Yet, a closer look at Douglass's speech to Bethel indicates a more critical and nuanced perspective on what a rising black intellectual at the time, W. E. B. Du Bois, called in 1903 "ever an unasked question": "How does it feel to be a problem?" Du Bois answered "seldom a word."[21]

In the 1890 speech, Douglass expresses reservations over the question itself. "I object to characterizing the relation subsisting between the white and colored people of this country as the Negro problem, as if the Negro had precipitated the problem, and as if he were in any way responsible for the problem." The problem with the "Negro Problem" discourse was the "offensive associations" of the words *Negro* and *problem* that downplayed full truths, played up half-truths, interspersed utter lies, and thereby, with the help of the powerful in US society, succeeded in "confusing the moral sense of the nation and misleading the public mind." Douglass describes it more poignantly when he concludes: "Problem, problem, race problem, negro problem, has ... f[l]itted through their sentences in all *the mazes of metaphorical confusion*" (my emphasis).[22]

Combining at once the modes of rebuke and intellectual inquiry, Douglass's "criticism" of the ideological language, metaphors, rhetoric, and creativity of racism does not overstate the political power of "sentences." Rather, his criticism measures exactly their influence both within and without the literary societies, monuments, schools, and institutes that had been working to shape the way blacks understood and accessed the political process. Again, at the level of sentence, Douglass recommends "employing the truest and most agreeable names to describe the relation which at present subsists between ourselves and the other people of the country." But terminological revision is not enough. The revised language and ideas must correspond to a reformed political psyche in which the majority of whites could live alongside emancipated blacks. This nation must deal with the legal abolition of corporal slavery not by, consciously or subconsciously, devising unwritten laws that instituted ideological slavery, but instead by developing "sufficient moral stamina to maintain its own honor and integrity by vindicating its own Constitution and fulfilling its own pledges."[23]

Douglass's unwavering, patient faith that "truth, justice, liberty, and humanity will ultimately prevail"[24] could have been seen – and, today, still might be seen – as too idealistic and out of touch with the contemporary realities of African America. His moral and political philosophies, however, ended up sustaining him from his early youth to his death – through the eras of bondage and emancipation, through the amendments and rollbacks of the Constitution, through the Congressional changes in party leadership, through the ideological persistence of slavery. And, at every moment, he was a stalwart leader in the political war on the laws of racism, both written and unwritten.

NOTES

1. Indeed, literary scholarship on Douglass's postbellum writings tends to coalesce around discussions of his third autobiography, *The Life and Times of Frederick Douglass* (1881, 1892), which does not cover the breadth of issues he explored in his letters, speeches, and essays. What is more, such writings are the subject principally in biographies of Douglass, such as William S. McFeely's definitive *Frederick Douglass* (New York: W. W. Norton, 1991). Excellent scholarly comments on the relationship between formal and informal black politics include Steven Hahn, *A Nation under Our Feet: Black Political Struggles in the Rural South from Slavery to the Great Migration* (Cambridge, MA: Harvard University Press, 2003); Michael C. Dawson, *Black Visions: The Roots of Contemporary African-American Political Ideologies* (Chicago, IL and London: University of Chicago Press, 2001); and Robin D. G. Kelley, *Race Rebels: Culture, Politics, and the Black Working Class* (New York: Free Press, 1994).
2. Dawson, *Black Visions*, 4.
3. I use the term *racism* as the shortened substitute of *anti-black racism*. Racism is a broadly Western phenomenon, not only an American one, extending back to the seventeenth century, proven by the shared ideological perspective of both British and American Enlightenment philosophers on Africa and its descendants and on Native American citizens. See Thomas F. Gossett, *Race: The History of an Idea in America* (New York and Oxford: Oxford University Press, 1997), 3–31.
4. For the discussion of "kinship, labor, and circuits of communication and education," see Hahn, *A Nation under Our Feet*, 7; for the policy of emigrationism, see Douglass, "The United States Cannot Remain Half-Slave and Half-Free" (1883, LW 4:354–71); for the right of blacks to bear arms, see Douglass, "The Need for Continuing Antislavery Work" (1865, LW 4:166–69). While Douglass acknowledged the social importance of the black church, he was quite critical of theological hypocrisy.
5. Hahn, *A Nation under Our Feet*, 3.

6. For a thorough study of the Reconstruction era, see Eric Foner, *Reconstruction: America's Unfinished Revolution, 1863–1877* (New York: Harper and Row, 1988).

7. Barbara McCaskill and Caroline Gebhard, Introduction to *Post-Bellum, Pre-Harlem: African American Literature and Culture, 1877–1919*, ed. McCaskill and Gebhard (New York: New York University Press, 2006), 1–14.

8. For Douglass's discussion of state versus federal constitutions, see "The Need for Continuing Anti-Slavery Work," 167, and "Reconstruction" (LW 4: 198–204), 199.

9. Douglass privileged the struggle of black men over the struggle of white women for elective franchise. The black men's endurance of slavery, in his eyes, entitled them to vote more than white women, who already possessed indirect elective representation through their fathers, brothers, and husbands. See "Letter to Josephine Sophie White Griffing" (LW 4:212–13).

10. For my discussion of racial uplift, see Gene Jarrett, *Deans and Truants: Race and Realism in African American Literature* (Philadelphia: University of Pennsylvania Press, 2007), 54–59.

11. Deak Nabers, *The Victory of Law: The Fourteenth Amendment, the Civil War, and American Literature, 1852–1867* (Baltimore, MD: Johns Hopkins University Press, 2006), 7.

12. The plenitude of black social, cultural, and intellectual activities in which political consciousness arose undermines the suggestion that a direct path existed between literacy and political action, a suggestion made in Elizabeth McHenry's invaluable book, *Forgotten Readers: Recovering the Lost History of African American Literary Societies* (Durham, NC: Duke University Press, 2002). Elsewhere, I imply that this possible critique of McHenry has been broadened in recent scholarship on African American literature and politics, which argues that the connection of intellectual culture to political action was strained at best in the postbellum era; see Jarrett, "New Negro Politics," *American Literary History* 18:4 (2006): 836–46. This essay belongs to my ongoing effort to show that the path between black intellectual culture and political action was, according to Douglass, also a wonderfully complex articulation of activities and institutions by which blacks accumulated and distributed social power in their communities.

13. Dawson, *Black Visions*, 10. For discussion of the variety of grassroots mobilization in meetings, see Hahn, *A Nation under Our Feet*, 2, 174, 328; for the conventions, see Hahn, 199, 262.

14. On the importance of written communication and the prevalence of literacy in black communities, see Hahn, *A Nation under Our Feet*, 3, and McHenry, *Forgotten Readers*, 5.

15. Eric Sundquist, *To Wake the Nations: Race in the Making of American Literature* (Cambridge, MA: Harvard University Press, 1993), 83–112.

16. Dawson, *Black Visions*, 15.

17. The best-known example of such scholarship is Henry Louis Gates, Jr., *Figures in Black: Words, Signs, and the "Racial" Self* (Oxford: Oxford University Press, 1987). Gates has argued that "the Afro-American literary tradition was generated as a response to eighteenth- and nineteenth-century allegations that persons of African descent did not, and could not, create literature" (25).

18. McHenry, *Forgotten Readers*, 151.

19. Douglass, "The Race Problem" (1890), "Library of Congress: American Memory," http://memory.loc.gov/cgibin/query/r?ammem/murray:@field(DOCID+@lit(lcrbmrp toc13div1), 20.
20. Douglass, "The Race Problem," 3, 5.
21. W. E. B. Du Bois, *The Souls of Black Folk*, in *Writings* (New York: Library of America, 1996), 363.
22. Douglass, "The Race Problem," 5, 8.
23. *Ibid.*
24. *Ibid.*, 16.

I2

VALERIE SMITH

Born into Slavery: Echoes and Legacies

For several generations, students and scholars of African American history and literature (and those of US history and literature more broadly defined) have considered Frederick Douglass's 1845 *Narrative of the Life of Frederick Douglass, An American Slave, Written by Himself* to be something of a foundational text. Although it is not the first narrative written by a former slave, it has long been the narrative to which teachers and students of African American autobiography and history turn to illustrate the impact of "the peculiar institution" upon virtually every aspect of the lives of enslaved people and to display their capacity for resistance. In part, the text has earned this reputation because of Douglass's legendary stature as a statesman, orator, abolitionist, author, editor, and reformer. And in part, the *Narrative* has achieved its elevated position in the canon of American letters because it is a rhetorical *tour de force*; its emotional complexity, memorable characterizations, and vivid imagery testify eloquently to the human capacity to triumph over oppression and illiteracy.

Moreover, many of us who teach and write about American literature admire Douglass's *Narrative* because it does a lot of work for us. Not only does it engage concerns with which his contemporaries wrestled, including the meaning of freedom and American democracy, and the contradictions of American religion. It also anticipates themes that have recurred in twentieth- and now twenty-first-century literature, including the relationship between narrative and political authority, the mutually constitutive nature of constructions of race and gender, the relationship between self-making and national ideologies, and the status of the black body within the institution of antebellum slavery. Indeed, neo-slave narratives – modern novels that take the story of slavery as their subject – such as Gayl Jones's *Corregidora* (1975), Ishmael Reed's *Flight to Canada* (1976), Octavia Butler's *Kindred* (1979), Charles Johnson's *Oxherding Tale* (1982), Sherley Anne Williams's *Dessa Rose* (1986), Toni Morrison's *Beloved* (1987), Lorene Cary's *The Price of a Child* (1995), and Edward P. Jones's *The Known World* (2004), to name but a few – can all be read as texts that respond in some way to Douglass.

The Evolving Legacy

In recent years, scholars have begun to question the primacy of Douglass's *Narrative* in the tradition of African American letters. In her landmark essay entitled "In the First Place: Making Frederick Douglass and the Afro-American Narrative Tradition," Deborah E. McDowell critiques the ways in which scholars have accepted and reproduced the notion of Douglass as the progenitor of a literary and cultural legacy, principally because, she argues, this use of Douglass and his *Narrative* has masculinized the canon of African American literature. As she puts it:

> It is this choice of Douglass as "the first," as "representative man," as the part that stands for the whole, that reproduces the omission of women from view, except as afterthoughts different from "the same" (black men). And that omission is not merely an oversight, but given the discursive system that authorizes Douglass as the source and the origin, that omission is a necessity.[1]

In *Forgotten Readers: Recovering the Lost History of African American Literary Societies* (2002), Elizabeth McHenry argues that by focusing on the antebellum narratives, scholars have trained our attention on the regime that enforced illiteracy and turned our attention away from the efforts of freed people in the North to cultivate literacy within their own communities.

In *The Great Escapes: Four Slave Narratives* (2007), Daphne A. Brooks anthologizes four slave narratives that have enjoyed a resurgence of critical interest during the past decade, but have yet to receive the attention that has been directed towards either Douglass's *Narrative* or Harriet Jacobs's *Incidents in the Life of a Slave Girl, Written by Herself* (1861). She acknowledges William Wells Brown's, William and Ellen Craft's, and Henry "Box" Brown's debt to Douglass's *Narrative*, especially "its conversion ideology, its scathing critique of Christian slaveholders' hypocrisy, and its diligent and persistent engagement with willful and exhilarating self-creation." Yet, as she points out, Wells Brown, the Crafts, and "Box" Brown differ from Douglass in that their narratives emphasize the means by which they escaped. At least in the *Narrative*, Douglass, of course, chose to conceal the details of his escape in order to ensure that that route would be available to those who remained enslaved. As Brooks writes:

> Where these narratives diverge from Douglass's formidable example, however, is in their buoyant emphasis on the skillful and ingenious strategy of escape itself and the spectacular lengths to which captives would go to obtain their freedom. Each work ... celebrates the extreme craft involved in engineering escapes, and each outlines the various material and performative tools involved in organizing tacit flight. By foregrounding the escape itself, all of the texts ... make plain the

quotidian bravery and extraordinary artistic gifts on which these fugitives relied in order to secure their liberty.²

Through their disclosures, their performances on the transatlantic abolitionist circuit, and their interpellation of a variety of genres into their narratives and performances, they helped shape the future of African American letters in ways that are comparable to, yet distinct from Douglass's contributions. As Brooks puts it:

> The Browns and the Crafts no doubt contributed to an aesthetic legacy in American letters that preserved and documented the resourceful innovations of people who, like their ancestors in the legendary African folktale, discovered their ability to fly, and who passed on the story of their flight as a source of inspiration to all those who would come after them to imagine, create, and do the seeming impossible.³

McDowell's, McHenry's, and Brooks's observations suggest that in order to appreciate Douglass's contributions to African American and American letters and history, we must assess his achievement in relation not only to the full range of narratives written by freed and fugitive slaves, but also to other forms of cultural production. Yet even as we contextualize the contributions of his writings about slavery, we find that Douglass has much to teach us about the impact of racial ideology and the "peculiar institution" on blacks and whites, Northerners and Southerners, freed and enslaved people.

Douglass's Call

The strikingly understated opening paragraphs of the *Narrative* introduce the reader to one of the central themes of the text: that the system of slavery withheld from enslaved people access to the protocols and institutions by which humanity and citizenship are typically defined. Denied knowledge of the precise date and place of his birth, Douglass is consigned to the status of livestock, as the comparisons with which the text begins make clear:

> I was born in Tuckahoe, near Hillsborough, and about twelve miles from Easton, in Talbot county, Maryland. I have no accurate knowledge of my age, never having seen any authentic record containing it. By far the larger part of the slaves know as little of their ages as horses know of theirs, and it is the wish of most masters within my knowledge to keep their slaves thus ignorant. I do not remember to have ever met a slave who could tell of his birthday. They seldom come nearer to it than planting-time, harvest-time, cherry-time, spring-time, or fall-time. (N 15)

Douglass is denied access as well to the parental relationships that often ground identity. The son of a black enslaved woman and (probably) her white master, his very existence derives from the conflation of sexual and property rights that the system of slavery endorsed. His account, like those of so many of his counterparts, reminds us that by raping their women slaves, masters simultaneously gratified themselves sexually and increased their store of human property. To his father/master, Douglass is, therefore, little more than chattel with no claim to parental attention or affection.

He knows for certain who his mother is, but in keeping with "common custom," he was separated from her geographically, a condition that distanced him from her emotionally as well (N 15). He explains that she was hired out to work for a Mr. Stewart, whose home was twelve miles away from theirs. A field hand, she was only able to visit with him at night, and only on rare occasions. She died when he was seven; his dispassionate account of that loss signals the depth of his emotional distance from her:

> I was not allowed to be present during her illness, at her death, or burial. She was gone long before I knew any thing about it. Never having enjoyed, to any considerable extent, her soothing presence, her tender and watchful care, I received the tidings of her death with much the same emotions I should have probably felt at the death of a stranger. (N 16)

Denied a connection to his mother and father, Douglass did enjoy nevertheless the benefit of extended familial ties. During his childhood, he lived with other slave children in his grandmother's cottage on the outskirts of the plantation. As a result, he remained ignorant of the brutalities of slavery until he was old enough to work.

He dates his initiation into the meaning of his enslavement from the first time he watched his Aunt Hester being beaten for daring to visit her lover, Ned Roberts. This scene explicitly enacts the violence to which enslaved black bodies were submitted and the tortured, yet unacknowledged ways in which masters sought to assert sexual claims on enslaved women. Not surprisingly, this scene has received considerable critical attention and bears quoting at some length here:

> Before he commenced whipping Aunt Hester, he took her into the kitchen, and stripped her from neck to waist, leaving her neck, shoulders, and back, entirely naked. He then told her to cross her hands, calling her at the same time a d——d b——h. After crossing her hands, he tied them with a strong rope, and led her to a stool under a large hook in the joist, put in for the purpose. He made her get upon the stool, and tied her hands to the hook. She now stood fair for his infernal purpose. Her arms were stretched up at their full length, so that she stood upon the ends of her toes. He then said to her, "Now, you d——d b——h,

I'll learn you how to disobey my orders!" and after rolling up his sleeves, he commenced to lay on the heavy cowskin, and soon the warm, red blood (amid heart-rending shrieks from her, and horrid oaths from him) came dripping to the floor. I was so terrified and horror-stricken at the sight, that I hid myself in a closet, and dared not venture out till long after the bloody transaction was over.   (N 19)

After this incident, he was often awakened by his aunt's cries. Powerless to stop the beatings he overhears, he feels implicated in them, describing himself as "a witness and a participant" (N 18). This scene forces the young Douglass to confront the physical and emotional horror of slavery. As he describes it: "It was the blood-stained gate, the entrance to the hell of slavery, through which I was about to pass."

If Douglass is initiated into the meaning of his condition when he watches his aunt being beaten, he becomes conscious of the meaning of freedom when he learns to read and write. During his first stay in Baltimore, he links the acquisition of literacy to both the act of rebellion and the achievement of freedom, an experience that has become a prototypical situation for later African American writers. Douglass begins to learn to read because his naïve, originally well-intentioned mistress, Mrs. Auld, does not realize that, as a slave, he is to be treated differently from a white child. Just as she discourages his "crouching servility" (N 37) in her presence, she also teaches him to read upon discovering his illiteracy. More sophisticated in the ways of the slave system than his wife, Mr. Auld puts an abrupt end to Douglass's education. As Douglass recalls it, Auld tells his wife:

> "If you give a nigger an inch, he will take an ell. A nigger should know nothing but to obey his master – to do as he is told to do. Learning will *spoil* the best nigger in the world. Now," said he, "if you teach that nigger (speaking of myself) how to read, there would be no keeping him. It would forever unfit him to be a slave. He would at once become unmanageable, and of no value to his master. As to himself, it could do him no good, but a great deal of harm. It would make him discontented and unhappy."   (N 37)

By revealing that literacy would "unfit him to be a slave," Auld kindles Douglass's nascent rebelliousness and yearning for freedom. The young boy does not yet understand the explicit connections between freedom and literacy, but he is inspired to learn to read and write by every means available to him, precisely because his master denies him this privilege and associates these two forbidden fruits with each other. Douglass acknowledges that although he has lost his means of education, he has acquired an "invaluable instruction" about his condition from the very master who tries to keep him ignorant (N 38).

The acquisition of literacy facilitates Douglass's achievement of freedom in two ways. The text that was available to him – Caleb Bingham's 1797 *The Columbian Orator* including Richard Brinsley Sheridan's speech on behalf of Catholic emancipation – taught him his letters as well as the civic virtues of freedom and abolition. In *The Columbian Orator*, a collection of political essays, poems, and dialogues used in American schoolrooms in the early decades of the nineteenth century to teach reading, oratory, and patriotism, he found a dialogue between a master and a slave in which the slave, who has a history of running away, refutes the master's defense of slavery so effectively that the master emancipates him. From Sheridan, the Irish playwright and Member of Parliament, he learned "a bold denunciation of slavery, and a powerful vindication of human rights" (N 42). Indeed, his new skill apprises him of so many notions that he comes to consider literacy a mixed blessing:

> The reading of these documents enabled me to utter my thoughts, and to meet the arguments brought forward to sustain slavery; but while they relieved me of one difficulty, they brought on another even more painful than the one of which I was relieved … In moments of agony, I envied my fellow slaves for their stupidity.

As if in anticipation of the power of the word in his future career in public life, he learns to manipulate the language of his super-ordinates to his own advantage. By means of his own ingenuity he learns to write, through competitions with white boys in his neighborhood, by copying letters he had learned on fences, walls, and pavement, and by tracing over the letters in his young master's used copybooks. Moreover, during his first escape attempt, described later in the *Narrative*, he writes passes or protections for himself and two fellow slaves. Indeed, the *Narrative* itself has been read as a symbolic, self-authored protection, for in the process of presenting and organizing his experiences, Douglass celebrates his achievement of autonomy.

After the independent-minded, newly literate Douglass returns to the plantation from Baltimore, his owner, Master Thomas, sends him to work for Covey, a man known as "'the nigger-breaker'" because of his reputation for beating enslaved men and women into submission (N 54). Suffering under Covey's persistent abuse, Douglass temporarily loses much of his independence of mind and slips back into the emotional lethargy he associates with mental and physical enslavement. But if the acquisition of literacy first enabled him to feel free, the act of physical resistance precipitates his second and lasting period of liberation. Indeed, if the sight of his aunt's wrongful punishment initiated him into slavery, he emancipates himself by revising that earlier episode and refusing to be beaten himself:

This battle with Mr. Covey was the turning-point in my career as a slave. It
rekindled the few expiring embers of freedom, and revived within me a sense of
my own manhood. It recalled the departed self-confidence, and inspired me
again with a determination to be free … My long-crushed spirit rose, cowardice
departed, bold defiance took its place; and I now resolved that, however long I
might remain a slave in form, the day had passed forever when I could be a slave
in fact … From this time I was never again what might be called fairly whipped,
though I remained a slave four years afterwards. I had several fights but was
never whipped.   (N 65)

Douglass's *Narrative* thus celebrates both explicitly and symbolically a
slave's capacity for resistance and liberation in a system that conspires to
deprive him of his humanity. Whether through indirection or explicit denunciation, he exposes the fundamental contradictions of the slaveholding system
that make a mockery of American principles and Christian mores. He reveals
the various ways in which the slavocracy seeks to undermine the sanctity of
family relations. Furthermore, his countless descriptions of the conditions
under which slaves live rebut any theories that slaves love the station to which
they are assigned or are humanized by the system of slavery. He discredits
the apologists' evidence of the slaves' contentment by decoding the misery the
sorrow songs convey. And he reveals the misuses to which slaveholders
put their religious beliefs. Indeed, when faced with white caulkers in
Massachusetts who refused to allow him to practice his trade because of his
race, and in light of Northern compliance with the Fugitive Slave Law, he
debunks the myth of the North as a promised land of freedom.

Modern Echoes

Although Douglass is best known for his *Narrative*, in recent years many of
his other writings have received heightened attention. Increasingly, scholars
and students have begun to assess the impact of *My Bondage and My
Freedom* (1855) and *Life and Times of Frederick Douglass* (1881, 1892).
Likewise, the speech he delivered on July 5, 1852 at the request of the citizens
of Rochester, New York as part of their July 4 celebration has inspired critical
scrutiny. In light of the issues surrounding the 2007–8 election cycle, it is
perhaps worth considering briefly the ways in which contemporary oratory
echoes Douglass's rhetoric.

During the historic 2007–8 presidential election cycle – when for the first
time a white woman and a black man were the leading candidates for the
nomination of a major political party, a black man went on to become his
party's nominee, a white woman was the vice-presidential nominee for only the
second time, and of course an African American won the presidency for the first

time in the history of the United States – issues of gender, socioeconomic status, and especially race entered public discourse as never before. An early (but not the only) example involved accusations concerning Barack Obama's association with his former pastor, the Reverend Jeremiah Wright. When excerpts from the Reverend Jeremiah Wright's sermons began to circulate in the media, pundits, as well as many average Americans, denounced Wright (and Obama, by association) for being unpatriotic, if not blasphemous. Wright was castigated for his outspoken criticisms of the contradictions of American democracy, especially of the ways in which these contradictions exclude African Americans and other disfranchised groups from the fruits of democracy. He was criticized in particular for the sermon he preached in the aftermath of September 11, 2001, in which he asserted that US foreign policy was largely to blame for the attacks in New York and Pennsylvania, and on the Pentagon.

In the now-famous speech delivered on March 18, 2008, a speech known as "The More Perfect Union" speech, Barack Obama describes Reverend Wright's "incendiary language" as "divisive" and "distorted" because it "sees white racism as endemic, and elevates what is wrong with America above all that we know is right with America." He asserts that "many of the disparities that exist in the African American community today" – inferior education, wealth and income disparities, unemployment, and inadequate basic services – "can be directly traced to inequalities passed on from an earlier generation that suffered under the brutal legacy of slavery and Jim Crow." Nevertheless, Obama describes Wright's rhetoric as an anachronistic throwback, a function of the fact that he came of age in the late 1950s and 1960s, when "segregation was still the law of the land and opportunity was systematically constricted." As he puts it:

> For the men and women of Rev. Wright's generation, the memories of humiliation and doubt and fear have not gone away; nor has [sic] the anger and the bitterness of those years. That anger may not get expressed in public, in front of white co-workers or white friends … [Occasionally] it finds voice in the church on Sunday morning, in the pulpit and in the pews. The fact that so many people are surprised to hear that anger in some of Rev. Wright's sermons simply reminds us of the old truism that the most segregated hour in American life occurs on Sunday morning.[4]

Those familiar with the strain of social gospel of which Reverend Wright's rhetoric is characteristic understood his critiques of the contradictions in American democracy not as a throwback, but rather as part of the long history of black oratory where political critique and Biblical exegesis are intertwined.

Numerous commentators invoked the memory of the Reverend Dr. Martin Luther King, Jr. in discussions of Reverend Wright's sermon. So often associated with the speech he delivered on the steps of the Lincoln Memorial at the 1963 March on Washington, Dr. King became increasingly incisive, indeed radical, in his critiques of US domestic and foreign policy in the last years of his life. In a sermon entitled "A Time to Break Silence," delivered at the Riverside Church in New York City on April 4, 1967, a year to the day before he died, King asserted that the soul of America will only be redeemed when it ends the oppression of the disfranchised at home and its military aggression abroad. Although he had been criticized for his denunciation of the Vietnam War, he defended his right to speak out against the American refusal to recognize a post-independence Vietnam, the American support of French efforts to re-colonize Vietnam, the American support of a long line of military dictators in that country, and American military aggression.

Dr. King declaimed against capitalist greed and disregard for the poor and vulnerable and enumerated the atrocities for which US foreign policy is responsible. While he did not go so far as to say that our national tragedies are retribution for our national sins, he did warn of the consequences of those sins, such as the brutalization of US troops and the expansion of a foreign policy motivated by a desire to protect its overseas interests no matter the human cost. As he asserted:

> We can no longer afford to worship the god of hate or bow before the altar of retaliation. The oceans of history are made turbulent by the ever-rising tides of hate. History is cluttered with the wreckage of nations and individuals that pursued this self-defeating path of hate.[5]

Like Dr. King, Frederick Douglass was also unafraid to speak to the contradictions that lie at the heart of American democracy. In the Appendix to the *Narrative*, he acknowledges that some of his readers may believe that he is irreligious because of his denunciations of slaveholding Christians. Yet he takes pains to clarify that his critique extends only to those Christians who condone slavery, Northerners and Southerners alike. As he writes:

> Dark and terrible as is this picture, I hold it to be strictly true of the overwhelming mass of professed Christians in America. They strain at a gnat, and swallow a camel. Could any thing be more true of our churches? They would be shocked at the proposition of fellowshipping a *sheep*-stealer; and at the same time they hug to their communion a *man*-stealer, and brand me with being an infidel, if I find fault with them for it. They attend with Pharisaical strictness to the outward forms of religion, and at the same time neglect the weightier matters of the law, judgment, mercy, and faith. They are always ready to sacrifice, but seldom to show mercy. They are they who are represented as professing to love God whom they have not seen, whilst they hate their brother whom they have seen. They love the heathen on the other side of the globe. They can pray for him, pay money to have the Bible

put into his hand, and missionaries to instruct him; while they despise and totally neglect the heathen at their own doors. (N 99–100)

The speech Frederick Douglass delivered on July 5, 1852 has come to be known by the title: "What to the Slave Is the Fourth of July?" In language that is even more forceful than the rhetoric of the Appendix to the *Narrative*, he decries the hypocrisy that underlies the rhetoric of American patriotism and depicts the extent to which blacks are excluded from the national body. His critique, relentless and unapologetic, reminds us of the long history of African American denunciations of the gap between national rhetoric and state-sanctioned practices and policies. As he puts it:

> Whether we turn to the declarations of the past, or to the professions of the present, the conduct of the nation seems equally hideous and revolting. America is false to the past, false to the present, and solemnly binds herself to be false to the future. Standing with God and the crushed and bleeding slave on this occasion, I will, in the name of humanity which is outraged, in the name of liberty which is fettered, in the name of the constitution and the bible, which are disregarded and trampled upon, dare to call in question and to denounce, with all the emphasis I can command, everything that serves to perpetuate slavery – the great sin and shame of America! "I will not equivocate – I will not excuse." I will use the severest language I can command, and yet not one word shall escape me that any man, whose judgment is not blinded by prejudice, or who is not at heart a slaveholder, shall not confess to be right and just. (MB 432)

NOTES

1. Deborah E. McDowell, "In the First Place: Making Frederick Douglass and the Afro-American Narrative Tradition," in *Critical Essays on Frederick Douglass*, ed. William L. Andrews (Boston, MA: G. K. Hall & Co., 1991), 208.
2. Daphne A. Brooks, "Introduction," *The Great Escapes: Four Slave Narratives*, ed. Daphne A. Brooks (New York: Barnes and Noble, 2007), xix.
3. *Ibid.*, lx.
4. Barack Obama, "The More Perfect Union" (2008), quoted at: http://my.barack obama.com/page/content/hisownwords.
5. Martin Luther King, Jr., "A Time to Break Silence," in *Testament of Hope: The Essential Writings and Speeches of Martin Luther King, Jr.*, ed. James M. Washington (New York: HarperCollins, 1991), 242.

GUIDE TO FURTHER READING

A full list of important scholarship on Douglass would be too lengthy to include here and might be more overwhelming than useful to all but the most specialized readers. What follows is limited to book-length studies of particular relevance to the topics addressed in this volume.

Andrews, William L. *To Tell a Free Story: The First Century of Afro-American Autobiography, 1760–1865*. Urbana: University of Illinois Press, 1986.

Andrews, William L., ed. *Critical Essays on Frederick Douglass*. Boston, MA: G. K. Hall & Co., 1991.

Baker, Houston. *The Journey Back: Issues in Black Literature and Criticism*. Chicago, IL: University of Chicago Press, 1980.

Berlin, Ira. *Generations of Captivity: A History of African-American Slaves*. Cambridge, MA: Harvard University Press, 2003.

Blassingame, John. *The Slave Community: Plantation Life in the Antebellum South*. New York: Oxford University Press, 1979.

Blight, David W. *Frederick Douglass' Civil War: Keeping Faith in Jubilee*. Baton Rouge: Louisiana State University Press, 1989.

Castronovo, Russ. *Fathering the Nation: Genealogies of Slavery and Freedom*. Berkeley: University of California Press, 1995.

Crane, Gregg. *Race, Citizenship and Law in American Literature*. Cambridge: Cambridge University Press, 2002.

Davis, David Brion. *Inhuman Bondage: The Rise and Fall of Slavery in the New World*. New York: Oxford University Press, 2006.

Davis, Reginald F. *Frederick Douglass: A Precursor of Liberation Theology*. Macon, GA: Mercer University Press, 2005.

Ernest, John. *Resistance and Reformation in Nineteenth-Century African-American Literature: Brown, Wilson, Jacobs, Delany, Douglass, and Harper*. Jackson: University Press of Mississippi, 1995.

Fisch, Audrey, ed. *The Cambridge Companion to the African American Slave Narrative*. Cambridge: Cambridge University Press, 2007.

Fisher, Dexter, and Robert B. Stepto, eds. *Afro-American Literature: The Reconstruction of Instruction*. New York: Modern Language Association, 1979.

Foner, Philip S. *Frederick Douglass: A Biography*. New York: Citadel Press, 1964.

Foster, Frances Smith. *Witnessing Slavery: The Development of the Antebellum Slave Narratives*. Westport, CT: Greenwood Press, 1979.

Gates, Henry Louis, Jr. *Figures in Black: Words, Signs, and the "Racial" Self*. New York: Oxford University Press, 1987.

Giles, Paul. *Virtual Americas: Transnational Fictions and the Transatlantic Imaginary*. Durham, NC: Duke University Press, 2002.

Gilroy, Paul. *The Black Atlantic: Modernity and Double Consciousness*. Cambridge, MA: Harvard University Press, 1993.

Hall, James C., ed. *Approaches to Teaching Narrative of the Life of Frederick Douglass*. New York: Modern Language Association of America, 1999.

Lampe, Gregory P. *Frederick Douglass: Freedom's Voice, 1818–1845*. East Lansing: Michigan State University Press, 1998.

Lawson, Bill E., and Frank Kirkland, eds. *Frederick Douglass: A Critical Reader*. Malden, MA: Blackwell, 1999.

Lee, Maurice S. *Slavery, Philosophy, and American Literature, 1830–1860*. Cambridge: Cambridge University Press, 2005.

Levine, Robert S. *Martin Delany, Frederick Douglass, and the Politics of Representative Identity*. Chapel Hill: University of North Carolina Press, 1997.

Levine, Robert S., and Samuel Otter, eds. *Frederick Douglass and Herman Melville: Essays in Relation*. Chapel Hill: University of North Carolina Press, 2008.

McBride, Dwight A. *Impossible Witnesses: Truth, Abolitionism, and Slave Testimony*. New York: New York University Press, 2001.

McDowell, Deborah E., and Arnold Rampersad, eds. *Slavery and the Literary Imagination*. Baltimore, MD: Johns Hopkins University Press, 1989.

McFeely, William S. *Frederick Douglass*. New York: W. W. Norton, 1991.

McHenry, Elizabeth. *Forgotten Readers: Recovering the Lost History of African American Literary Societies*. Durham, NC: Duke University Press, 2002.

Martin, Waldo E., Jr. *The Mind of Frederick Douglass*. Chapel Hill: University of North Carolina Press, 1984.

Moses, Wilson Jeremiah. *Creative Conflict in African American Thought: Frederick Douglass, Alexander Crummell, Booker T. Washington, W. E. B. Du Bois, and Marcus Garvey*. Cambridge: Cambridge University Press, 2004.

Nwankwo, Ifeoma. *Black Cosmopolitanism: Racial Consciousness, National Identity, and Transnational Ideology in the Americas*. Philadelphia: University of Pennsylvania Press, 2005.

Preston, Dickson J. *Young Frederick Douglass: The Maryland Years*. Baltimore, MD: Johns Hopkins University Press, 1980.

Quarles, Benjamin. *Frederick Douglass*. Washington, DC: Associated Publishers, 1948.

Riss, Arther. *Race, Slavery, and Liberalism in Nineteenth-Century American Literature*. Cambridge: Cambridge University Press, 2006.

Rowe, John Carlos. *At Emerson's Tomb: The Politics of Classic American Literature*. New York: Columbia University Press, 1997.

Smith, Valerie. *Self-Discovery and Authority in Afro-American Narrative*. Cambridge, MA: Harvard University Press, 1991.

Stauffer, John. *The Black Hearts of Men: Radical Abolitionists and the Transformation of Race*. Cambridge, MA: Harvard University Press, 2002.

Giants: The Parallel Lives of Frederick Douglass and Abraham Lincoln. New York: Twelve, 2008.

Sundquist, Eric, ed. *Frederick Douglass: New Literary and Historical Essays.* Cambridge: Cambridge University Press, 1990.

Sundquist, Eric. *To Wake the Nations: Race in the Making of American Literature.* Cambridge, MA: Harvard University Press, 1993.

Walker, Peter F. *Moral Choices: Memory, Desire, and Imagination in Nineteenth-Century American Abolition.* Baton Rouge: Louisiana State University Press, 1978.

Wallace, Maurice O. *Constructing the Black Masculine: Identity and Ideality in African American Men's Literature and Culture, 1775–1995.* Durham, NC: Duke University Press, 2002.

Williamson, Scott C. *The Narrative Life: The Moral and Religious Thought of Frederick Douglass.* Macon, GA: Mercer University Press, 2002.

INDEX